The New Complete

BASSET HOUND

by Mercedes Braun

Fourth Edition . . . Second Printing

1982

HOWELL BOOK HOUSE INC.
230 Park Avenue
New York, N.Y. 10169

Ch. Jesse James of Eleandon was the author's choice for Best of Breed at the Pilgrim Basset Hound Club Specialty in 1965. He was handled to this good win by Paul Saucier. Club President Doris Hurry (right) presents the trophy.

Shafer

Library of Congress Cataloging in Publication Data

Braun, Mercedes.
    The new complete basset hound.

    Published in 1969 under title: The complete basset hound.

    1. Basset-hounds.   I. Title.
SF429.B2B7   1979   636.753   79-4465
ISBN 0-87605-021-6

To those who really care;
        to whom the Basset of tomorrow
        is more important than the wins of today
This book is respectfully dedicated.

Ch. Strathalbyn Shoot To Kill (Lyn-Mar Acres Radar ex Tantivy Blond Sidonia), owned by J. J. J. McKenna, Jr. and Eric F. George (breeder). This dog is a remarkable specimen on two counts. He is one of the country's most outstanding pack hounds having been named Grand Champion at the Bryn Mawr Hound Show and has caused considerable excitement in the conformation ring. As this book goes to press, this impressive hound has garnered multiple Group wins and placements and was BB at the 1979 Westminster and International Kennel Club shows. He is shown here with his handler, Joy S. Brewster in a relaxed moment. *Ashbey*

Contents

About the Author

HOUNDS and Sporting dogs have always held an important place in the life of Mercedes Braun. As a small child she often followed her father and their dogs on hunting trips. Here she learned the ways of the field, lessons she has used through the years.

Mrs. Braun and her family were avid Beagle fans, but she became captivated by "Morgan," the famous Basset that frequently appeared on the *Gary Moore Show* during the early 1950s. Soon afterward, while the Brauns were out hunting, they met a Basset for the first time. From that day on they were "hooked."

Eventually Braun's Hoot'n Annie joined the family. When Annie was ready to be mated, Mrs. Braun visited the Toledo Kennel Club show. Here she saw some of the best dogs of the day and learned about Annie's relationship to some of them. A stud dog was recommended and a breeding was done. Later, a male dog was purchased that would form the basis for a breeding program with stock from that first litter. The Braun love affair with the Basset was now launched in earnest.

Mrs. Braun's successes as a breeder are reflected in the honors her Bassets have earned in the field, in conformation competition and in obedience trials. The Braun Bassets were always bred for utility and beauty. They have won their place in the record books.

The Basset Hound Club of America tapped Mrs. Braun in the early 1960s. Originally appointed Club trophy chairman, she was later named to the important posts of BHCA columnist in *Pure-Bred Dogs—American Kennel Gazette* and editor of *Tally-Ho*, the official BHCA publication. In 1965 Mercedes Braun was elected secretary of the BHCA and continued in this important office for three years.

Both Mrs. Braun and her husband, Joseph, also took an active part in local all-breed and Specialty club affairs in and around Toledo, Ohio. They became obedience instructors for the Toledo

Kennel Club with Mrs. Braun also serving as the Club's hospitality chairman and corresponding secretary. They were also active members of the BHC of Greater Detroit, Western Michigan BHC and helped organize the Maumee Valley BHC. Maumee Valley honored the Brauns with life memberships in recognition of their many efforts on behalf of the Club. Additionally, Mrs. Braun was also the secretary of the Ohio Dog Owners' Association. Her interests and energies helped dogs and dog owners in and out of the Basset Hound fancy.

For a number of years, Mrs. Braun was a professional handler, resigning in 1966 to become a judge. She is now approved for all Toy breeds, some Sporting and Non-Sporting and, of course, Basset Hounds. Mr. Braun is approved to judge a number of the Hound breeds.

Mrs. Braun and her husband are now retired to a life of ease in Florida, but they have two Bassets which they show sparingly when they are not either fishing or swimming.

Mercedes and Joseph Braun have given the Basset fancy a forward thrust through their involvement with and love of the breed. Their chief pleasure now is to observe the successes of newer fanciers they have helped in the breed.

—ELSWORTH HOWELL

Introduction

OVER THIRTEEN years have passed since Mercedes Braun introduced the first edition of *The Complete Basset Hound*. It was good news and only fitting that Merce be called upon to update her book and reflect what has happened to our breed since the middle sixties.

Many new, serious breeders have joined the ranks of the more experienced. With the development of our interstate system of highways, allowing more and more breeders to participate in activities previously beyond a day's travel, regional differences in type and preferences have changed dramatically. The author does a remarkable job in helping the reader appreciate the effects of this change over the last decade.

Merce demonstrates the unique versatility of the breed and the breeders responsible for the development of the Basset in the areas of field, show, tracking, and obedience.

The author is well qualified as an authority to present and document this valuable information. Her experience as a judge, AKC licensed handler, obedience teacher, and as a breeder of conformation and field trial dogs, which brought to the breed one of our few dual champions, has given her a complete understanding of all aspects of the breed. Merce's years of dedication to the Basset Hound Club of America as Secretary and editor of *Tally-Ho,* the BHCA newsletter has given her an in-depth knowledge of the breeders by sharing with them their experiences in the development of our breed. Whether the reader is an experienced breeder or a beginner, this is the one book on Basset Hounds that is a must reference for the library.

FINN BERGISHAGEN

Finn Bergishagen has been active in the Basset Hound Club of America since 1962 and served as President in 1976 and 1977.

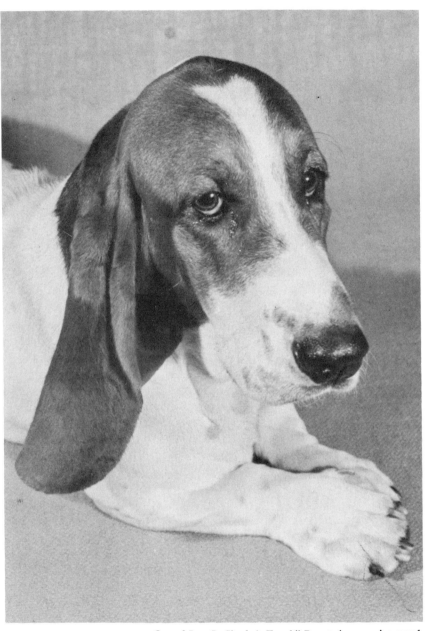

One of Jean L. Sheehy's Topohil Bassets in a pensive mood.

Acknowledgments

WITHOUT many wonderful people, there would be no book at all. To all of them, I wish to express my gratitude. I knew there was little reference material on the Basset and huge gaps in the history of the American bloodlines when I accepted the task of writing. There was a great need for a compilation of known facts, if nothing more, so that what was known would be accessible to all. What I did not know was that I would be invited to use books that were tucked away in private libraries so that I could compare the opinions of many authors. I also did not know that fanciers around the world would be eager to assist because they were just as anxious as we in America to see this book in print.

We must first thank Elsworth Howell who realized our need for such a book and expressed his desire to publish it if I would write it. It is impossible to thank adequately George Pugh of Xenia, Ohio, a judge who is wholeheartedly interested in any breed. His personal interests involve Obedience, the Springer Spaniels, Gordon Setters, Toy Manchester Terriers, and Bassets. When he learned of my un dertaking, he graciously threw open the doors of his private library where I found many old, out-of-print volumes that contained refer- ence to the Basset. Here I was able to review information and form a

11

theory on the origin of the breed. He loaned me his nearly-complete set of American Kennel Gazettes so that I was able to piece together the American bloodlines.

The officers of The Basset Hound Club of America were generous in their contribution. John Eylander, Norwood Engle, and Loren Free never tired of lengthy correspondence and discussions on pedigrees, pictures, and breeders. Darrielyn Oursler checked the club records. The secretaries of the regional clubs, for the most part, supplied the data on their clubs.

Many breeders were most helpful. Jean Sanger Look, especially, contributed a great deal of material and loaned pictures of many early Bassets. Clarence, "Clip," and Helen Boutell offered the scale drawing for the Standard chapter and a copy of the De Penne painting. Dr. & Mrs. Leonard Skolnick sent microfilm of French books. James S. Jones, Master of the Tewksbury Foot Basset Pack, volunteered to write the chapter on the packs in America. Alfred Bissell sent further information about the packs. Others sent pictures of them. Fred Carter assisted with the bloodlines in Canada. There were many more, too numerous to mention, who answered my plea for information and pictures. Mark Washbond, Chris Teeter, Richard Basset, Doris Hurry, and the Kenneth Eldridges were very helpful.

From overseas, help was given without restraint. George Johnston and Gerard Kemp of England supplied most of the material on modern Basset affairs in Great Britain. M. Hubert and M. Abel Desamy painstakingly translated my letters to them and sent the information on modern French Bassets as did M. Jean Rothea. Keith Goodwin contributed the Australian chapter. Peggy Blakeney wrote of the New Zealand Club

I am not schooled in the French language. Dr. Tryggve Baak of Waterville, Ohio, whose Bulldogs I handle, spent many hours translating the French writings. A friend, William Gravesmill, took some of the French correspondence to an associate at the Toledo Museum of Art where he was supervisor of music. Dale Fleming and the Dal-Tex Basset Hound Club sent action photos of field trials.

It is impossible to thank all who offered so much. Nothing could have been accomplished without the help of my most severe critic, staunch supporter, and husband, Joe. We are deeply indebted to

12

those who loaned their cherished photographs. Every little bit helped to make this a complete book. To all who contributed, even a small amount, the appreciation of the publisher, the author, and the Basset fanciers is gratefully acknowledged.

MERCEDES BRAUN

The author with Ch. Braun's Jenny Diver

1

What Is a Basset?

TECHNICALLY, he is a long, low dog of the scent-hound category, known for his pensive expression and easy-going manner. He was bred to hunt small game, and because this is his primary purpose, the following pages are filled with material concerning this function of the breed.

We must not forget, however, that it is the Basset's versatility that brought him fame. He is perhaps best known for the lovable nature which led him to be dubbed "the armchair clown." Do not be fooled when you see him sound asleep on his back or sprawled on his favorite chair (which he has taken away from you). Put a lead on this same dog, take him to a show, and he can give a polished performance with a "Don't you love me, Mr. Judge?" attitude that will command applause from the ringside. Take him to the field, and he can show you how a scent-hound should perform—over, under, and through rough ground, never tiring all day long.

At home, the Basset will assume his subtle manner of "ruling the roost." He refuses to accept the fact that he is a dog by devious methods. He can affect poor hearing when he doesn't want to obey or pretend to sleep so soundly that you do not have the heart to disturb him. But his alertness miraculously returns if you open the refrigerator door ever so stealthily. He is a built-in baby-sitter, an ideal family pet. A Basset needs firm convincing that his big, brown eyes will get him nowhere. But first convince yourself of this, if you can. He is smart enough to be very adept at playing dumb. He will do his best to outmaneuver you to gain his own way, and he will make you like it. You need only one Basset to fill the house with laughter, the woods with beautiful music, and the show with an approving ovation. Small wonder the breed has attained such popularity and owners readily admit, "I am owned by a Basset."

Sir Everett Millais's "Model."

2

History of the
Basset Hound

THE origin of the Basset Hound is somewhat elusive. Until the writing of this book, I accepted the common belief set forth in most 20th century publications that the Basset Hound was a direct descendant of the St. Hubert Hound. The verity of this contention has been doubted since the uncovering of information in certain rare, old volumes. I shall present the facts I have discovered. The reader may draw his own conclusions, as I have done.

Though the many varieties of Basset Hounds are included in this book, we are chiefly concerned with the type that is known in America today. M. Jean Rothea, president of the Club du Basset Artesien Normand in 1964, states that since this was the line that produced the British Basset, and few other importations were made, we must conclude that the American Basset is descended predominantly from the Basset d'Artois, now called the Basset Artesien Normand in France. As you will read in the following pages, the Basset d'Artois had become nearly extinct at one time. Comte le Couteulx de Cantelue, Monsieur Lane, and a few other men were largely responsible for the revival of this variety. Genealogy before their time is of little importance to breeding programs though the early history is interesting. A letter from M. Abel Desamy, president of the Club du Griffon Vendeen, further substantiates and enlarges this theory: "Here is my personal opinion on the origin of the 'Basset Hound.' It is a descendant of the French Bassets 'le Couteulx' and 'Lane.' There are, moreover, common points between the 'Basset Hound' and our 'Artesien Normand.' M. Megin assures me that about 1880 the English (a certain Mr. Krehl) imported a Basset of M. le Couteulx (Fino) and several females (Gunera and Theo), next a Basset of M. Lane (Romano). These dogs took root and the English obtained their characteristic type; more heavy dogs, with head of a Bloodhound. It is possible, evidently, that in order to establish this stock, one or the other called upon the ancestry of the Basset Ardennais (the Basset of St. Hubert). This remains to be proven."

One must bear in mind that prior to the later years of the Napoleonic era, all dogs lower than sixteen inches were called Bassets (*bas* meaning low-set) in France. Each province and each breed had its Basset. To ask a Frenchman for a Basset, without stating which variety, was like asking for a horse without indicating if it should be a race-horse, plow-horse, or cart-horse.

One must realize that terms, though they may fit *our* visualization of a dog, may not give us the description as it was in the mind of the writer. Words often do not compare with available pictures and data. For an example, refer to the drawing of one of the earliest English imports, Sir Everett Millais's Model. While reading the delineation, one envisions great depth of muzzle, many folds of very loose skin, and great ear length. The dog in the picture, however, if compared to the modern American Basset, would be described today as having a snipey muzzle, a dry head, and short, heavy ears. In another publication, the Basset was said to be "broader in chest than a Bulldog" of that era, but he was certainly not broader than the Bulldog which is familiar to us today.

According to early writers, the original German Dachshund and the Schweisshund were indistinguishable from the Basset in structural characteristics though they were either copper-red or black-and-tan. Since the ancient origin of the Basset is of little value to a present-day breeding program, we will not go into the evolution of these hounds.

On the monument of Thothmus III, who reigned over Egypt

more than 2000 years B.C., were found figures of a dog of the same proportions as the Basset. The inscription states that this animal was his favorite companion. Those familiar with the ancient arts will agree that figures are not always representative of their real-life subjects. However, the same characteristics were found on early Assyrian dog sculptures. This information fairly well establishes the existence of a dog of a long, low structure. An early Indian breed was pictured in much the same manner.

About 125 A.D., Arrian described dogs sent out by the Roman Procurator Cynegii. These were the Segusian hounds, a small Basset named after a Celtic tribe inhabiting the western banks of the Rhone district in Western France to which they were sent. He wrote of the hounds that were favored by the Segusiani as being shaggy and ugly, the most highbred being the ugliest. The writer's description implies that these animals were of the structure, and used for the work, of the historical Basset. If we study the course of the history of the Segusiani tribe, we may conclude that these dogs were the ancestors of the Basset Griffon varieties. The Vendee district is east of the Rhone. The rough-coated Basset that developed there is known as the Griffon Vendeen. The Fauve de Bretagne was named for Brittany, the province in which it was popular.

Oppian, in 200 A.D., tells of another variety which was also sent out from Rome to the Rhone area. These dogs were called the Agasaeus. They were no less clever at hunting on scent than the Carian or Cretan types, but structurally, they were sorry brutes. In pursuit and recovery, they were only inferior on one point—speed. The Agasaeus was later linked, by other authors, with the Beagle. The Beagle of this era, however, was a long, low, heavy dog, compared to the Beagle as we know it. It is quite conceivable that the smooth-coat Bassets are descended from the Agasaeus which was used to drive game within reach of the bowman's shaft.

A pack of Spartan hounds were described by Darcius in this manner: "From thence we have the dogs that are prized, from Achaian, Lacedeomon, dwelling in woods, precipitating themselves on wild beasts, tracking them throughout their dens and deep valleys, and encountering them everywhere; making their teeth meet in their rigid hides; always able to track what has at any time been indicated to them. The broad river that flows among the winding hills does not impede them, nor does its boundary arrest their course. Their mouths may be broken by their constant barking, and they may drag their weary limbs after them, but they are still constant to pursue the prey." We are all familiar with the line from Shakespeare's *Midsummer Night's Dream,* "My hounds are bred out of the Spartan kind. . . ." Major Heseltine, writer and owner of the famous Walhampton pack in England, praised Shakespeare's discourse highly. Yet, in the same article containing this praise, he stated that the Basset came from France, and, in the sixteenth century, was known to De Fouilloux, an early authority on dogs. He offered no reason why he felt the breed had its origin in France, yet referred to Bassets as being bred out of the Spartan hounds.

On the subject of the St. Hubert Hound, which was called the "dog of Flanders" in the eighth century, authors wrote of its existence in the time of the Gauls. The appellation was derived from the patron of the monks of the same name who are credited with breeding them. St. Hubert obtained his hounds from the south of Gaul (France) in the sixth century, using them for hunting at his abbey in Ardennes. There were two varieties. The Abbots preferred the black-and-tans for hunting boar and wolf. The white variety was later known as the Talbot Hound. Although no direct reference to the size of the St. Hubert Hound can be found, it is known that the Talbot was twenty-eight inches high. During this era, the King of France collected annual tribute. The Abbots of St. Hubert paid their taxes with dogs contributed to the King's kennels. These dogs, thus, became known to the noblemen who hunted with them.

Reference was made by Sir Thomas Cockaine, in 1591, recommending that a breed known only as the "heavy Southern-type hound" in southern France be bred with a Kibble Hound of the broken and crook-legged Basset type, to be used as Lymehounds. This establishes that the Kibble Hound was a type of Basset.

In an 1879 volume, the Swedish Beagle was described as being larger than the English Beagle, possessing a nice head, long, folding, soft ears, good dewlap, and being black, tan, and white in color. In this same book, the Dachshund head was said to resemble the Bloodhound, with ears thirteen to fourteen inches long, weight of dog, eighteen to twenty pounds. This type of Dachshund, according to the writer, was later crossed with terriers to produce the breed as it is known today. There was also mentioned the Rostaing Bassets with long bodies, short crooked legs, and owned by a French marquis. This variety had grand Otterhound heads with rough coats and were, undoubtedly, the type known as the Basset Griffon today. We will discuss the Griffon varieties in later chapters.

Most of the information on Bassets in modern books has been taken from the writings of English authors. Many of them admit openly that the true origin of the breed was not known to them. They knew only that the dogs were bred by M. le Couteulx and M. Lane. Sir Everett Millais was one of the earliest English breeders and writers. Others often referred to his theory. This in turn came from le Couteulx who believed that *all* French hounds were derived from the St. Hubert. He alludes to twelve different varieties of Bassets which appeared to have been known up to the time of the French Revolution. He concluded that, since all hounds had similarly shaped heads, long ears, and dewlap, they were related. Being certain that the Hounds of St. Hubert dated back to the eighth century, he theorized that all similar animals descended from them.

Sir Everett Millais further elaborated on this supposition by stating that the rickety-type Bloodhounds, descendants of the St. Hubert Hound, could have developed short, crooked legs. Millais believed that sportsmen who followed their hunting dogs on foot set to work breeding specimens with the shortest legs, and the Basset was the result. He was further convinced by the name, which he interpreted to mean "dwarf." However, Cassell's dictionary defines "bas" as "not high; low; lowered; inferior," depending on the context.

Sir Everett's theory is possible, though geneticists of today would call the process he describes selective breeding. They would attribute the formation of the legs to genetic makeup rather than to poor nutrition and rickets. If we accept the "direct descendant of the St. Hubert Hound" theory, we must suspect that these dogs carried genes capable of producing short legs which appeared in certain specimens when they were inbred. St. Hubert had taken dogs from the Rhone district in southern France to his abbey and kennels in the Ardennes province of northern France. We have previously ascertained that the Agasaeus, referred to by Oppian, had been sent to this district by the Roman Procurator Cynegii.

St. Hubert could have bred dogs that were approximately twenty-eight inches high but which were carrying short-leg genes.

A fact that is little known is that there was also a Basset of St. Hubert which was either shiny black or uniformly copper in color. Without perusal of possible records kept by the Abbots of St. Hubert, one cannot reach an indisputable conclusion about the origin of this type, but it seems feasible that St. Hubert took more than one breed to his kennel along the Belgian border. From the Agasaeus he bred the Basset of St. Hubert.

Undoubtedly, as later writers called upon the works of those before them, they neglected to realize that the St. Hubert Hound was a variety under the broader title of "Basset Hounds." At least, they failed to make the point clear. As time went on, there was confusion between the St. Hubert Hound and the Basset of St. Hubert.

The Bleu de Gascogne was another variety mentioned in early writings. This type was smooth-coated, heavily mottled, with longer ears than the St. Hubert. It was developed in the Gascony area along the Bay of Biscay, west of the Rhone district. It is very possible that these dogs were also descendants of the Agasaeus.

Undoubtedly, fanciers of each district called upon the little Bassets along the Rhone, selected those best suited to their topography, and developed their distinctive types. The same breeding process would hold true for dogs of similar structure, known by different names, in other countries.

3

Modern Smooth Coats

IN 1887, Stonehenge wrote, "In France, about twelve distinct breeds of hounds are met with, including the St. Hubert, the smooth hounds of La Vendee, the Brittany Red Hound, the grey St. Louis, the Gascony, the Normandy, the Saintogne, the Poitou, the Breese, the Vendee rough-coated hound, the Artois, and the little Basset, coupled with the Briquet. Of these, the grey St. Louis is almost extinct, and all the others, with the exception of the Basset, may be grouped with the St. Hubert and the Red Hound of Brittany. . . . The varieties of the Basset are innumerable some being black-and-tan, and common throughout the Black Forest and Vosges, while the others are either tricoloured or blue mottled. The tricolour has lately been introduced into England in large numbers, having been first shown to the English visitors at the French show of 1863. . . ." He called upon the earliest French authority, De Fouilloux, to deal with the "Basset d'Artois," with which we are chiefly concerned, for a description of this dog: "The Artesien, with full-crooked fore-legs, smooth coats, brave, and having double rows of teeth like wolves." Stonehenge continued, "In the many political storms that have swept over France, carrying away her monarchial pageantry and the impressing ceremonies of the chase, many of

23

that country's ancient breeds became almost extinct. Amongst them, the basset-hound fared a little better than its blood neighbors— the hounds of Artois, Normandy, Gascony, and Saintogne. Thanks to the sporting and patriotic instincts of the descendant of the old noblesse, Count le Couteulx de Canteleu, who spared neither trouble nor expense in his purpose, the smooth tricolour basset-hound of Artois has been preserved in all its purity. The breed was not revived; it had never died out, but it was necessary to search all over the 'basset' districts to find, in sportsmen's kennels, the few true typical specimens, and to breed from them alone. In these efforts on behalf of the old breeds he was greatly benefited by the valuable assistance of M. Pierre Pichot, editor of the 'Revue Britannique.' These are inseparably connected with the famous kennel of Chateau St. Martin, and hounds of Count Couteulx's strain are now as highly prized and eagerly sought for in England as in France. They are aptly described by the French writer De la Blanchere as 'large hounds on short legs.' " The remainder of this work is an account of their field work and standard.

George Krehl, one of the earliest English fanciers, wrote for Vero Shaw's *The Book of the Dog*, in 1881, ". . . The Basset par excellence, though, is the beautiful smooth-coated · tricolour of Artois, and this is the type with its rich and brilliant colouring of black, white, and golden tan, its noble Bloodhound-like head so full of solemn dignity, and long velvet-soft ears, the kind and pensive eye, the heavy folds of the throat, the strange fore-limbs, the quaint and medieval appearance—this is the type, I say, that will stand first in the estimation of an intelligent dog-loving public. The type will always be associated with the name of Comte le Couteulx de Cantelue, and all the Bassets at present (1881) in this country (England) are descended from, or are direct importations from, his celebrated kennel. To this Nobleman, inspired with a hereditary love of the chase and all its accessories, is due the credit of, in a manner, resuscitating this breed, which twenty-five years ago, by careless rearing and the freakish crosses that Continental sportsmen affect, had become well-nigh extinct. The Count has been kind enough to supply me with the particulars of that period. Observing the growing scarcity of good and pure tricolour Artesien Bassets, he set about to do for them what he had already accomplished for other ancient and moribund breeds of Gaul. He started to find a pair of true and pure specimens to revive the breed. After purchasing some thirty dogs, he at last acquired a grand dog, Fino (the first of the name), in Artois, and a lively bitch, Mignarde, in another part of the country. Their produce were true and level to their parentage, showing no signs of throwing back to misalliances; the pups only differed in being more or less crooked, as is still the case in modern litters. The Count continues that he bred in and in to perfect the breed, and that his dogs were sturdy and vigorous enough to permit this means. Ten years later he endeavoured to find another stud-dog for new blood. His huntsman travelled the North of France through to find one, and the experiment made with a superb Basset that he bought in the Saumur, having produced yellow pups, he destroyed them and continued to rely on his own strain. The Count, in his description of the head, lays great stress upon the occipital protuberance, which he calls 'la bosse de chasse'; the head long, narrow and thin in the muzzle, the ears very long; the head of the dog being much heavier and stronger than the bitch's. He gives about four inches for the height of the crooked legs. Colour, tricolour, sometimes ticked with black spots. He goes on to say that some of them have more teeth than dogs usually have, and that many have the 'bec de lievre' i.e. the lower jaw a little shorter than the upper. He states that two of the best bitches in his pack have this formation of the jaw.

"Of the dogs chosen for the coloured plate, Jupiter shows most of the Bloodhound type head; the bitch Pallas is but little short of perfection, and it was the eulogistic description of her qualities in 'The Field,' when she won at Brussels, that induced the writer to find her out in France, and buy her and her mate, Jupiter. Fino de Paris, the third dog in the picture, is demi-torse; he is own brother to Mr. Millais's Model, which is full-torse. He was, until I purchased him from the Jardin d'Acclimation, Paris, the stud-dog of Europe; and Count Couteulx considers him a 'particularly good and pure stud-dog, a perfect specimen of the breed, low on the legs, very strong, well-knit loins, and head typical of the breed, long and thin.' "

Mr. Krehl's article is very interesting. I suggest you compare his description with the copy of this picture of Jupiter, Pallas, and Fino de Paris.

During this period, Monsieurs Couteulx, Masson, and Lane bred from the same original stock, but each got different results. In 1881, M. Louis Lane, of Francqueville, near Boos, exhibited several large, strong, heavy-boned hounds with a decided family likeness. The head was of good length, the ear long, but the faces lacked the Bloodhound character and expression that was seen in the Fino de Paris type. The Lane hounds became very much in demand when the two Couteulx types were much inbred and in need of an out-cross.

To better understand the difference in types, let us elaborate on them. There were eventually two Couteulx types, Fino de Paris and Termino (or Masson):

Fino de Paris Type

COLOR. Rich tricolor, harepie, lemon and white. The markings were even and brilliant, the tan deep, the black saddle-shape on the back running into tan on the buttocks.

COAT. Thick, strong, and, at times, crimped even to coarseness; stern, feathered.

HEAD. In those unallied to the Termino hounds, flattish; ears set high and small; skull domed. In those containing Termino blood, the head was large, well shaped, ears hung low and of good size, with well-developed flews, nose slightly inclined to Roman.

EYE. Dark, sunken, and showing a prominent haw.

BONE. Good; in those not too closely inbred, massive.

LEGS. Torses (full crooked), demi-torses (half crooked), droites (straight).

GENERAL APPEARANCE. A fine hound, a powerful physique.

EXAMPLES: Fino de Paris, Fino V, VI, Pallas II, Fresco, Forester, Merlin, Clovis, Eve, Texas Fino, Wazir, Aryan, Laelaps, Fancy, Fiddler & Flora.

Termino or Masson Type

COLOR. Tricolor (light), lemon and white, harepie, blue-mottled. The tricolor was far less briliant than the Fino de Paris type, the tan not so rich, the back distributed in uneven patches over the body, frequently ticked or blue-mottled.

Jupiter, Pallas, and Fino de Paris.

COAT. Short and fine; no crimping.

HEAD. Domed, though in many of the best specimens this was not apparent.

NOSE. Strongly Roman and finer than the Fino de Paris hounds.

EARS. Hung very low and immensely long.

FLEWS. Well marked.

EYE. Sunken, dark, hawed.

BONE. Somewhat light, except in one or two specimens.

LEGS. Torses, demi-torses, droites with an inclination to height.

GENERAL APPEARANCE. A fine, upstanding hound, well put-together, and of high breeding.

EXAMPLES: Termino, Guinevre, Bellicent, Bourbon, Chopette, Zues, Beau, Beauclerc, Narcissus, Colinette, Blondin, Desia.

It would be well to understand how the difference in Couteulx types came about. In the following table of production, C indicates Couteulx's Fino de Paris type, M is for Masson or Termino type.

Fino de Paris (C) ex Trouvette (C) produced Mignarde (C)

Fino de Paris (C) ex Mignarde (C) produced Finette (C)

Termino (M) ex Finette (C) produced Guinevre (M)

Fino de Paris (C) ex Guinevre (M) produced Bourbon (M) & Fino V (C & M)

Fino de Paris (C) ex Ravende II (C) produced Fanfaro (C)

Fanfaro (C) ex Theo (M) produced Vivien (C & M)

Although Guinevre and Theo were bred from Fino de Paris stock, on the dam's side, they were quite different from Fino de Paris, or any other hound from Comte Couteulx's kennels. They resembled Bellicent, a hound from M. Masson's kennels, which is proof that this peculiar type is indigenous in his line. They must have resembled their sire, which belonged to M. Masson.

Guinevre was mated with Fino de Paris. Had she proved true to common rules of breeding, she should have given birth to his type. She did not; her pup, Bourbon, resembled the Masson dogs. Fino V was similar to his sire but carried some of his dam's qualities.

Bourbon was mated with his aunt, Theo, and produced Chopette, a bitch excelling even her sire in points which made him so different from his brother Fino V.

Vivien was very weak Masson, or Termino, type. She threw both types which ever way mated, and threw in her own, as in the case of Jupiter, a poor type-producer.

Fino de Paris was bred from brother and sister. His pedigree before his grandparents is unknown. Termino as a sire was more prepotent, stamping the character of his family against odds in favor of Fino de Paris.

Lane Type

COLOR. Light tricolor, lemon and white, harepie with ticking.
COAT. Short and thick.
HEAD. Domed, large and coarse, lacking Bloodhound expression.
EARS. Long, heavy, broad, hung low.
EYES. Light.
FLEWS. Well-marked.
LEGS. Torses.
BONE. Enormous.
GENERAL APPEARANCE. A very big, heavy Basset; coarse and clumsy, with enormous chest development.
EXAMPLES: Romano II, Gavette, Blanchette II, Champion, Bavard, Chorister, Hannibal.

An interesting piece on field workers was written by "Wildfowler" in 1879: "He is the slowest of hounds and his value cannot be overestimated. His style of hunting is peculiar, inasmuch that he will have his own way, and each one tries for himself; and if one of them finds, and 'says' so, the others will not blindly follow him and give tongue simply because he does as some hounds, accustomed to work in packs, are apt to do; but, on the contrary, they are slow to acknowledge the alarm given, and will investigate the matter for themselves." He further tells how they work in Indian file, "each one speaking to the line according to his own sentiments on the point, irrespective of what the others may think about it, each working as if he were alone." How true.

All of these writers go on and on about their experiences in the field. Some used field dogs for vermin-killing (badger, fox, etc.);

others employed them for pheasant shooting, woodcock, etc., while some were trained to retrieve from water. The most unusual use was for truffle-hunting. Many peasants employed the dogs' extraordinary scenting power to assist them in finding tubers. All the peasant had to do was dig the potato-shaped delicacy from the ground. How versatile can a breed get?

Others in France had begun to take a serious interest in the breed. M. Leon Verrier started his kennel of Bulins in 1874. M. Verrier wrote that his finest Bassets reproduced themselves no matter what. The ancestry of le Couteulx was in their background, though he had no proof. Pedigrees were not kept on record in these days.

M. Verrier was a great admirer of the Lane type but desired to escape its lighter coloring without loosing the type. He purchased the best dogs he could find. He attempted to breed dogs with straighter legs but had many disappointments because he never kept records of the lines of his brood bitches or of the studs he employed. M. Verrier later left the country of Bray and moved near Rouen where he had the opportunity to work more closely with M. Lane and M. Bardin. He bred Brin d'Or, a fine stud hound, to Revaude and Timbale I, and many fine hounds resulted: Ch. Musquetaire, Cocardas, & Merville II. Timbale is associated with Ch. Caressant, Chimere, Gouveneur, Indescrete, Ch. Megere, and Ch. Tenebreau. All of these dogs measured twelve to fourteen inches and had half-crooked legs, which M. Verrier had by then, decided, was an essential characteristic. He also found that it was very difficult to maintain this type of leg in breedings due to the variations in backgrounds. He felt that another important feature of the Basset was the roundness of the hindquarters and noted that many were becoming slack in this point because amateur breeders did not agree on the importance of this characteristic.

In the 1920s he wrote that most Bassets were crosses between the dogs of Gossalin, le Couteulx, Marchart, and his own, the best coming from crosses between Lane and le Couteulx.

M. Machart of Somme had beautiful animals related to the Lane and le Couteulx lines. The dogs were enormous in type, with large ears, deep dewlaps, and some of grey-badger color. After his death, most of Machart's best dogs were purchased by the Colonel de Champs and M. le Baron de Segonzac.

30

Another resident of Somme was M. Gosselin. His dogs were thought to be products of a cross with le Couteulx, though the type was altered. Unfortunately, he did not keep many records. In an attempt to establish type, he sent a bitch, Sonnaute, to another kennel in the area to be bred. In the account of this mating, no further information about the sire was given. The puppies resembled Machart's lines. They carried a small part of the Couteulx and de Briey characteristics, but were different in type. At the exposition of d'Amiens, there were representatives of M. Gosselin and M. de Guilbon, and the types were established as Sonnaute, Gosselin, and Machart.

At many shows in Paris, M. Hannoire exhibited dogs whose ancestry appeared to go back to M. le Couteulx.

M. Mallart was known as an exhibitor of Briquets d'Artois, but he also bred Bassets. According to Leon Verrier, they were of excellent type.

M. Baillet lived in Villenauxe and later moved to Rouen where he acquired the eagerness of other Basset breeders. He preferred the smaller dogs.

A frequent exhibitor in Paris was M. Segonzac. He showed Chs. Troubadour and Intendante with success, but as he crossed the different sizes and leg structures, his dogs lost the uniformity for which the earlier examples had been known.

Col. de Champs showed several dogs of excellent quality. His Hourvari gained a championship and was a dependable producer. Justice de Fremont was a daughter of Ch. Hourvari. This lovely bitch was owned by le Vicomte de Peufeilhoux who exhibited a few Bassets. Verrier judged her at de Lyon and awarded her the highest honors.

Dr. Leseigner bred some of his le Couteulx bitches to various studs. His dogs were solid, robust, and admirable in the field. Leseigner became well known because he conducted his own hunt, uncoupled eight or ten dogs, and handled them in this manner, himself, to high awards. They would drive any kind of game to be killed. A friend, M. George Pariset, whose dogs had the same origin as Leseigner's, adopted the same manner of field work.

These were the earliest French breeders. Though they kept no records and had little knowledge of genetic theory, they were dedicated in their work. By trial and error, eliminating undesirable producers, they established the individual types for which they became known. Several breeders joined their ranks by the 1920s, but most of the importations in the days when the Basset was introduced to England and America came from dogs that were bred by these gentlemen. If one considers the difficulties of communication and travel in those days, one can better appreciate the results of their efforts.

This brings us to the time of the first imports to Britain and the first recorded Bassets in the United States. The French continued to breed a more diminutive size than did the British and American fanciers. Further French history will be found in a later chapter.

Readers may find the first British Standard and comments upon it, in *British Dogs* written by Hugh Dalziel in 1879, most interesting:

Points of the Basset Hound

Head, skull, eyes, muzzle, and flews	15
Ears	15
Neck, dewlap, chest, and shoulders	10
Fore legs and feet	15
Back, loins, and hind quarters	10
Stern	5
Coat and skin	10
Colour and markings	15
Basset character and symmetry	5
	100

1. To begin with the HEAD, as the most distinguishing part of all breeds. The head of the Basset-hound is most perfect when it closest resembles a Bloodhound's. It is long and narrow, with heavy flews, occiput prominent, "la bosse de la chasse," and forehead wrinkled to the eyes, which should be kind, and show a haw. The general appearance of the head must present high breeding and reposeful dignity, the teeth are small, and the upper jaw sometimes protrudes. This is not a fault, and is called the "bec de lievre."

2. The EARS very long, and when drawn forward folding well over the nose—so long that in hunting they will often actually tread on them; they are set on low, and hang loose in folds like drapery, the ends curling, in texture thin and velvety.

3. The NECK is powerful, with heavy dewlaps. Elbows must not turn out. The chest is deep, full, and framed like a "man-of-war." Body long and low.

4. FORE LEGS short, about 4", and close-fitting to the chest till the crooked knee, from where the wrinkled ankle ends in a massive paw, each toe standing out distinctly.

5. The STIFLES are bent, and the quarters full of muscle, which stands out so that when one looks at the dog from behind, it gives him a round, barrel-like effect. This, with their peculiar, waddling gait, goes a long way towards Basset character—a quality easily recognised by the judge, and as desirable as Terrier character in a Terrier.

6. The STERN is coarse underneath, and carried hound-fashion.

7. The COAT is short, smooth, and fine, and has a gloss on it like that of a racehorse. (To get this appearance, they should be houndgloved, never brushed.) Skin loose and elastic.

8. The COLOUR should be black, white, and tan; the head, shoulders, and quarters a rich tan, and black patches on the back. They are sometimes harepied.

Dalziel's comments follow: "In refusing to accept the above as a correct description of any dog, I take strong exception to the dogma that 'the head is the most distinguishing feature of all breeds.' It is not so in either the Basset or Dachshund, both of which are more distinguished from other hounds by the disproportion between their length and height, than any other feature.

"Whether we take dogs, sheep, or cattle, the head as distinguishing breeds does not go far, but in marking groups, each including many breeds, it comes into prominence. But what are we to say of an animal constructed as Mr. Krehl does the Basset, opining, unintelligible terms, a prodigy from his inner consciousness or abortive imagination?

"What would a English MFH say to a hound whose ears are worth all the rest of his head, including nose? What can anybody say to a dog of any kind, unless it be a fancy toy, whose hide, tail, and ears make nearly half of him and are reckoned at one-seventh more value than all the rest of him, except head and a something undefined, and called character—which latter quality, it is hinted, if not distinctly stated, is only visible to a judge? Certainly a dog 40% nice seems best fitted for the tanyard.

"The fact is, the description is absurd, and can only be accepted as a caricature of any hound; and it seems to me impossible that the Basset Club, or at least, those members of it who desire to use the Basset for his legitimate work, can, on reflection, continue to accept it as the standard by which their hounds shall be judged: even if indisposed to criticise too keenly, they liberally give their own definition to the obscurities of its involved sentences."

These comments are priceless. They continue to apply. Again, I urge you to compare the description with the drawings of Model, Jupiter, Pallas, and Fino de Paris.

Hartshead Red Dust

Roxey and Pearl Cumberland
when they were puppies.

4

The Basset Hound in America up to 1950

THE history of the Basset Hound in America dates back to a surprisingly early period. It is common belief that George Washington's diary indicates that his friend Lafayette sent these hounds to the United States after the Revolution. Undoubtedly, others were brought here in the company of the more prosperous immigrants who enjoyed the sport of the chase.

According to *The American Book of the Dog*, Lord Aylesford imported a brace by Jupiter in 1883 which he used for rabbit hunting on his ranch near Big Springs, Texas. This same year, Mr. Chamberlain purchased Ch. Nemours from George Krehl, Hanover Square, London, and brought him to Lawrence Timson's Maizeland Kennels at Red Hook, N.J. Nemours was whelped March 21, 1883, sired by Ch. Jupiter out of Vivien. The following Spring of 1884, Westminster Kennel Club made a class for the Basset Hound and Ch. Nemours made his bow to the American public, just one year after the Basset Hound Club of England was formed. He was shown at Philadelphia and the National Breeders Show the same year. In 1885, he was first at New Haven, Boston, and New York, gaining his championship at Boston in 1886.

Mr. C. B. Gilbert of New Haven, Conn. Soon followed Mr. Chamberlain's and Lord Aylesford's interest in the breed. He imported Bertrand (by Bourbon) and Canace (by Jupiter) in 1885. From these he bred Jose and Juan.

The first Bassets registered with the American Kennel Club were Bouncer and Countess in 1885. Bouncer: 3234; male; sire, Major; dam, Venus; black, white, and tan; whelped, March 18, 1881; breeder, Pottinger Dorsey, Newmarket, Md.; owner, Colin Cameron, Brickville, Penna. Countess: 3235; bitch; sire, Nero; dam, Lotta; whelped April 1880; breeder, E. S. Krecht, Germany; owner, B. F. Seitner, Dayton, Ohio.

In 1889, Charles Porter of Philadelphia introduced Babette, by Merlin, at the New York show. Porter later adopted the Upland prefix. Cornelius Stevenson's Chasseur, by Farmer, was also shown this same year.

It is interesting to note that, according to the *American Kennel Gazette* of 1916, Bassets were listed as a recognized foreign dog and one of the breeds not eligible for the Winners classes. By 1917, reclassifications were as follows: large dogs, medium dogs, small dogs, and cage dogs. Basset hound-smooth coat and Basset hound-rough coat, were under the heading of medium dogs.

Gerald Livingston made his first importation in 1921. His Kilsyth line became well known near his Georgia plantation and his home at Huntington, Long Island. It was an important contribution to the breed.

In 1925, Erastus Tefft exhibited Simillante at the Westminster show under Walter Reeves in a combined sex class. He, as did Livingston, drafted heavily on the Walhampton pack. In 1925, Musique, another of Tefft's bitches, was Best of Breed over Simillante and Livingston's Pandora and Crescent. Classes were divided this year. Livingston's Vanneur took the Open Dog class, defeating Runt, owned by Tefft, and Vanneur's kennel mates, Rattler and Rector.

During 1925 and 1926, Tefft imported Ch. Lavenham Pippin 422999; Pippin's tricolor niece Walhampton Passion 651344; Ch. Leader, and Baillet's Reveuse. Gerald Livingston imported the Walhampton pack leader, Walhampton Dainty 476679, and Eng. & Am. Ch. Walhampton Andrew. Lewis Thompson imported Eng.

Ch. Amir of Reynalton 943437 and Walhampton Nicety 943438. Both were tricolor. During this period Carl Smith imported the French dogs Baillet's Trompette II and Fr. Ch. Baillet's Corvette, also known, erroneously, as Cornette. He purchased Baillet's Brano from Gerald Livingston who had imported him. Smith's brother, George, and a friend, imported Walhampton Aaron and Walhampton Lively. There were more imports that were not registered with the AKC. Tefft and Smith were among those who had trouble getting the dogs recognized by AKC so they turned to the UKC and the American Field for registration. Caviar 476677, Dalby Hall Drifter 651342, Dalby Hall Diligence 665043, tricolored Walhampton Abbot 988268, Governor, and Tapageur De L'Hermite also came to this country in the 1925–26 period. Consuelo Ford imported the tricolor Ch. Westerby Vintage A339140. Another import of the era was Walhampton Lively, owned by Loren Free of Bainbridge, Ohio, whose kennel was much later known by its Shellbark prefix.

The February 1928 issue of *Time* carried a picture of a Basset puppy, the youngest creature ever to appear on its cover up to that time. The puppy, from Gerald Livingston's Kilsyth kennel, bred from Int. Am. & Eng. Ch. Walhampton Andrew and Walhampton Dainty, helped to bring the breed before the public.

Few were exhibited during this period and for several years to follow. They appeared sporadically at shows. By 1928, the American Kennel Club reclassified Groups, and the Basset was listed as a Sporting dog. At the Atlantic City show, Walhampton Linguist was Best of Breed over kennelmates, Brookmead Merchant, Mixer, Medley, Mindful, and Minnow, all owned by Mrs. G. Sloane of Locust Valley, Long Island, N.Y. Winners gained three points, and Linguist gained his championship in the same year. The following year, the same entries, plus Brookmead Mullet, Mollie, and Walhampton Alice, all owned by the Brookmead kennels, were the only Bassets at several eastern shows including Westminster where Mixer captured the honors. W. Fritz introduced Smith's True Boy at the Detroit show. S. A. Mitchell, of Oyster Bay, N.Y., offered a litter for sale. Walhampton Alice, Brookmead Mixer, Medley, and Mullet gained their championships in 1929.

About this time, the Basset was selected for use in experiments dealing with inheritance of coat coloring. A few new names began to appear. F. A. Ostendorf exhibited his Broadaxe and Blaze in Ohio. H. O. Putnam entered Trompette Chief in the same area. At Detroit, in 1929, the following were seen: G. W. King's Maple Drive Concertone, Carmelita (Walhampton Aaron ex King's Patches) dam of the first Field Champion, and Bugler. W. Fritz entered King's Fan All, Baillet's Trompette II, and Maple Drive Maxim (Walhampton Aaron ex Corvette). E. Krahn exhibited Carry on Michigan, and H. L. Cotton showed Peggy Leach (Ch. Walhampton Andrew ex Belle of Kilsyth).

The following year Fritz purchased Carry on Michigan. Carl Nottke showed his puppy bitch called Nottke's Bonnett.

Carl Smith took over the Starridge pack in 1930. Names connected with this pack are Smith's Yankee Lad, Lavinham Pippin, Walhampton Passion, and Woelk's Brigadier.

Entries continued to be small and scattered. At most shows, all entries were from one kennel. Many championships were gained in this manner. Westminster had no representatives of the breed at the 1930 show. In 1931 and 1932, Marvey's Sam, owned by W. H. Attwood, was the only entry. G. M. Livingston's Kilsyth Broker was Best of Breed over his kennelmates, Bramble and Famous, in 1933. None were entered in 1934. At other shows in this era, a few names appeared. The Cheston Kennels showed Dalby Hall Dormouse, Kilsyth Freddy, and Kilsyth Felix at Boston. J. F. Freeland entered his Freeland's Tarzan, Judy, Ginger, and Dinah at Baltimore. In Pennsylvania, Mrs. W. N. Ely exhibited Mrs. Ely Binki and Kilsyth Bracelet. The Irish Hills prefix appeared at Flint, Michigan. At Delaware County, Pennsylvania, W. P. Klapp, of Radnor, Penna., showed Klapp's Queen, Joy, and Mable, and the Stockford Kennels exhibited Diamond Rosebank. Klapp entered Rebecca at Devon, Penna., showing against Lewis Thompson's Amir of Reynalton, Stanco Joan, and Stanco Koto, and the Stockford Kennel's Kilsyth Bracelet. Rebecca 784043 gained her championship in 1934.

There was a noticeable rise in activity between 1935 and 1940. Ownership was changed on several dogs. In 1935, no Bassets were entered at Westminster or Chicago, which was not yet known as International. Carl Nottke showed Smith's Red Powder, Maple Drive Perk, and Nottke's Capaneus who was sold to B. F. Chaney

Walhampton Lively, English import owned by Loren Free.

Ch. Mon. Philippe of Greenly Hall, result of one of the early breedings by the Fogelsons, of Maple Drive Marlin and Coquette of Greenly Hall.

that year. Irish Hill's Candidate and Senator, plus Jigilo's Blondy were exhibited by W. Fritz. Thompson's entries were Stanco Koto, Weedy, Dagget, and Chuck. Maple Drive Scorch Smith was shown by T. E. Seavey, and Ann Levy brought out Irish Hills Troubadour. Al's Accurate, Woelk's Beauty and Judy, Al's Famous, Ancient, and Chief of the North, plus Rentschler's Colonel were some of the notable dogs shown by Alfred Kannowski. Emil and Effie Seitz appeared with Hillcrest Poyntair. Carmon Klink showed Maple Drive Rhythm, Dare Devil Babe, Raven Duke, and Ring Leader. Roy Smith began exhibiting Michigan Maestro. O. A. Grigsby had Nottke's Venus. This was the year that Stanco Liz was whelped.

Fanciers had begun to take a keener interest in serious breeding. 1936 saw the formation of the Basset Hound Club of America. The group of organizers was comprised of the Alfred Bissells, B. F. Chaney, Harold Frazee, William Fritz, George Gregg, Carmon Klink, Alfred Kannowski, W. P. Klapp, Jr., James Lee, Ann Levy, Gerald Livingston, Carl Nottke, Emil Seitz, and Lewis Thompson. Appearances at shows were still infrequent. None at all were entered at Westminster in 1936.

In 1937, Kilsyth Frills took Westminster's Best of Breed over seven kennelmates. At Boston, A. R. MacDonald exhibited Smith's Armac Auldscout. Maple Drive Maxim, now owned by F. J. Brookhiser, took a Group placing. Smith's Buena and Woelk's Mike were exhibited by J. Chenoweth in Michigan, and G. B. Woods appeared in St. Louis, Missouri with Michigan Don.

The Basset Hound Club of America held the first trial in the United States at Hastings, Michigan, in 1937. Entered were: Hillcrest Charley Boy, Hillcrest Peggy, Woelk's Lady Peterson, Taylor's White Collar, and the Michigan Maestro. Emil and Effie Seitz had adopted the Hillcrest prefix which was later changed to Hartshead. Theirs was an important contribution to the American bloodline. Hillcrest Peggy became the first Field Champion.

Best of Breed at Westminster went to B. Lippincott's Raffer A170434 in 1938. The only other entry was his Fallowfield Thunderer. Detroit had a large entry and five points went to Agawa Judy owned by H. W. Langrill. The Harold Fogelsons came forth with Venus Black Mischief and Peg O' My Heart. They were to become famous under the kennel name of Greenly Hall. Kannowski entered Al's Empress, Bess, and Chief Topic. Nottke showed his Red Gracious and Al's Ancient. Grigsby exhibited Northwood's Babe and

40

Nottke's Venus. Two new exhibitors appeared: H. D. Abbot, showing Smith's Red Actor at Cincinnati, Ohio, and T. C. Brown, with Boots at Chattanooga, Tenn. J. E. Lee took an interest in showing Wanadoga Wallingford in the Michigan area as did the Seitz's with their new entries Hillcrest Fryball and Belle of Hillcrest. In the East, Livingston exhibited Kilsyth Frills and Freckles, while the Thompsons entered Stanco Flit, Chuck, Toby, Cocoa, and Molly of Lincroft. Fred Bayliss brought the famous Chausseur and Edwina. Edwina and her sister, Stanco Liz, were daughters of Walhampton Nicety ex Reddy II (Reddy I ex Kilsyth Brevity). Chausseur was a son of Maple Drive Maxim ex Topsy Edwina and Chausseur produced Bijou Pearl, Rhinestone, and Moonstone of Banbury, and Kiernan's Mitz. Pearl was the dam of Pepper Comstock. Bred to Sears Saratoga, Stanco Liz produced Roxey, Bell, and Pearl Cumberland for her owner Charles Sears. Maygold Bebe and Bijou Amethyst of Banbury were her offspring by Kilsyth Banker. All of these dogs are pillars of the breed as you will see by referring to the production chart of Walhampton Nicety.

A field trial was held at Kimberton, Penna., in 1938. Note that the following were the same entries that were being shown: Stanco Chuck, Koto, and Dagget, Hillcrest Peggy, Chausseur, Maple Drive Trude, and Queen Ruby. Dr. J. P. Honey, of Danville, Ill., ran his dogs at the Michigan trial and began to take a keen interest in both the show and the field under the Honey prefix.

Production Chart of Walhampton Nicety

The following is a partial list of the offspring of Walhampton Nicety (Walhampton Grazier ex Walhampton Nicknack) when bred to the studs Eng. Ch. Amir of Reynalton (Amant ex Dignity of Lohair) and Ch. Reddy II (Reddy I ex Kilsyth Brevity).

Offspring of Nicety & Amir	*Grandchildren*
Music of Woodleigh	Fallowfield Reaper (ex Walhampton Abbott)
	Fallowfield Contralto (ex Walhampton Abbott)

Fallowfield Thunderer (ex Walhampton Abbott)
Stockford Lady (ex Walhampton Abbott)

Al's Chief of Geneseo

Honey Girl of Geneseo (ex Wally)
Bard of Geneseo
Al's Janet (ex Woelk's Beauty)
Hess's Bold Buccaneer
Al's Gretchen (ex Woelk's Beauty)
Hess's Dignity of Devonshire (ex Wally)
Al's Chief Topic (ex Snitzel)
Al's Freda (ex Al's Accurate)

Offspring of Nicety & Reddy II	*Grandchildren*
Edwina	Bijou Pearl of Banbury (ex Chasseur) Bijou Rhinestone of Banbury (ex Chasseur) Bijou Moonstone of Banbury (ex Chasseur) Kiernan's Mitz (ex Chasseur) Bijou Sapphire of Banbury (ex Chasseur)
Stanco Liz	Roxey Cumberland (ex Sears Saratoga) Bell Cumberland (ex Sears Saratoga) Pearl Cumberland (ex Sears Saratoga) Maygold Bebe (ex Kilsyth Banker) Bijou Amethyst of Banbury (ex Kilsyth Banker)

Nicety's Grandchildren and Some of Their Get

Fallowfield Reaper

Hartshead Pepper, Hartshead Masked Knight, Hartshead Duchess, Hartshead Huntsman, Hartshead Firegirl

Fallowfield Contralto

Ben's Black King

Fallowfield Thunderer

Pearl, Malone

Honey Girl of Geneseo

Red Musette of Belbay, Neleigh's Ada, Eingle's Red Tim, Lady Belle, Freckles of Belbay, Belbay Saddler

Roxey Cumberland

Arbter's Rose, Dapple Queen, The Bricker's Belle, Engle's Cumberland Diana, Greer's Cumberland Dainty, Blue Ticked York

Bijou Sapphire of Banbury

Bijou Rutile of Banbury

Bijou Rhinestone of Banbury

Basso of Banbury

Hess's Dignity of Devonshire

Reisers's Tusc-o-Sport

Pearl Cumberland

Bricker's Betty, Rex Cumberland

Al's Chief Topic

Al's Bonnie Girl

43

Kiernan's Mitz

Melancholy Baby, Simone of Greenly Hall, Duchess of Greenly Hall

New names appearing in 1938 were: J. R. Bream, F. J. Brookhiser's Esseff Drivette, G. R. Davis with Smith's Princess Royal and Big Wager, all in the New York area. In South Carolina, J. W. Beckman and M. C. Crowder showed Peco Black Ranger and Smith's Pennellas. T. W. Landskroener exhibited Pensfield Bess in New Jersey. An important name to appear was Friar of Woodleigh owned by F. B. Carter of Devon, Mass. H. W. Langro's Agawa Judy gained her championship in 1938.

There were 134 stud book registrations in 1939. By 1940, these registrations were up to 241. Irish Hills Senator, owned by James E. Lee of Battle Creek, Mich., gained his field title. He was the second Field Champion; the first male. Sixty hounds were run at this trial in Pottersville, New Jersey. Besides Senator, entries were: Mrs. A. W. Porter's Stockford Duke, James S. Jones's Westerby Dreadnought, L. Thompson's Stanco Boy, Dagget, Chuck, and Koto, Consuelo Ford's Bijou Pearl of Banbury, Bijou Opal of Banbury, Livingston's Kilsyth Baronet and Bright, Fred Bayliss's Lasha, and Al Michel's Queen. Queen took first in the all-age bitch class, and Al was an enthusiastic breeder for the next twenty years. A stake was introduced for packs comprised of three couples. Consuelo Ford offered the Banbury Cross Challenge Cup won by the Brandywine Bassets of Mary Mather's kennel. At Hastings, Mich., Dr. J. P. Honey's Maple Drive Marlin defeated his Honey's Andy, Seitz's Ch. Hillcrest Charley Boy, Roy Smith's Michigan Maestro, and Nottke's Ajax in a combined-sex all-age class.

Stud book registrations were 214 in 1941. The breed had only one representative at Westminster, Mrs. E. W. Mile's Belle Chanson of Neverland. Bassets appeared for the first time at the Chicago International show. Carl Nottke's Harvey Prince was Best of Breed over the Fogelson's Sir Guy and Promise of Greenly Hall, and J. E. Lee's Ojibwa of Wanadoga and Nottke's Venus. The Fogelson's campaigned under their Greenly Hall prefix, showing Glamour Girl, Count, Promise, Baron, Serenade, and Sir Guy. C. V. Bickelman purchased Count and entered him at Bucks County, Penna., together with his Bick's Luck, Parnee's Jasper, and Bassette's Royal Wager. Talla's Black Duke of Valhalla was shown at Ravenna, Ohio. M. A. Vance bought Bugle Ann of Greenly Hall which was exhibited at Dayton, Ohio. Sir Rusty Boy, owned by R. H. Beckman, was at Syracuse, N.Y.; C. J Carr's Red Bear was at eastern Ohio shows; and H. R. Morrison showed Prancer of Gogo in western Pennsylvania. Alf Kannowski's Al's Chief Topic and Fogelson's Glamour Girl of Greenly Hall were the only entries at Detroit. In the Delaware area, Porters showed their Upland Master, Fancy, and Fresh. Another important dog was whelped this year, Samuel Smith's Roxey of Cumberland.

This is the year that Leslie Kelly, of Alexandria, Penna., introduced his Bassets to the ring. Among them were Kelly's Chief Hareman, Kelly's Kanjur, Kelly's Model Huntress, and Smith's Pantasota. Kelly later adopted the Neleigh and Belbay prefixes which gained fame. Kelly's Chief Hareman had gained his championship by Fall. Promise of Greenly Hall was also finished about the same time.

The war severely curtailed extensive travel in 1942. Only Upland Fresh, Master, Topsy, Beauty, Tattler, and Fancy from the Porters' kennels were shown at Westminster in a combined-sex class. Fresh was Best of Breed for five points. Ch. Promise of Greenly Hall, Ch. Duchess of Greenly Hall, plus W. A. Davis's Davis King and Queen were at International. The Banbury Bassets of Consuelo Ford were entered at Winchester and E. Newcomb showed Schlegel's Conesus at Rochester, N.Y. There were 202 stud book registrations.

The following year, 1943, the Fogelsons joined the Upland entries at Westminster. Ch. Promise of Greenly Hall was Best of Breed. Their Duchess was also entered against Porter's Upland Spot, Sue, Spook, Laff, Lucky, Fred, and Mike who was Best of Winners. Duchess appeared later that year at Plainfield, N.J., shown by her new owners, Mr. & Mrs. M. Lynwood Walton who became well-known through the years for their Lyn-Mar Acres line. The Upland dogs were victorious over Duchess at Bryn Mawr and Devon, Penna. She was shown to her championship in Wisconsin, Indiana, and Illinois. Ch. Promise of Greenly Hall took the high honors at Westminster again in 1944.

In 1946, Ch. Duchess of Greenly Hall was Best of Breed at this show. The Waltons had adopted the Lyn-Mar prefix and showed Joliecoeur, Future, and Maitri of Lyn-Mar. The Belbay kennel of

Hartshead Debutante, Hartshead Blackboy, Hartshead Melodie, Hartshead Duchess, and Hartshead Beauty.

Ch. Anthony of St. Hubert, first Basset to go Best in Show; owner-breeder, Mark Washbond.

46

Leslie Kelly was represented by Envy, Ginger, Bubbles Debut, and Model Huntress who took the points.

More serious breeders joined the ranks as interest in the breed continued to grow. One of these fanciers was Mark Washbond who purchased Jacqueson of St. Hubert from the Fogelsons in 1946. He later purchased Rossita of Greenly Hall. From Ch. Duke of Greenly Hall and Rossita he produced Ch. Anthony of St. Hubert. Tony was brought out in May of 1949. By September he had gained his championship with a Group I already on his record. It must be remembered that judges were still hesitant about their evaluation of the Basset because entries were still small and scattered. Something about this dog, however, caught their fancy, and they carried him to fame. He was seldom defeated as a Special and gained many Group Firsts. In 1952 he brought glory to the breed by capturing the first Basset Best in Show in the country at the Egyptian Kennel Club show. Mark attained his goal of producing approximately one litter a year and finishing one of each sex from each litter. He later dropped from competition, as did many other serious fanciers, when too many unconscientious breeders began commercializing at the expense of better breedings.

Samuel J. Smith of New Cumberland, Penna., became an active breeder in this period. He owned Roxey and Pearl Cumberland out of Stanco Liz ex Sears Saratoga, Peg Cumberland (Ch. Westerby Vintage ex Bijou Pearl of Banbury), Pepper Comstock, out of the same breeding, Sailor Comstock and his son, Prince Comstock, out of Bell Cumberland, a sister to Roxey and Pearl. Pepper was the dam of Duke of Greenhill. In the early days Sam Smith showed his dogs as well as ran them in the trials. The Cumberland type was very much like the Basset of the 1960s, playing an important part in American bloodlines.

In 1946, Norwood Engle purchased Dapple Queen from Smith. She was a red-and-white out of Roxey and Peg Cumberland. Queen was bred to Darwin's General, a son of Hartshead Pepper and Ch. Beryl of Lyn-Mar Acres. The litter consisted of five females and one male. The male died at the age of eight months. Engle's Peg, Lady, and Mitz were sold, Patsy and Belle were kept. He then purchased Belbay Xtra Handsome (Ch. Belbay Design ex Ch. Belbay Treasure), and with the help of Frank and Dorothy Hardy, showed him to his championship. Then Engle, and a friend, Dr. Hughes, repurchased

Engle's Peg and bred her to Handsome. In 1952, this mating produced two males and two females which bore the prefix of En-Hu derived from the first two letters of both owners' names. One male, Reddy of En-Hu, was sold to Ruth Turner in California; the other, Sport of En-Hu, went to Mr. Hatton in Kansas. Both gained their championships. Reddy died in 1961. Jill of En-Hu was sold to Dr. Mahon of New Cumberland, Penna. Although her quality was as high as the others, her new owner showed her only once, preferring to keep her as a pet. In 1954, Chris Teeter bought Fanny of En-Hu, the first bitch in his kennel. Fanny gained her championship and fame as the dam of a long line of champions. Thinking Peg and Handsome could be bred again, all of the puppies had been sold. However, Peg died during her next whelping and all the puppies were lost. Her name will live on through the bloodlines of her famous offspring. Her sister, Patsy, was bred to Handsome and produced Ch. Engle's Primrose Patsy. Dr. Mahon was persuaded to breed Jill of En-Hu to Engle's Black Jack. The two female puppies, named Engle's Jenny of Nor-Mil and Engle's Jill of Nor-Mil, were sold to Chris Teeter. One of the males, En-Hu's Tick On, went to the western part of the country. Others in the Engle kennel were Rose M, litter mate to Al Michel's Trailer M, and Engle's Miss Mitzie, dam of Ch. Tulpehocken Trailer and granddam of Field Chs. Tulpehocken Til and Hepsy. There are twenty-seven field champions bearing the name of Engle breedings up to this time.

During the year 1946, three exhibitors appeared with the first entries at California shows. J. W. Robinson exhibited Robinson's Red Bird, Robinson's Gold Nugget, Black Knight, and the English imports Maytime, Moonlight and Maytime the Pudding. He had the only entries at Santa Cruz, Vallejo, and San Rafael. At Harbor Cities he had a competitor in the puppy class where A. Morris showed Belbay Quintina. Grace Greenburg of Camarillo, adopting the Belleau prefix, entered Belleau Adjutant, Belleau Jet, Kelly's Patches, Parker's Hi Watha, Neleigh's Skippy, sister to Neleigh's Pennsylvania Lady, and Belleau's Apagliacci. She had the only entries at Ventura.

During this year, Al Michel was showing Ben's Black King. Kelly showed Butz's Yankee Boy, Belbay Model Huntress, Kanjur, Envy, Ginger, Quaint, and Qualitee of Belbay. Fogelson's representative was Coquette of Greenly Hall. The Fowlers showed Buckeye Bill's

Ch. Belbay Triumph.

Ch. Belbay Xtra Handsome.

```
                                                                Smith's Red Pathfinder
                                        Ch. Kelly's Chief Hareman
                        Ch. Butz's Yankee Boy                   Smith's Pantasota

                                        Kelly's Jet Girl        Smith's Major Le Havre

          Ch. Belbay Design                                     Woelk's Pebble

                                        Duke of Blackhawk       Maple Drive Trimmer

                Pattern of Belbay                               Ch. Lady Cinderella
Ch. Belbay Xtra Handsome                                        Ch. Kelly's Chief Hareman
Ch. Belbay Chevalier            Neleigh's Pennsylvania Lady
Ch. Mr. Cyclops of Belbay                                       Neleigh's Ada
Belbay Cloud
                                                                Smith's Red Pathfinder
                                        Ch. Kelly's Chief Hareman
                        Ch. Butz's Yankee Boy                   Smith's Pantasota

                                        Kelly's Jet Girl        Smith's Major Le Havre

          Ch. Belbay Treasure                                   Woelk's Pebble

                                        Ch. Kelly's Chief Hareman   Smith's Red Pathfinder

                Neleigh's Pennsylvania Lady                     Smith's Pantasota

                                        Neleigh's Ada           Bard of Geneseo

                                                                Honey Girl of Geneseo
```

Ch. Belbay Design and Ch. Belbay Winning Look were brother and sister

Ch. Belbay Treasure and Ch. Belbay Triumph were brother and sister

Tomboy Tootsie and Victory Queen, Fowler's Franco, and Glenmaire's Red Bear Tongue. Waltons entered Maitri of Lyn-Mar (dam of Ch. Lyn-Mar's Clown), Luvlee, and Queen-O-Trump. A dog named Luke, owned by the Barabon kennels, appeared in Seattle, Wash. Topsy of Westerfield and Thompson's Trailer were shown by the Thompsons while R. Bossard exhibited Thompson's Helper. Championships were gained by H. R. Morrison's Braggelonne of Belbay, Fowler's Buckeye Bill's Victory Queen, Fowler's Franco, and Buckeye Bill's Tomboy Tootsie, Kelly's Butz's Yankee Boy, Envy of Belbay, and Kelly's Kanjur.

In 1947, Ch. Braggelonne of Belbay was Best of Breed at Westminster. Best of Opposite Sex went to Ch. Envy of Belbay. Hartshead Pepper took the points in a combined class of dogs and bitches including Soubrette of Lyn-Mar, Belbay Treasure, Hartshead Ginger, Belbay Triumph, Talmai, Model Huntress, Buckeye Bill's Victory Toddles, Thompson's Ginger and Trailer, Chanson of Lyn-Mar, and Al's Chief Topic.

During this year the Lyn-Mar kennels covered the shows in the vicinity of New Jersey and eastern Pennsylvania. Ira Shoop showed in Pennsylvania, as did Kelly with the Belbay breedings and E. W. Graham bearing the Stregraham prefix. One of this line was sent to J. Barringer in the Chicago area. At Louisville, Ky., C. S. Furio appeared with Shaw's Corky. In Michigan, R. F. Smith's Major and Queen Elizabeth competed with Melancholy Baby, all owned by Roy Smith. R. L. Wilson entered Davis King, Trim's Joy, Ruppert's Royal Ace, Forester of Belbay, and Belbay Casandra at Bremerton, Washington.

In California, J. W. Robinson and Grace Greenburg were joined by M. Carney who had purchased Belleau's Apagliacci, and Cordelia Skapinski (Jensen) with Gun Major of Belleau.

During this year, Maitri of Lyn-Mar, Belbay Triumph, Hartshead Pepper, Stregraham's Patricia, and Robinson's Red Bird gained their championships.

This was also the year that Johnny Bose's name began to appear. Johnny's primary interest was in the field. Often missed is the fact that his Bose's Princess Patty was bred to Al Michel's Ben's Black King, producing Webb's Black Amanda, dam of Chs. Siefenjagenheim Lazy Bones, Dominoe, Calico, and Gremlin, all bearing the same prefix. Amanda's sister, Antoinette, was bred to the son of their brother, Adam. A female of this litter, Braun's Hootn' Annie, was the dam of Ch. Braun's Humpty Dumpty CD and behind other champions in the Braun's kennel.

Jean Sanger Look became interested in the breed at this time. She was the first to exhibit Bassets in North Carolina. Residing in Greensboro, Mrs. Look became an ardent fancier producing a long line of champions as well as attending the trials. Her name gave her an ideal prefix. Hers is an interesting breeding pattern to study. Four matings of Ch. Andre of Greenly Hall and Ch. Belbay Winning Look, sister of Belbay Design, produced Ch. Look's Choice, Pensive, Agreeable, Winning Streak, Handsome, Nice, and Bashful. All but Look's Bashful gained their championships.

Ch. Look's Choice sired Champions Millvan's Design, Millvan's Blondie, Millvan's Blissful, Millvan's Cherub, Jeffery of Forest Bay, Antique's Little Nutmeg, Byron of Brookville, Monsieur Beaucoup, and Best in Show-winning Long View Acres Blaze By.

Ch. Look's Handsome produced Ch. Rockingham Cooper King when bred to Rockingham Red out of Ch. Belbay Winning Look ex Ch. Belbay Triumph. He also sired Ch. Anastasia Hubertus, Ch. Miss Murgatroid of Elvalin, and Ch. Eulenspiegel's Deb Crescent.

Ch. Look's Pensive's offspring were Ch. Reluctant Rachel of Elvalin and Ch. Kathenette of Elvalin. Look's Bashful was bred to Ch. Millvan's Casper and produced Ch. Look's Good of Pioneer. Her offspring by Ch. Belbay Triumph were Chs. Look's Special, Smooth, and Fancy. She was also the dam of Ch. Hartshead Micky when bred to Ch. Hartshead Top Hit. Triumph and Belbay Winning Look produced Ch. Edelham's Queen Bess, Rockingham Red, and Rockingham Echoe.

Ch. Belbay Design and Ch. Belbay Winning Look were both out of Ch. Butz's Yankee Boy ex Pattern of Belbay. Yankee Boy was bred to Neleigh's Pennsylvania Lady when he sired Ch. Belbay Treasure and Ch. Belbay Triumph, purchased at the age of three by Jean Look. Triumph succumbed to cancer of the liver in 1957, at the age of ten years. This red-and-white dog had been one of the first Bassets handled by Dorothy Hardy. Winning Look died the following year of kidney failure.

Most of the aforementioned dogs were shown in the 1950s. Dr. and Mrs. Vincent Nardiello owned Choice who gained approximately 100 Best of Breed awards. The Nardiellos adopted the Mill-

51

van kennel name and had such notables as the Best in Show-winning Ch. Millvan's Deacon. The Elvalin prefix was used by Elva and Franklin Heckler. Mrs. Heckler carried on after the death of her husband in 1956. The Hubertus name, of course, belonged to the kennel of Frank and Dorothy Hardy who have contributed so much to the breed.

Late in 1947, Mrs. Walter P. Houchin took a serious interest in the breed. She obtained Belleau Jet of Little Gate from Mrs. Walter Monroe, who had brought her from the Belleau kennels of Mrs. Greenburg. All three ladies were active in Dachshunds. Mrs. Monroe's kennel prefix was Little Gate. Jet had been whelped in 1946, sired by Hess's Drum Major by Belleau Jet. The Houchins adopted the kennel name Jet Foret when they moved to New Lennox, Ill., in 1944, describing the large trees (black forest) surrounding their home. Millie's interest in the breed continued to rise. She was secretary-treasurer of the Basset Hound Club of America from 1954 to 1957 and became a breeder-judge.

Walter and Marjorie Brandt became interested in the breed in 1947. They purchased French Belle in Woonsocket, R.I., and hunted her for the following thirteen years. Soon after acquiring Belle, their affection for the breed prompted them to obtain Lulu's Patches and Lulu's Red from Matthew Moore of Windber, Penna. These litter brothers were out of Ridenhour's Sport ex Lulu Saddler. The Brandts were the pioneers of Bassets in Obedience. Though the instructor at the training club was not very encouraging, the dogs did respond to the work. Red was the first Basset to receive a Companion Dog degree, soon followed by Patches, which was the second. Meantime, the Bench Show beckoned. Patches went on to a CDX and a championship, the first Basset in the country to hold all three titles. Lulu's Red was struck by a car while driving a rabbit across a road. The Brandts became serious breeders, gaining championships, obedience titles, and hunting. Walter was another to become a breeder-judge. His death in 1963 was mourned by fanciers throughout the country.

Charles E. Gillespie fell in love with his Grandfather's Basset in his early days in Western Pennsylvania. He and his wife, Priscilla, began raising Bassets in 1948. Their kennel name, Hunting Horn, has become well known. Among their first dogs were Ch. Duff of Red House, purchased from Ira Shoop, and Ch. Belle of Scabbard

Ch. Look's Choice.

Ch. Look's Winning Streak.

Look's Bashful.

Ch. Look's Handsome.

53

raised by Isabel Holden. Belle was a litter sister of Ch. Slowpoke Hubertus out of Ch. Hartshead Pepper ex Abigail of Woodleigh. She was bred to Ch. Lyn-Mar's Clown producing Hunting Horn Burma.

Mrs. Elizabeth Streeter, who later became well known for her Skycastle dogs, purchased her first Basset, Regiomontanues, sired by Bijou Onyx. She lived in New York at that time.

The Westminster entry in 1948 included Darwin's Leander and Katrinka, Lyn-Mar's Glamour, Lyn-Mar's Charm, Lyn-Mar's Joliecoeur, Belbay Aaron and Treasure, Kilsyth Longfellow and Lucky, and Ira Shoop's Ch. Hartshead Pepper which took Best of Breed. Belbay Treasure gained her championship that year. Only eight males and females were entered in a combined stake at the trial in Jackson, Michigan, with Snowfall Shorty, Queen Elizabeth, and Melancholy Baby placing in that order.

In 1949, there were seven dogs and two bitches under Walter Reeves at Westminster. Ch. Hartshead Pepper repeated his win of the year before. Ch. Belbay Treasure was Best of Opposite Sex. Best of Winners went to Belbay Design, and Derbydach's Belle de Beaupre took the points in bitches. At the Brighton, Mich., trial, Snowfall Shorty, Trigger Triumph, Lucky Boy, Hartshead Bold Venture, and R. F. Smith's Major were run in all-age dogs, placing in the order mentioned. All-age bitches were Queen Elizabeth, Snowfall Sadie, Hartshead Melanie, Hartshead Peggy Again, and Meyer's Black Queen. The Dog Stakes at Dubois, Penna., in October were: Shebe's Mingo, Trigger Triumph, Lucky Boy, Graham's Ring, and Hartshead Bold Venture. Bitches were: Graham's Jill, Melancholy Baby, Shebe's Lady, Hartshead Melanie, and Hartshead Jet.

This brings us to the close of the first half of the 1900s when most fanciers participated in both show and field endeavors. Interest had steadily grown. New names appeared each year. One must keep in mind that this information was compiled from records of activities. It must be presumed that there were others attracted to the breed who did not enter into competition. One does have perceivable data, however, on the progress of the principal dogs and breeders who were the foundation of the American bloodlines.

5

The Basset Hound
in America after 1950

POPULARITY of the Basset began to grow by leaps and bounds. By the latter part of the decade, he was doomed to become a celebrity. I say, "doomed," because once a breed becomes so attractive that there is a great demand for it, there are those who breed for quantity, to supply this demand, with little thought for quality. Further degeneration is brought about by those who breed-up certain "winning traits" to the point of overexaggeration, caring nothing for utility. Others, desiring to have "the fastest dog at the trial," breed for lighter bone and more height, ignoring the fact that the dog was intended to be a *slow trailer*. Fortunately for the breed, there remain the sincere enthusiasts who concentrate their efforts to produce *good* Bassets that are both beautiful and useful.

In the Northwest, perhaps Richard and Evelyn Bassett are the best known of the pioneers. In 1950, they purchased Ch. Jones's Virginia Jim and Jones's Virginia Jean. Both of these dogs were bred by Franklin W. Jones of Fairfax, Va., from his Upland stock. Jim was entered in Obedience, eventually at a trial, and in conformation.

Ch. Fanny of En-Hu.

Ch. Bassett's Josephine, Ch. Mattie's Quercus C.D., and Ch. Bassett's Jody.

He gained his CD, the third Basset in the country to do so, but had no competition in conformation at his first nine shows. He was bred to Bonny's Cissy Sue (Hartshead and Greenly Hall bloodlines) and produced the grand old dog, Ch. Mattie's Quercus CD, the first Basset on the West Coast to capture a Hound Group. He later became the third in the country to go Best in Show. Quercus sired thirteen champions and was grandsire to many more. Jean was bred to Sir Hubert II, a double grandson of Ch. Hartshead Pepper, producing Ch. Bassett's Jody and Josephine. Among Jody's offspring were Ch. Bassett's Miss Wrinkles, dam of eight champions, and Ch. Bassett's Eloise, who was sold to Jean Dudley. Josephine was the dam of Ch. Bassett's Roustabout, who, upon retirement in 1961, had won seven Best in Show awards, and thirty-four Hound Group Firsts. By this time, Rousty had sired eight champions. In 1955, the Bassetts imported Rossingham Barrister who gained his championship in 1957 and was the sire of twenty champions.

Another dedicated enthusiast joined the breed in 1950, though he had been in "dogs" with his father, Ed, since 1924. John Eylander acquired Danny Boy from the Pine Gables kennels of Gerald and Leona Harding. He bought and finished Ch. Etalle of St. Hubert, owned Am. & Can. Ch. Hoosier Linda's Bonnie and Ch. Siefenjagenheim Calamity. Among his field champions were Bose's Initiative, Shellbark's Michie, Ed's Jo Jo, Olson's Mitzie, Little Lady Tammy, and Max's Happy Hunter. Ch. Eylander's Red Rose was sold to Milton Stringer of Algonac, Mich. "Rosie" was the dam of Am. & Can. Ch. Whistle Down's Commando and other fine dogs. Though, in time, both Ed and John devoted most of their efforts to field work, John continued to breed for the points desirable in the show ring believing that the show and field dog should be of one and the same quality. The present Standard was approved during his term as President of the Basset Hound Club of America and the groundwork was laid for Field Trial rules for Bassets.

The Lyn-Mar name had risen to great heights by now. Ch. Lyn-Mar's Clown (Kilsyth Lucky ex Ch. Maitri of Lyn-Mar) was Best of Breed at Westminster in 1950–1953.

In 1950 and 1951, the trials were followed by the entries of the Hartshead kennel, Greenly Hall, Roy Smith, Claude Smith, Johnny Bose, Al Michel, Norwood Engle, Meyers, Snowfall kennel, and the Tulpehocken kennel.

Am. and Can. Ch. Bassett's Roustabout with owner-handler, Richard Bassett, under judge, Percy Roberts.

Ch. Notrenom's Encore Rebel (Am. & Can. Ch. Bassett's Roustabout ex Bassett's Bagatelle) with owner, breeder and handler Richard E. Bassett. At five years of age, Rebel has won 36 Best of Breeds and 10 Hound Group firsts.

By 1952, a Dachshund breeder, Doris Hurry, was so impressed with Ch. Lyn-Mar's Clown that she purchased one of his daughters, Lyn-Mar Intrigue, who gained her championship by the time she was a year old. Mrs. Hurry adopted the Blue Hill prefix. She is well-known for her home-bred champions, Miss Randolph, Fire Cracker, Carosel (who produced four champions in one litter), Daiquiri, Senator, Buccaneer, Ivy, Guzzler, and Intoxication, all bearing the Blue Hill name. American & Canadian championships were gained by Boozer of Blue Hill CD, and Cherry Blossom of Blue Hill, while the Canadian titles went to Imperial and Ivan who had five Best in Shows in Canada. Am. & Can. Ch. Boozer of Blue Hill was purchased as a young dog by the Kenneth Eldriges of Reading, Mass. Ken took an interest in conformation while Louise preferred Obedience work. Boozer was the first Basset to gain an Obedience title in both the United States and Canada as well as a championship. His son, Ch. Guzzler of Blue Hill sired Ch. Aberjona of Great Oak, the kennel name adopted by the Eldridges. Perhaps the most notable was Doris's Ch. Ike of Blue Hill. He was the first male Basset to gain a Bermuda championship; the first to carry a Bermuda, Canadian, & American title. Ike captured a Best in Show before he was a year old at the Basset Hound Club of Canada's first Specialty in 1961. Bred and handled by Doris, owned by her daughter, Barbara, Ike was the product of a mating of Ch. The Ring's Ali Baba ex Am. & Can. Ch. Cherry Blossom of Blue Hill.

In California, Ruth Turner had become interested in Bassets and purchased Reddy of En-Hu from Norwood Engle. Paul Nelson had also joined the Mac Carlisles, Bill Morris, and Cordelia Skapinski in that area.

The Brandts, Doris Hurry, and the Frank Hardys were joined in the East by the Joseph Kulpers, Isabel Holden, Janet Yontz, Gladys Clement, Jeanne Millett, Dr. Pierre Morand, and Mrs. L. P. Gillespie.

Ruth and Helen Fox, Harry Gill, Lester Webb, and the John Siefens became Midwest breeders in this period.

Webb's Black Amanda was purchased by the Siefens. She was out of the Johnny Bose litter of Ben's Black King ex Bose's Princess Patty. Siefen bred Amanda to Ch. Lyn-Mar's Clown (Kilsyth Lucky ex Ch. Maitri of Lyn-Mar). From these matings came such dogs as

59

Am., Can., and Ber. Ch. Ike of Blue Hill, with breeder, Doris Hurry; owned by Barbara Hurry.

Am. and Can. Ch. Boozer of Blue Hill holds an American and Canadian Companion Dog degree; shown with breeder-trainer, Louise Eldridge.

Ch. Boozer of Blue Hill (Ch. Abbott Run Valley Rockett ex Carousel of Blue Hill), Ch. Guzzler of Blue Hill ("Boozer" ex Ellen of Blue Hill), and Ch. Aberjona of Great Oak (Ch. Ike of Blue Hill ex Glamour of Blue Hill).

60

Calico, Calamity, Dominoe, Gremlin, Glory Be, and Lazy Bones, all carrying the Siefenjagenheim prefix.

Queenie Wickstrom purchased Dominoe. He was bred to her Oakdale Sue (Lord Tietge ex Ferge's Gypsy Girl: breeders, Mr. & Mrs. Everett Ferge, Webster, N.Y.) and her daughter by Ch. Slow Poke Hubertus, Wickstrom's Cozette. From these matings, Queenie produced many fine Bassets, which in turn, threw quality. Dominoe was first shown in the East at the time the competition was high. His career began at the age of seven months, when he was shown in Puppy classes except at Westminster, where he finished at nine months of age. He had his first Best in Show at thirteen months of age. Ch. Siefenjagenheim Dominoe was used sparingly and only on very select bitches. His percentage of champion offspring was high, however. He was bred to bitches of dissimilar backgrounds, and he is considered one of *the* great sires.

Walter and Marge Brandt bred a litter from Lulu's Red and French Belle producing Cesar and Lulu's Belle. Belle was eventually sold to Gladys Clement. Cesar was trained in Obedience and gained a CDX by 1957. They bred Lulu's Patches to Dr. Morand's Beaver Brook's Booby Haide and got Ch. Alexander the Great, CDX. In 1952, Lulu's Belle was bred to Beaver Brook's Basso Profundo and they acquired Abbot Run Valley Amy, Abbot Run Valley Amos CD, and Abbot Run Valley Asa, who became a bench champion. Dr. Morand kept Tete Rouge as pick of the litter. With this litter the Brandts began the use of the Abbot Run Valley prefix. Lulu's Belle was bred to Ch. Alexander the Great, CDX to produce A.R.V. Andre, A.R.V. Suzzette, and A.R.V. Rascal who was the first Basset owned by Col. Julian and Betty Dexter. They adopted the Galway prefix. The Brandts rescued Greenore's Trumpeter from a boarding kennel. He was out of Ch. Lyn-Mar's Clown ex Suzette of Lyn-Mar Acres. Dr. Morand chose him to be bred to Beaver Brook's Tete Rouge. This mating produced A.R.V. Rocket who finished in 1958, and the Brandts purchased A.R.V. Gem from the same litter. Both dogs became top producers. Rocket sired four champions in one litter bred to Doris Hurry's Carosel of Blue Hill. Mrs. Hurry bred her Ch. Miss Randolph of Blue Hill to Greenore's Trumpeter. This mating produced Ch. Driquire of Blue Hill. A.R.V. Rocket was bred to A.R.V. Amy to produce Ch. A.R.V. Rudy.

61

Ch. Slowpoke Hubertus.

```
                                                                Walhampton Lingerer
                                              Walhampton Abbot
                                                                Walhampton Arabel
                         Fallowfield Reaper
                                                                Eng. Ch. Amir of Reynalton
                                              Music of Woodleigh
                                                                Walhampton Nicety
         Ch. Hartshead Pepper
                                                                Stanco Dagget
                                              Duke of Rising Sun
                                                                Stanco Lady
                         Hillcrest Gigolette
                                                                Walhampton Aaron
                                              Maple Drive Murky
                                                                Peggy Leach
Ch. Slowpoke Hubertus
                                                                Walhampton Abbot
                                              Fallowfield Reaper
                                                                Music of Woodleigh
                         Hartshead Huntsman
                                                                Chausseur
                                              Hartshead Firefly
                                                                Hillcrest Fyrball of Hartshead
         Abigail of Woodleigh
                                                                Venus's Black Mischief
                                              Ch. Duke of Greenly Hall
                                                                White's Jaconde
                         Glamour Girl
                                                                Ch. Kelly's Chief Hareman
                                              Red Musette of Belbay
                                                                Honey Girl of Geneseo
```

62

In 1952, Nancy Evans established her kennel in Pheonix, Arizona. Some of her well-known dogs are: Am. & Can. Ch. Sujumar's Yogi Barr, Ch. Nancy Evans King Leo la Belle, and Ch. Nancy Evans Falstaff, all Best in Show winners, Ch. Standpine's Siesta Pancho, Ch. La Z Dee J's Johnny Be Good. Ch. Nancy Evans Fair Exchange, Ch. Nancy Evans Double Cross, Ch. Nancy Evans Billy the Kid, Ch. Nancy Evans Daisy of Yarroe, Ch. Ferge's O'Connor's Bugle, Ch. Belbay Chevalier, Ch. Nancy Evans Sir Galahad, a BIS winner, Ch. Capers of Queen-Wicke, and Ch. Nancy Evans Jasper of Tamara, another BIS winner.

Norwood Engle became more and more active. He had attended his first national Specialty in 1950 and entered competition at the 1951 BHCA Specialty. The En-Hu breedings were his but he became better known under the Nor-Mil kennel name, for Norwood and Mildred.

In 1954, Chris Teeter, who was already a familiar figure at the shows, decided he wanted a pair of Bassets that could be top winners. With the help of Frank Hardy, he purchased Fanny of En-Hu from Norwood Engle, and Slowpoke Hubertus. In the next nine years he finished fifty-one champions. Among the progeny of Pokey and Fanny, were: Chs. Long View Acres Frannie, Long View Acres Sweet Talk, Long View Acres Night and Day, Stringer's Napoleon the Beau, Long View Acres Smokey, and Long View Acres Venture On who was the eighteenth champion produced by Fanny. Only two of these eighteen were not sired by Pokey. Chris Teeter purchased Siefenjagenheim Lazy Bones from John Siefen. He became the top winning dog in the country, siring fifty champions before his death in 1962. Among these was Ch. The Ring's Banshee, bred by Bob and Mary Lees Noerr out of Ch. Lyn-Mar Acres Flirtatious (Ch. Lyn-Mar Acres Scalawag ex Duchess of Lyn-Mar). Banshee brought more fame to her owner's Long View Acres Kennels by topping her sire's record. She was first in the Hound Group at Westminster in 1960. Another Lazy Bones son, Am & Can. Ch. Rocky of Long View Acres took several Best in Show awards, sired Chs. Long View Acres Repeater and Belle Patty of Barlindall, and later gained obedience titles for his new California owner. The Long View Acres prefix can be found on the pedigrees of many dogs throughout the country and their influence was great indeed.

Ch. Lyn-Mar Acres Flirtatious with handler, Alfred Murray; owned by Robert and Mary Lees Noerr.

Ch. The Ring's Banshee; handler, Dorothy Hardy.

Ch. Siefenjagenheim Dominoe.

Ch. Siefenjagenheim Lazy Bones.


```
                                         Kilsyth Baronet

                       Kilsyth Lucky

                                         Kilsyth Mitzie

     Ch. Lyn-Mar's Clown

                                         Ch. Promise of Greenly Hall

                       Ch. Maitri of Lyn-Mar

                                         Ch. Duchess of Greenly Hall

Ch. Siefenjagenheim Lazy Bones
Ch. Siefenjagenheim Dominoe

                                         Kishacoquillas Trailer

                       Ben's Black King

                                         Fallowfield Contralto

     Ch. Webb's Black Amanda

                                         Duke of Greenhill

                       Bose's Princess Patty

                                         Freckles of Belbay
```

Am. and Can. Ch. Rocky of Long View Acres C.D.

Ch. Long View Acres Smokey.

Loren Free began to enter competition in 1954, though he had obtained Walhampton Lively in 1927 and soon thereafter added Abbott's Girlie and Starridge Partner. He campaigned Belbay General Sno-Sheen (Belbay Triumph ex Larghetto of Belbay) to his championship. The field trials beckoned and Free began running his dogs. Among his field champions were: Eingle's Beckie, Queen Bee, Shellbark's Atomic Blue, Shellbark's Michie, Little Mac, and Kanode's Sally Nell. Beckie, in turn, produced more field champions and, by the 1960s, Loren claimed every dog in his Shellbark Kennel to be her descendant. The Eingle prefix was used by Clarence Eingle of Carey, Ohio, and not to be confused with Norwood Engle of Pennsylvania. Free remained active until his death in 1977.

Ruth Turner traveled to her first national meeting and trial, in New Philadelphia, Ohio, in 1955. After that, she became a well-known figure in the Parent Club. This was seven years after she had purchased her first Basset. Ruth was the first to put the Club's newsletter into magazine form. She later served as a Director of the BHCA. Abbot Run Valley Perdita was one of her foundation bitches.

In 1954, Howard Smith bought his first Basset from a mating of Yukon Eric ex Spotted Lady. In honor of his wife, Rosie, he immediately adopted his kennel name and named the puppy Rosie's Queen. Howard had hunted most of his life and was pleased that Queen turned out to be a good hunting dog. John Eylander talked Howard into attending a field trial in 1957. He has been "hooked" ever since. His first big break came when he obtained Fld. Ch. Behney's Bill from Bob Taber. Bill produced good running pups that were easy to handle. Ed Eylander brought Fd. Ch. Miss Mitzie to breed to Bill. From this mating, Howard received Rosie's Ed's Miss Mitzie. He also obtained Hartshead Sportsman from J. C. Cunningham. This was a good looking, slow running hound. He bred Miss Mitzie to Sportsman and raised four puppies. The best of these, Rosie's Miss Mitzie, was lost during her first whelping. Ken McWilliams had another of this litter, McWilliams Buckineer. He never finished but left his mark on later litters. Rosie's Sportsman, better known as Herk, contributed greatly to the running ability of dogs that are descended from him. Rosie's Bill was Howard's favorite and produced many champion offspring before his death in 1970.

Ch. Belbay General Sno-Sheen.

Fd. Ch. Queen Bee with owner, Loren Free.

Ch. Anastasia Hubertus and Dorothy Hardy.

Ch. Look's Pensive of Elvalin taking Best of Opposite Sex at Westminster in 1957. Her brother, Ch. Look's Choice, was Best of Breed.

Doris and Bill Hurry bred Ch. Cook's Killbuck Chief to their Ch. Lyn-Mar Acres Intrigue. The Gillespies purchased a bitch from this litter and named her Hunting Horn Chloe.

Barbara Dunning, of California, bought Gordon's Boy Sockratese (Ch. Belbay Chevalier ex Shula's KaNeima) bred by Raymond E. Gordon. Cordelia Jensen suggested she show him. Benj and Sally Harris encouraged her and helped her become acquainted through the BHC of Southern California. She soon finished her first bitch, Ch. Wilhelmina of Salt Box Farm (Sir William ex Annabelle of Marben) whom she had purchased from Mrs. Oliver Adams. This became her foundation brood bitch.

At about the same time, Ray Wells' son purchased Double B's Grand Duchess (Ch. Knight Errant of Willow Road ex Dame Daphne of Double B) from Clarence and Helen Boutell. She finished with Ray Wells and Christy Boutell alternating handling.

We began to see such names as the Buchers with the Warwick breedings, the Meadow Park prefix of the Wolfs, the King's Trojan Echoes line, the Julian Dexters with the Galway prefix, Bob and Mary Lees Noerr, Dorothy Shula, breeder, and Frank Inn, trainer of Cleo of television fame, the Robert Lindsays and their Lime Tree dogs, the Bob Ellenbergers, Ken Hirst, the Lester Cabbage's Southwind breedings, and the Donald Batemans, Helen Boutell's Double B prefix, and many more including the author's within the next few years.

By 1957, Nancy Evans purchased Ferge's O'Connor's Bugle from the Everett Ferges. The following had taken a Best in Show: Ch. Sport of En-Hu, Ch. Lenfield's Juliana, Ch. Lyn-Mar Acres Top Brass, Ch. Greenore's Joker, and Ch. Siefenjagenheim Lazy Bones.

In the mid 1950s, Benj and Sally Harris purchased their first Basset, and soon became very active fanciers. By 1957, Benj was elected president of the BHC of Southern California. They were to become important national figures. Their interests led Benj to become associated with several Obedience clubs. This eventually led to his becoming a Tracking and Obedience judge. Their Pierre's Bonne Joie was the first UDT Basset, the third UD, and the third TD.

One of the early Colorado breeders was Jane Austin. She bought her first two Bassets from Nancy Evans. They were Judge (Ch.

Rebel's Red Dandee ex Cheyenne's Black Rose) and Chevalier's Lazy Susan (Ch. Belbay Chevalier ex Melanie of Cypress). The Robert Mahaffey's bitch, Clancie Crockett, out of Davy Crockett, arrived with Lazy Susan. The McChesneys were showing Hartshead Jake, CD and Ch. Hartshead Dinah, CD.

Bill Barton had a kennel of hunting Beagles. His cousin, Jean Williams Watts, purchased a bitch, from the Paul Nelsons, named Miss Clancy of Canoga Park. She was out of Ch. Huey of Cypress ex Ch. Darwin's Blondy. Captain Watts bred her to Dr. and Mrs. Duane Newton's Ch. Newton's Imperial, a California dog out of Ch. Long View Acres Uncle Ed ex Newton's Tina Marie. This breeding produced six puppies, one being Ch. Sir Angus of Reno. Subsequently Captain Watts was ordered overseas. Her parents took Clancy, and all but one pup was sold. Captain Watts pursuaded Bill Barton to keep one puppy. He was named Mister Tandy of Coralwood, and after attempting to run him, unsuccessfully, Barton was encouraged to show him. Once the two learned to show, Tandy gained his championship in just eight shows.

Mr. and Mrs. Ronald Scholz became interested in the breed in 1957. Between 1957 and 1961 they bought several bitches for breeding and showing that were not good enough for either. They had many disappointments until they bought Manor Hill Penny Candy (Ch. Double B's Ishmael ex Alpha of Double B) from Helen Boutell. Their success in Bassets began with the purchase of this bitch.

Joe and Pinkie Navar went to their first field trial this same year. Bob Taber, whom they had met at Elizabeth Streetter's, encouraged them to attend with a running bitch, Darwin's Celena (Ch. Hartshead Pepper ex Bryl of Lyn-Mar), owned by a friend. The trials gained avid enthusiasts when the Navars came in second. They had actually owned their first Basset in 1955. She was Engle's Xmas Cheer, out of a mating of Engle's Big Chief ex Engle's Mag Pie, given to the Navars' son by Frank Hardy. In 1956 they bred her to Tulpehocken Shorty, owned by Bob Taber and kept five of the nine resulting pups. Joe Joe, Heather, and Jolly made their field championships. Joy was used as a brood bitch. Both she and Jester were good running dogs but did not quite make their field titles. Fld. Ch. Navar's Joe Joe only lacked a major to become a dual when he was injured by a car and could be shown no more. Although Xmas

Ch. Abbot Run Valley Brassy, owned by Marjorie Brandt,
one of the breed's most influential modern sires.

Ch. Gladstone of Mandeville.

Cheer would never run a rabbit, and Shorty never ran at a trial, they produced good running dogs. The Navars' first field trial, with their own dogs, was at Buckeye in 1957. Their first national entries were at Holland, Michigan, in 1958.

The Musicland Kennels were started when Jeanne Dudley, later Mrs. Wade C. Hills, purchased Ch. Bassett's Eloise at the age of three months from Dick and Evelyn Basset. Eloise was a daughter of Ch. Mattie's Quercus, CD and Ch. Bassett's Jody. In 1958, she got Ch. Look's Musical of Musicland from Jean Look. With the assistance of such breeders, who supplied her foundation stock, the Musicland name became famous. Look's Musical was bred to Eloise and produced Ch. Musicland's Demure Danseuse. The following year, the same mating produced Ch. Musicland's Mountain Music who became a top winner and the sire of ten champions.

Roger Fredette had heard of the Abbot Run Valley Kennels from a handler. He approached the Brandts to breed his Duchess of Diamond Hill to their A.R.V. Rocket. This mating produced an outstanding bitch, Ch. Ro-Fre la Reine de la Balle. Fredette and Walter Brandt co-owned her. Roger then bought interest in Ch. A.R.V. Rudy and trained him as a brace with Reine. They were a well-received, Group winning brace at Westminster in 1961. The Brandts bred A.R.V. Gem to Ch. Milvan's Deacon who was owned by Mary Nardiello. From this litter of two, the male, A.R.V. Prankster finished. The bitch was sold to Charlotte Larson (Nicklaw), later bred to A.R.V. Brassy, producing Ch. Battenkill Brass Echo, a top-winning bitch in 1964 and 1965. Ch. Driquire of Blue Hill was bred to Ch. Longview Acres Smokey. A.R.V. Gabby was one of the favorites from this litter.

Sandra Campbell Craigwood Bassets had their start in 1958. Sandra and her husband obtained a pet bitch, named Pongi Fongi, who was bred once to Clinch River Hercules and produced Ch. Campbell's Shoo Fly. This dog began Sandra's interest in showing. After Shoo Fly, she showed Ch. Campbell's Hobo for a time.

Lena Wray bought her first Basset as a pet and companion for her husand, Billy. The hound was obtained from a Fort Pierce breeder, George Bell, out of a mating of Tom Fool Houston ex Chloe the Coy Charmer. Lena had grown up, in Wisconsin, with dogs of other breeds but became taken with the Basset. When she

Ch. Musicland's Mountain Music, owned
and bred by Jeanne Dudley Hills.
Olson

Ch. Sir Clarence of Queen Wicke, a fine example of father and daughter
breeding (Ch. Siefenjagenheim Dominoe ex his daughter, Wickstrom's
Dominelle).

saw a magazine article featuring the Richard Bassets her desire to own one had become stronger, though she had no intention of showing. Her vet suggested, after Humphrey Jo became quite large, that she take him to an obedience school. This led to obedience competition where James Daniels, then a handler, asked to try him in the conformation ring. He soon had both his conformation championship and his CD degree.

Mrs. Mildred Buckholz got Lena interested in tracking and, in 1962, Humphrey also gained his tracking degree. This set the pattern for the Wrays' future. In 1960, they bought BeeLee's Pruneface Prudence (Sambolino of Great Promise ex Adam's Red Gal). Prudie was not shown in conformation but was one of the earliest to earn all obedience degrees. Lena became an avid enthusiast of tracking, even getting degrees on her champions. She trained and tracked twelve dogs, by 1977, and had become a tracking judge. She earned degrees on: Ch. Humphrey Jo, CD, TD; BeeLee's Pruneface Prudence, UDT; Ch. Sir Tomo's Party Doll, TD; Ch. Party Doll's Geraldine, TD; BeeLee's Mister Fred, TD; BeeLee's Miss Tricia, TD; Ch. Julie of Rockin-Pas, TD; Ch. Lady of Pine Manor, TD; Ch Bret Mavrick of Rockin-Pas, TD, his son, BeeLee's Bruiser the Behemoth, TD; Ernest's Shirley Black Kettle, TD, and Slippery Hill Bonnie Parker, TD.

Jean Look moved to East Randolph, N.Y., in 1958. Ch. Bassett's Roustabout, Ch. Millvan's Deacon, Ch. Rocky of Long View Acres and Ch. Long View Acres Blaze By all had Best in Show wins in 1958. By this time, Warwick Squire, Anastasia Hubertus, Double B's Ishmael, Hubertus Dark Josephine, and many others had gained their championships, including Chs. The Ring's Ali Baba, Arthur North, and Aleric out of the Noerr's mating of Ch. Long View Acres Smokey ex Ch. Miss Linda Lovely of Elvalin.

Doris Hurry bred her Ch. Cherry Blossom of Blue Hill to Ch. The Ring's Ali Baba. From this litter, the Gillespies bought a pup that was to become their Ch. Imperial of Blue Hill II. When this bitch was bred to Nancy and Robert Lindsay's Ch. Lime Tree Micawber (Ch. Seifenjagenheim Lazy Bones ex Ch. Lyn-Mar's Zephyr), they kept Am. & Can. Ch. Hunting Horn Noah who won at the national Specialty. Noah produced many offspring, two of which were retained as brood bitches. Hunting Horn Regina was bred to Ch. Galway's Meshak, owned by Julian and Betty Dexter, producing Hunting Horn Chloe II, who was bred back to Noah, giving them Hunting Horn Frederica.

Barbara Dunning finished Ch. Bon-Et-Bas Napoleon Bonaparte who was owned by Fawn and Paul Harris. He was the sire of Barbara's Bar-B Dapper Dan as well as Ch. Bar-B Ringside Gossip and Bar-B Buckets of Love. These were out of her bitch, Wilhelmina. Barbara was limited to taking only one dog to a show because she traveled with Rex Cain and Ben Brown, so only Ch. Bar-B Ringside Gossip finished. When bred to Ch. Nancy Evans Billy the Kid, she produced Ch. Bar-B Endless Gossip. Barbara handled for the Paul Nelsons, showing Ch. Santana-Mandeville Ichabod and Ch. Santana-Mandeville Just Fred, Maj. William Kelly, Jeffrey Schwinn, Hub Robinson and took Richard & Mitzie Hiett's Sir Richey of Hubey High to Westminster. She also handled Ch. Picolo Pierre and Ch. Fassett's Uncle Ed.

Ray Wells was stationed at Ft. Bliss, Texas. He bred his Ch. Double B's Grand Duchess to Nancy Evans' Billy the Kid. One of the pups from this mating was Duchess' Porkchop of Cape Cod. "Chopper" was retired from the show ring before he finished but he did get his field trial championship and sired some nice running dogs. In the meantime, Helen Boutell, of the Double B Kennels, was having space problems. American & Bermudian Ch. Double B's Lucky Libertine (Ch. Hubertus Playboy ex Ch. Double B's Veronica) went to live with Ray Wells. At that time, this dog knew nothing about the woods, but he learned and became the breed's fourth dual champion. He was also a popular stud. Bred to Nancy Evans' Valentina, he produced Fussbudget of Cape Cod, another that became a field champion.

In the Texas area, Ch. Sherlitt's Lemon Drop Kid was being shown. He was a product of Sherlitt's Kennels owned by Marge and Bob Frazier. They had bred their Sherlitt's Bona Dea (Ch. Longview Acres Smokey ex Santana's Pocahontas) to Am. & Mex. Ch. Gladstone of Mandeville (Ch. Huey of Cypress ex Ch. Homlin's Missie). In seven outings, he was never defeated. He went on to many Group placements.

In 1960, Paul and Suzanne Mohr purchased Nancy Evans Socrates (Ch. Belleau's Davy Crockett ex Ch. Bernadotte of Petite

Roche). They campaigned him to a CD. It was not until 1966, how-ever, that they were successful with their breeding program. Ch. Supai's Aunt Jemima finished for them that year.

Tom and Medora Harper of Omaha, Nebraska, bought their first Basset in 1960. He was Harpo Von Haus Harper (Ch. Pioneer's Prince Charming ex Agony of Bosque Redondo). He was a disap-pointment in the show ring so they sought to purchase one of better quality. Breeders suggested a good bitch. They finally pur-chased Moore's Prissy Sissy (Ch. Millvan's Deacon ex Moore's Mascot Mistress) from Elmer Moore in Kansas City. They felt she was a good choice as a brood matron because her grandfather, on her dam's side, was Ch. Siefenjagenheim Dominoe. Although she did not enjoy showing, she was bred successfully to Ch. Tyburn's Indian Emperor. They kept and finished Ch. Hugo Von Haus Harper from this mating. Sissy died at an early age, and Hugo became their stud dog. The Harpers purchased Ch. Musicland's Polka v.h. Harper (Ch. Musicland's Bill Bailey ex Musicland's Tico Tico) from Jeanne Hills. She was purchased as a puppy, and later produced two litters.

Jean Spaulding began entering field trial competition, in 1960, after she attended a meeting of the Kentuckiana BHC. Her husband, Bill, had bought her a two-and-a-half-year-old bitch for her birthday after having set out to buy a puppy. Jean bred this bitch, Sissy, several times but, by then, realized that this was not the trial quality she desired. She bought a four-month-old, black and tan bitch and named her Trick or Treat because she was bought on Halloween. She was obtained from Howard Smith who also sup-plied Jean's Bishop's Duke of Long Run (Fd. Ch. Shellbark's Atomic Blue ex Rosie's Peggy). Both became field champions. Duke sired Fd. Ch. Bluegrass Belle. Jean and Bill adopted Bluegrass as their kennel name. Jean became an enthusiastic figure at the field trials during the next few years. In 1966, the BHCA appointed Mrs. Spaulding publicity director and editor of *Tally-Ho*.

Hettie Page Garwood had lived in New York. In 1961, after she moved back to Texas, she obtained her first Basset, out of Bobby Crutchfield's stock. The background was mostly Belleau as were most area dogs about that time. Margranita's Captain Sambo was out of Ch. Crutchfield's Antoine ex Francine of Le Chenil. She later purchased a female, Margranita's Sparkle Daisy (Ch.. Crutch-

Ch. The Chocolate Soldier of Glyn, bred and owned by Ruth Bateman, was 1966 International K.C. Best of Breed and Group 3, has five Group Firsts, and was Best in Show at Peoria, Ill. Judge, Hollis Wilson; handler, Dick Cooper.

Ch. Harper's Rhett Butler (Ch. Orangepark Dexter ex Ch. Molly Bea v.h. Harper), owned and handled by Medora Harper. "Toby" is shown winning BB at the 1971 Timberline BHC Specialty under judge Harold Hardin.

Bennett

field's Beaujac ex Robindris Acres Sammy). These two produced Het's Daisy's Miss Bun Rabbit who was later bred to Ch. Glenhaven's Lord Jack. Het, however, suffered a broken leg in an auto accident and could not exhibit until 1965. She acquired Beaujac, Mama Sam, and Ch. Bloomer's Big Red from Tom Bloomer, and a small bitch out of Ch. Nancy Evans Biff who had been owned by Bob and Mary Jane Booth.

Clare Clowe acquired a puppy bitch out of Ch. Millvan's Deacon ex Ch. Lindley's Lucky Lindy Lou. She named her Sweet Clowver. Claire's name provided her with her Clowverleaf prefix.

Entering at the second Northern California field trial were: the Hagopians with dogs named Gus and Desmeralde Diablo; the Jeffreys with Ch. Belleau's Daniel Boone and Ann Hagop; the Mutimers with B. J.'s Brett and Sassy of Cypress; the Rubensteins with Sherman's Skylark; and Laumeister with Monsieur Cornelius.

June Hanns Moiseff finished her homebred Hanns Acres Piccolo Pierre at the Golden Gate KC show in 1960. Ch. Bassett's Roustabout, owned by Dick and Evelyn Bassett, won the Hound Group there to make it a real occasion. This was probably the first time a Basset had taken the Group at this show.

Ch. Hub's Chris Kringle, owned by W. H. Robinson, and Ch. Richy's Sir Hubey High, owned by Dick & Mitzie Hiett, were among the winning West Coast dogs. Dick eventually became an AKC field representative. Frank Lopez, of Sausalito, began to take an interest in obedience work. He later worked hard toward the lowering of the jump requirements for Bassets and other low-stationed breeds. Frank co-owned the following with David Devany: La Jolie Madam Tristesse, Monsieur Tristesse, Ch. Tristesse Beau Dandy, and Ch. Fair Lady Luck, CD.

Donald and Barbara Martin, and their children, Bryan, Peter, and Heidi, bought their first Basset, Sweet Violet Begonia Martin, from a pet shop. She was bred to Ch. Wickstrom's Gay Blade owned by Jean Fry. When the Martins took the puppies to the Fort Dearborn Specialty match, Catherine Cook and other club members advised that they were not show quality, should be sold, and that the Martins should start over. They then began with Barook stock which was strong in West Coast and Nancy Evans lineage. Later breedings introduced Abbot Run Valley Brassy lines. This produced Ch. Northwoods' Lady Esther, Ch. Northwoods' Erla-la, and North-

Ch. Margem Hills Mr. Brown, owned by Finn Bergishagen and Bette Williams. He is shown going BW enroute to his title at the Dal-Tex BHC Specialty under judge Joseph Braun, handler Roy Murray.

Twomey

Ch. Glenhaven's Lord Jack (left) with Het Garwood winning the Stud Dog class at the Dal-Tex Specialty. His daughters are Ch. White Mountain Amorette, with John Hackley, and Ch. Het's Bunny's Daisy Too, owned by Anne Locker and handled by Louisa Myers.

Twomey

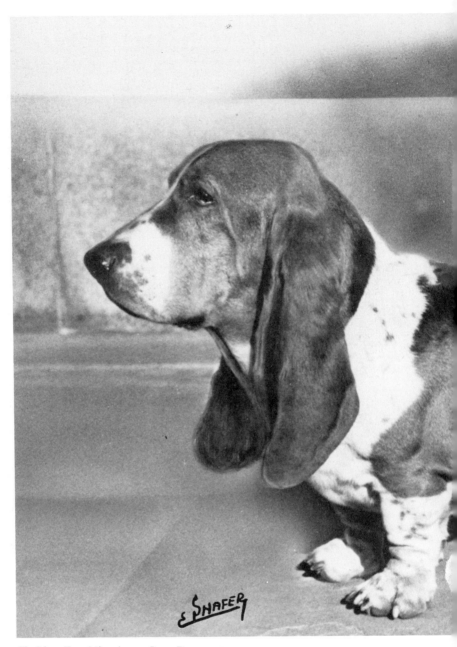

Ch. Lime Tree Micawber, a Lazy Bones son,
owned by Mr. and Mrs. Robert V. Lindsay.
Shafer

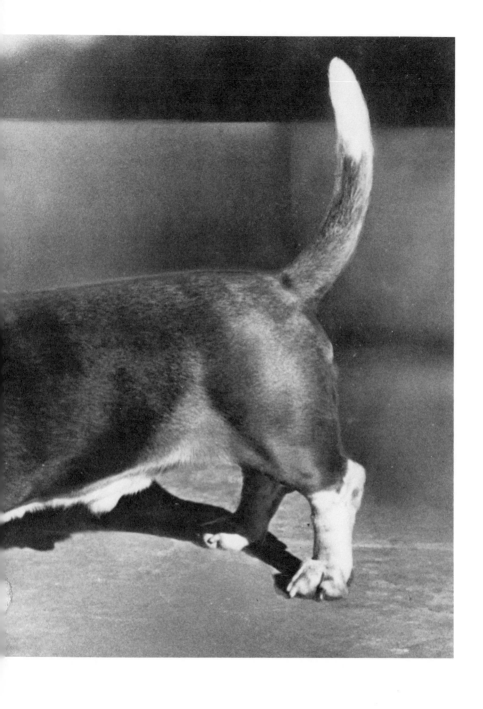

Ch. Tannenbaum's Funtastic, a top winner on the West Coast in 1963 and 1964; breeder-owner-handler, Lucille Barton; judge, Alva Rosenberg.

Ch. Kazoo's Flora Tina, owned by C. J. Collee, distinguished herself as the dam of 13 champions. She is shown in a win under judge Haskell Shuffman.

woods' Lazy Lizzy. They adopted the Northwoods' kennel name. Lizzy was bred back into the Brassy line through Ch. Gin Dic's Bit O'Brass.

Mickey Carter purchased Tulpehocken Morgan, in 1961, from David Angstadt. She was soon introduced to the sport of field trials at the Susquehanna club. Leonard "Buck" LaFollette took her under his wing and she learned much about the work. Les Crelin then offered her pick of some of his bitches. She bought Crelin's Fan Dancer from him in 1962. Bred back to Azul Rayo, owned by Bob Matthews, Mickey began a line that was to produce many good running dogs including Fd. Chs. Mickey's At Last, Almicks Cactus, and Almicks Glitter at Last. Almicks was adopted as the kennel name.

Joan and Ronald Scholz had kept Manor Hill's Dora out of their Manor Hill Penny Candy bred to Ch. Lime Tree Micawber. They purchased Bonnie Ridge Fire-Bird from her breeder, Arthur T. Fitzsimmons of Long Island. Fire-Bird was by Ch. Lyn-Mar Acres Barrister (Ch. His Lordship of Lyn-Mar Acres ex Ch. Headline of Lyn-Mar Acres) ex Bonnie Ridge Best Tip (Ch. Lyn-Mar Acres Brass Bound ex Ch. Pride of Lyn-Mar Acres). Fire-Bird was eventually bred to Ch. Abbot Run Valley Brassy (Ch. Lyn-Mar Acres Top Brass ex Ch. Ro-Fre la Reine de la Balle). Three breedings of Fire-Bird to Brassy produced Ch. Manor Hill Top Spot, Ch. Manor Hill Greta, Ch. Doc Floyd of Manor Hill, Ch. Forget-Me-Not of Manor Hill, and Ch. Forestbay Orvil of Manor Hill. Top Spot was bred to Manor Hill Dora and this produced the national Specialty winner Ch. Manor Hill Fringe Benefit. By 1975, Top Spot had already sired four champions. Among them was the all-time top-producing bitch, Ch. Kazoo's Question Mark, and Ch. Kazoo's Galloping Gitch, also a national Specialty winner.

Sonny and Tasi Collee became interested in purchasing something better than their first, Upsa Daisy Venus, who was obtained from Marvin Brandt of Holland, Michigan. From Mary Jo Shield's Kazoo Kennels, they bought Kazoo's Doctor Douglas and Kazoo's Flora-Tina. Both gained their championships. After a rather active breeding and showing program, finishing several champions, they adopted the kennel prefix of Tason. Flora-Tina produced thirteen champions for them. Her first litter was by Ch. The Ring's Cholmondeley. In it

Ch. Orangepark Roy (Ch. Orangepark Eustace ex Hartshead Maybelline), owned by Orangepark Kennels.
Norton of Kent

Ch. Hiflite's Tomfoolery, CD, owned by Tom Bloomer, III.
Graham

were: Am. & Can. Ch. Burrwood's Danifino, Ch. Whitebriar Easy Come, and Ch. Kazoo's Karmel Tassie. Ch. Kazoo's Dawn was out of Flora-Tina's second litter by Ch. Manor Hill Top Spot. The third litter was by Ch. Abbot Run Valley Brassy. In it were: Ch. Tason's Astro, Ch. Tason's Count Down, Ch. Tason's Gemini, Ch. Tason's Molly Brown, CD, Ch. Long View Acres Pride, Ch. Long View Acres Bonza, and Ch. Whitebriar's Winsome. Ch. Houndstown Tason's Sonny was from the fourth litter by Ch. Abbot Run Valley Brassy. In the fifth litter, sired by Ch. Talleyrand's Keene, was Ch. Tason's Lock Stock and Barrel. Tina died in 1970.

Louisa Myers met a lady, Mrs. C. L. Walter, who was walking a male Basset at the time. This lady happened to have a litter, at home, from Juliette of LaChenil who was down from Belleau's Pancho of Le Chenile and Georgette of Dauchau. Louisa, better known as Appie, obtained a bitch naming her Appie's Babette of Opelusas. Appie had shown in Junior Showmanship, as a youngster, and the bug bit again. She bred Babette to Mrs. Marge Frazier's Ch. Sherlitt's Lemon Drop Kid in 1963 and kept Appie's Aphrodite. She purchased Sherlitt's Mariebe's Bigg Daddy and bred him to Aphrodite getting Loma Caprice of My Lu. She adopted My Lu as a kennel name. After selling Caprice, the bitch was bred to Butcher Boy Tomo (Ch. Glenhaven's Butcher Boy ex Ch. Jolly Lane's Calamity Jane) producing My Lu's Sunshine Shirley, CD. Appie had become very interested in obedience work. With the help of Marge Frazier, Joan Urban, Het Garwood, and Bob and Mary Jane Booth, Appie became an avid breeder and competitor in the Texas shows. She bred her Sugar and Spice of My Lu to her Hiflite's Big John and produced My Lu's Blossom who became a top-producing bitch. Bred to both Ch. Glenhaven's Lord Jack and Ch. Tal-E-Ho's Top Banana, she tied for number two dam. Appie also eventually became interested in Tracking.

Marge and Len Skolnick raised their first litter at their Slippery Hill Kennels in 1961. Slippery Hill Chloe was one of this litter. Her sister, Pandora, became a progenitor of their field bloodline. The Skolnicks interests embraced both dog shows and field trials. Two bloodlines were developed, both strictly linebred. The bench bloodline was based on the Santana-Mandeville line through the foundation studs Ch. Santana-Mandeville Rodney and Ch. Santana-Mandeville Egghead. Later, Rodney's half-brother, Ch. Orangepark

85

Dexter was also bred into the line. Sisters, Chs. Slippery Hill Paprika, Nutmeg, and Cinnamon were granddaughters of Chloe.

Finn and Mary Lou Bergishagen founded their Jagersven Kennels when they purchased a tricolored bitch named Jagersven Samantha (Ch. Crutchfield's Andre Joseph ex Long View Acres Nancy J) from Chris Teeter. She completed her championship in 1964. Bred to Ch. Long View Acres Venture On, she produced Jagersven Hollyberry who was bred to Ch. Abbot Run Valley Brassy to produce Ch. Jagersven Harris Tweed, CD. Harris Tweed was the winner of several Hound Groups and the sire of Ch. Jagersven Gretchen and Ch. Jagersven Misa.

Bob and Mary Jane Booth were becoming well-known for their Hiflite Bassets at the shows in Texas. They later bought Kazoo's Question Mark from the Kazoo Kennels of Mary Jo Shields. She left an important mark on the bloodlines of the breed by producing: Ch. Hiflite's Tomfoolery, CD owned by Tom Bloomer, Ch. HiFlite's Trudy owned by Kazoo Kennels, Ch. Hiflite's Top of the Mark owned by Patricia Bellows, Ch. Hiflite's Big John, TD owned by Louisa Myers, Ch. Het's Hiflite Charlotte and Ch. Hiflite's Jodi owned by Het Garwood, Ch. Hiflite's Penny Bee owned by Laurie Jane Booth, and Ch. Hiflite's Sherrie Ann owned by the Booths.

From 1962 to 1969, Musicland kennels produced such dogs as: Chs. M. Tico Tico, Troubador, and Tambourine (Moore's Copper TKO ex Look's Doll Baby); Chs. M. Jubilee and John Henry (Ch. The Ring's Cholmondeley ex Moore's Minuet of Musicland); Chs. M. Calypso and Clare de Lune (Clowverleaf's Agamemnon ex Bassetts Eloise); Ch. M. Bill Bailey (Clowverleaf's Agamemnon ex Demure Danseuse); Chs. Marimba and Molly Darlin' (M. Mountain Music ex M. Tico Tico); Chs. M. Pearl Bailey, Perfidia, Poinciana, Pal Joey, Porgy, Polonaise, and Polka (M. Bill Bailey ex M. Tico Tico); Ch. Musicland Satchmo (M. Bill Bailey ex Molly Darlin'); Ch. M. Mountain Dew (M. Mountain Music ex Tico Tico); Ch. M. Count Basie (M. Mountain Music ex Pearl Bailey); and many more.

Some of the dogs bred at Musicland during the 1960s went to Blanche and Joe Schaeffer; Clare Clowe; Mellow Bay Kennels; Gra Vand Kennels; Ruth Turner; Maring Kennels; Sheilar Kennels; Bayroc Kennels, and Dixie Hall's Dixie Kennels.

Ch. Geronimo of Rockin-Pas, owned by Sandra Campbell and bred by Paul Saucier. He is shown with his handler Caroll James.

Graham

Ch. Santana-Mandeville Rodney, a Specialty winner, owned by Slippery Hill Kennels and shown with his handler Bobby Barlow.

Ch. Forestbay Montgomery (Ch. Forestbay Joshua ex Forestbay Manor Hill Mahalia), owned by Jean L. Sheehy and bred by Forestbay Kennels.
Ashbey

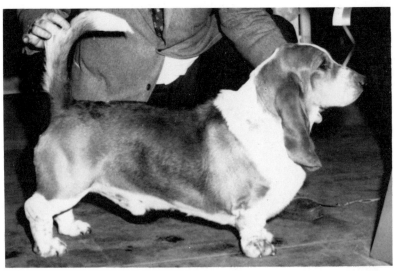

Ch. Manor Hill Top Spot, owned by Joan Scholz.
Shafer

Curt and Jean Sheehy purchased Woodville's Forester (Woodville's Chorus ex Woodville's Frolic in 1963. The following year they obtained Mischievous Molley from Mrs. Frances Scaife. Molly was out of Ch. The Ring's Ali Baba ex Hubertus Dolly Madison. Molly gained a CD and became a career girl in advertising. She was bred to Woodville's Forester producing Topohil's Andrea, CD and Topohil's Gros Chien Rouge. Her second litter, by Ch. Galway's Meshack produced only one puppy, Topohil's Cotton Candy, who also gained a CD. Candy was bred to Ch. Forestbay Montgomery giving the Sheehys' Ch. Topohil's Glory Bea and Ch. Topohil's Gypsy in 1972. Meanwhile they had purchased Abbot Run Valley Gayle (Abbot Run Valley Gabby ex Ch. Abbot Run Valley Brass Beauty) from Marjorie Brandt and Joseph Roan. Bred to Ch. Yclept Bruiser she produced Ch. Topohil's Kathy's Honey and Brazilian Ch. Topohil's Idoneous. By Ch. Forestbay Montgomery, she gave the Sheehy's Ch. Topohil Leader of the Pack. They also purchased Ch. Double B's Lord Chesterfield (Ch. Double B's B.M.O.C. ex Ch. Double B's Final Fling) from Helen Boutell and Ch. Forestbay Montgomery (Ch. Forestbay Joshua ex Forestbay Manor Hill Mahalia) from the Joe Kulpers' Forestbay Kennels. Montgomery finished easily and became a Specialty winner. He was among the top winning Bassets three years in a row although not extensively campaigned. By 1977, he had eight American and two Brazilian champions as his get.

The Beaureguarde Bassets began when Mary Bastable and Fran Gray purchased a pet, Mister Beaureguarde, from Nancy Evans. When they decided to show, they returned to Nancy Evans for Mister Bartholomew by Ch. Nancy Evans Double Cross ex Cactus Queen. He completed his championship and sired Ch. Beaureguarde's Red Baron. Shortly after, through Janis MacKimm, Amanda P. Beaureguarde (Ch. Nancy Evans' Jason ex Monique of Mar-Ray) was purchased. Their first litter of puppies was a linebred litter of Ch. Governor Chester Klutch and Amanda, producing Ch. Dickens P. Beaureguarde. They later bought Abagail P. Beaureguarde (Ch. Musicland's Mountain Dew ex MacKimm's Tabu). She became a foundation bitch. They decided to direct their breeding toward Musicland bloodlines, breeding Abigail to Ch. Musicland's Casey Jones, getting Ch. Pretty Patti P. Beaureguarde, Ch. Whitney P. Beaureguarde, and Mexican Ch. George Sundance Kid. Whitney was sold to Ross and Barbara Santino and became the foundation bitch for their Ro-Barbs Kennel. Abigail's second litter was by Ch. Dickens P. Beaureguarde, giving them only one puppy, Ch. Belvidere P. Beaureguarde who became the main stud behind future generations.

Henry and Ann Jerman became interested in showing while waiting for a puppy, from Robert and Kathryn Ellenberger of Northport, Long Island. They obtained a bitch, who became Ch. Talleyrand's Lynette (Ch. Abbot Run Valley Brassy ex Ch. Talleyrand's Relue Annie), the foundation bitch for their Tal-E-Ho Kennels. The Jerman's bred Lynette to four champions and concentrated on the best of the offspring of these matings. All of their later matings were linebreeding and inbreeding within this framework. When bred to Ch. Talleyrand's Keene, owned by the Ellenbergers, Lynette gave them a litter of nine. They kept two bitches, one named Tal-E-Ho's Ka-Ro and one named Tal-E-Ho's Funny Girl who is the granddam of Ch. Tal-E-Ho's Top Banana, top Basset of 1975, owned by the Martins' Northwoods Kennels. Ka-Ro was the dam of Ch. Tal-E-Ho Prancer. Ch. Tal-E-Ho's Hustler came from a mating of Lynette to Ch. Abbot Run Valley Brassy, a father-daughter mating. Bred to a Brassy son, Ch. Manor Hill Top Spot, she produced Tal-E-Ho George, the sire of Prancer. She produced another prepotent sire when bred to Am. & Bermudian Ch. Sir Tomo of Glenhaven.

In 1964, Fred and Stella Atwater and Les Crelin became interested in a new couple, Tom and Shirley Pettit, who would eventually contribute greatly to field trial bloodlines. These three people taught them how a field trial dog should perform. Les owned Rattle Dancer, Shimmy Dancer, and Van's Fantasy a great bitch who became the third Grand Champion. Les gave her to the Pettits when she was six years old. Pettit's first home bred field champions were a result of breeding "Fanny" to Fd. Ch. Rosies Sportsman. They then bought Fd. Ch. Rosie's Jeff, from Howard Smith's bloodline, and Fd. Ch. Dohrshires Twiggy from Pat and Jim Dohr's breedings. Jeff and Twiggy produced Dual Ch. Pettit's Ranger Ric who also gained the title of Grand Champion in the field. In 1975, Ric was Stud Dog of the Year, awarded by BHCA. He was number one dog in the *Field Producers Guide* for 1976. By 1977, Tom and Shirley had bred a total of seventeen field champions, finishing thirteen themselves.

Ch. Tal-E-Ho's Prancer (Tal-E-Ho's George ex Tal-E-Ho's Ka-Ro), owned by Henry and Anne Jerman, was BB at the 1971 Susquehanna BHC under Mrs. Eugene C. Urban. Mrs. Jerman handled Prancer from the classes to this good win.

Gilbert

Dual Ch. Pettit's Ranger Ric, owned by Dr. and Mrs. Thomas H. Pettit.

Gilbert

Jim and Wanda White had a few pet quality Bassets before they really founded their Windmaker Kennels. After losing a litter by Ch. Brigadier General Mark, owned by Al and Anna Tiedemann, they obtained Brigadier's Swamp Fox (Lyn-Mar Acres Goliath ex Ch. Vagabonds Brazen Brigadier) from this kennel. Twelve years later, he was still the favorite at Windmaker. Then they met Keith and Ann Haygood and purchased Keithann Rag Doll (Ch. Santana-Mandeville Rodney ex Ch. Hubertus Diamond Lil) who became a top producing bitch in 1973. The first breeding of any consequence came in 1967 when Swamp Fox was bred to Rag Doll. This gave them Ch. Keithann Windy and Ch. Windmaker's Summer Storm. In 1970, they took Summer Storm to Mrs. Walton's Ch. Lyn-Mar Acres M'Lord Batuff. This produced Ch. Windmaker's Storm Warning, Ch. Windmaker's Southern Storm, Windmaker's Black Storm, CD, Windmaker's Summer Breeze, and Windmaker's Windstorm. In 1971, Rag Doll was bred to Gorham's Southern Gentleman, giving them Ch. Windmaker's Great Thunder, TD, Gunstigg Morgan, and Spring Fever. In the early 1970s, Wanda saw Lena Wray tracking at the nationals and became interested in the work, later gaining TDs as well as CDs in obedience.

In 1963, the Bill Bartons obtained Abbot Run Valley Crackerjack (Ch. Abbot Run Valley Prankster ex Abbot Run Valley Sassy) from the Brandts. A few months later they went back and bought Abbot Run Valley Anita out of Ch. Abbot Run Valley Brassy ex Ch. Abbot Run Valley Gem. Crackerjack finished. He was bred to Anita who produced five lovely puppies. The Bartons purchased Richardson's Ann of Lime Tree (Ch. Lime Tree Micawber ex Ch. Richardson's Autumn Fire) from Nancy Lindsay's Lime Tree Kennels. Bred to Ch. Mister Tandy of Coralwood she produced Miss Mandelene of Coralwood. Mandy was later bred to Crackerjack and produced a beautiful bitch named Ch. Coralwood's Kadiddlehopper. In 1971, she became the number one bitch and ranked tenth of all Bassets being shown that year. The kennel name, Coralwood, was taken from the name of a particular section of the town in which they lived.

The Harpers obtained their second bitch, Marribea's Widget v.h. Harper (Ch. Santana-Mandeville's Tarzan ex Del Donna's Dian of Golden Bell) from the Merediths. They decided to linebreed toward Tarzan. Widget, bred to their Ch. Hugo Von Haus Harper, produced Ch. Molly Bea v.h. Harper. Molly was bred to Ch. Orange-park Dexter giving them Ch. Harper's Rhett Butler who was in the top ten Bassets for 1971, 1972, and 1973. By 1977, he had sired seventeen champions, one field champion, and one CD holder. He sired Can. & Am. Ch. Harper's Bart of Parkside and Can., Am., & Bermudian Ch. Parksides' Darby O'Gill owned by Ivan and Phyllis Macklin of Winnipeg, Canada.

The Orangepark Kennels of Mary and Wilton Meyer began with Hartshead Maybelline (Ch. Santana-Mandeville Gigolo ex Hartshead Looks Beautiful) and Ch. Santana-Mandeville Minnie (Ch. Santana-Mandeville No-Count ex Miss Jenny Magoo). They bred both bitches to Ch. Santana-Mandeville Tarzan. From Maybelline they got Ch. Orangepark Dexter and Ch. Orangepark Dotty. Minnie gave them Ch. Orangepark Eustace. This gave them an opportunity for close line breeding. Eustace was bred to Maybelline producing Ch. Orangepark Roy, the top winning dog for 1969 and 1970. When they bred to Helen Nelson Kellog's Ch. Santana-Mandeville Ichabod, they had even more that could be used for linebreeding. Some of the champions produced by Orangepark studs were: sired by Dexter; Ch. Orangepark Millicent, Ch. Musicland's Casey Jones, Ch. Knox's Kash McKall, Ch. Musicland's Crazy Rhythm, Ch. Harper's Rhett Butler, Ch. Tommy's Cousin Geo. O'Glenhaven, Ch. Musicland's Chairmain, Ch. Musicland's Country Music, Ch. Slippery Hill Quixote, and Ch. Arlo of Castlereagh; sired by Eustace; Ch. Orangepark Roy, Ch. Le Will's Sam's Son Le Clair, Ch. Orangepark Sabrina, and Ch. Orangepark Daffodil.

Al and Barbara Wicklund purchased their first Basset, Coralwood's Robin, from the Bartons. Robin was lost during surgery before she could have a career. At the suggestion of the Bartons, the Wicklunds went to Marge Brandt. Here they purchased Abbot Run Valley Pamela (Abbot Run Valley Gabby ex Am. & Can. Ch. Intoxication of Blue Hill), bred by Doris Hurry, on a co-ownership basis. She finished easily. In a mating to Ch. Abbot Run Valley Brassy, she produced Ch. Abbot Run Valley Bold n' Brassy, CD, Ch. Bar-Wick's Hey Sandy, Bar-Wick's Robbie, CD, and Bar-Wick's Dot's O.K., CD. Dot was their first obedience dog. Al trained her. Barbara gained a title on Bold n' Brassy. The Bar-Wick kennel name was adopted.

Marge Brandt held co-ownership on Sandy and Bold n' Brassy.

Sandy produced one litter sired by Ch. Ebenezer of Hampden Meadows who was co-owned by Marge Brandt and Betty Dexter. The Wicklunds and Marge Brandt kept Ch. Bar-Wick's Miss Met from this litter. Miss Met was bred to Ch. Tal-E-Ho's Charger producing Ch. Bar-Wick's First Baseman and Ch. Bar-Wick's Reba Ridge. Her second litter was by Ch. Forestbay Montgomery.

Out in Washington, Thor and Dorothy Sundberg had become interested in the breed. They obtained Notrenom's Cindy (Ch. Musicland's Mozart ex Ch. Bassett's Houseboater) from Dick and Evelyn Bassett's Notrenom Kennels. They later obtained their first champion from Bill and Lorraine Russell's Russtan kennel. This was Ch. Russtan's Taliesen Kilarney. After "Toby" attended his first national, in 1967, the Sundbergs decided that they must breed a different type if they wanted to win anyplace other than their own area where the dogs were much like theirs. They became acquainted with Norman and Connie Griggs, from Virginia. The Griggs' Bassets were heavy in Millvan background, and the Sundbergs began to incorporate these lines with theirs.

Ch. Nancy Evans Sir Galahad came into the spotlight about this time, and was a frequent winner in the Southwest. He was bred by Nancy Evans and owned, at that time, by the Carl Fuhrmans of San Antonio, Texas. In retirement, he was owned by Mrs. Joan Urban of Corpus Christi. Mrs. Urban bred him to her Ch. Sisu's Chere Amie producing Ch. Joan Urban's Peter Gunn and Ch. Joan Urban's Honey West. Alan Turner bred him to Ch. Glenhaven's Butcher Boy's littermate, Little Tear Drops, getting Ch. Glenhaven's Lord Jack.

Another Washington breeder was developing during this period. John Hackley had owned a Basset as early as 1954. When he moved to Washington, he purchased two pets, Chester and Samantha. Through his veterinarian and one of John's administrators in California, he located a contact for the BHC of Greater Seattle. Here he met the Bill Russells from whom he purchased Russtan's Flabellafera (Ch. Kelly's Major Topic ex Notrenom's Mozette of Russtan) who successfully completed her championship. Mr. Hackley's occupation makes for traveling. While in Durham, North Carolina, he visited kennels to obtain another bitch. There was nothing available but the Santana-Mandeville line was suggested to him. He was put in

Ch. Orangepark Dexter (Ch. Santana-Mandeville's Tarzan ex Hartshead Maybelline), owned by Mr. and Mrs. R. Wilton Meyer.
Ludwig

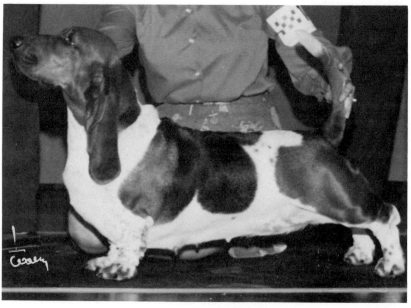

Ch. Southlake Adoration, CD, owned and handled by Freda Burks, a multiple Specialty winner.
Twomey

touch with Yvonne Ground who had J. P. Morgan. Here he bought a Morgan daughter named Moal Pierrette and finished her. John adopted the White Mountain kennel name. When he attended Chicago International, he was impressed with Ch. Long View Acres Winston and two of his sons, Ch. Braun's Grampagin and Ch. Braun's Herman of Rambling Road, litter brothers out of Rockin-Pas Cinder. He purchased a male, Ch. Braun's Prince John, from the next litter. Upon finishing, Flabellafera was bred to Ch. Glenhaven's Lord Jack. This mating gave him his first homebred champion, Ch. White Mountain Amorette, finished from the bred-by-exhibitor class.

As a result of his travels to other parts of the country and what he saw of other dogs, Mr. Hackley decided that he wanted to continue to incorporate more elegance into his line. He already had a start with Eleandon bloodlines behind Lord Jack and Prince John so he purchased a bitch from Mary Louise and Finn Bergishagen. She was Jagersven Blue Bonnet out of one of the matings of Ch. Margem Hills Mr. Brown and Ch. Shadow's Snow White. When the author moved to Florida, John Hackley obtained Ch. Deacon of Rockin-Pas from her. Deacon was heavily line bred from the Eleandon breedings.

Rebelglen kennels, John and Jo NewMyer, began when the New-Myers attended the BHC of Southern California show. They already owned a Basset but went shopping for one to show. They leased Jungfrau Fred (Ch. Flory's Houdini ex Flory's Gina Lowbridge) from Jim and Bonny Slayman who taught them how to show. The Jim Florys taught them about their bloodline based on a litter by Gallio of Belbay and Flory's Penelope. Gallio was the product of a father-daughter breeding on Ch. Mr. Cyclops of Belbay. Penelope was a Jet Foret-bred bitch and a granddaughter of Ch. Siefenjagenheim Lazy Bones and Ch. Mon Phillipe of Greenly Hall. She produced Ch. La Feu Mouche and Prince Valiant II, both extensively used as studs. Valiant produced Ch. Flory's Houdini. Gina Lowbridge was a La Feu Mouche daughter. The NewMyers bred their Jungfrau Fred to Am. & Mex. Ch. Kelly's Major Topic (Ch. Sujumar's Lone Ranger ex Am. & Mex. Ch. Belleau's Belle Jolie, CD) owned by the Major William Kellys. Major Topic's sire was by Ch. Belleau's Mr. Collier, a full brother of his dam, Jolie. As a result of the whelping, the NewMyers lost Fred but succeeded in raising the

Ch. Beartooth Victor (Sir Zachary of Margem ex Margem Hills Huslin Harriat), owned and bred by Dr. and Mrs. Byron R. Wisner. In two years of campaigning Victor built a superb show record that included 9 BIS, 24 Group firsts, 64 other placements and 124 BBs. In 1978 he was #1 Basset, #6 Hound and #25 among the top winners of all breeds on the *Kennel Review* system. He is shown here being awarded BIS at the Central Wyoming KC under judge Elaine Young, handler the late Marvin Cates.   *Kloeber*

puppies. Their first champion from this litter, Ch. Rebel's Frosty Topic, was breeder-owner handled. Am & Mex. Ch. Rebel's Major Calamity, CD was from the same litter. When Frosty developed cancer, one of his sons, Midnight Cowboy of Rebelglen took over as the kennel stud. His dam was Cinnamon Cinder Finale (Bar-B Theodore the Great ex Soupe's Rebel Abigail). Theodore was heavily linebred on Bar-B Dapper Dan. Abigail was linebred from Ch. Johnny Rebel, a Ch. Belbay Chevalier son. Midnight Cowboy produced Ch. Rebelglen's Missy of Rhineland and Ch. Priscilla of Rebelglen. Missy was co-bred with Bud and Diane Rinderneck of Rhinelan kennels. She took four majors and won all her points from the bred-by-exhibitor class. Priscilla was bred by Cynthia Curran.

Randy and Sue Sutfin, Ran-Su kennels, bought their first show dog, Casey of Wildwood (Ch. Margem Hills Dandy-Lion ex Wildwood's Gay Blade), from Jim and Jean Will. Their next was Marischen's Copper Coin (Margem Hills Diamond Jim ex Marischen's Mopey Lady). They brought out Ran-Su's Drummer Boy out of the Henry Peace's Ch. Frito Bandit of Margem Hills and Ran-Su's Cuddle Me. They obtained Orangepark Gidget (Ch. Orangepark Dexter ex Ch. Margem Hills Ginger Fizz. Bred to Am. & Can. Ch. Gin Dic's Bit O'Brass, she produced Am. & Can. Ch. Ran-Su's Carrien-On. They stepped into the spotlight when they brought out Am & Can. Ch. Ran-Su's Fanny Farmer, a beautiful daughter of Gidget by Ch. Coventry Rock Andy. Fanny finished and placed in the Group from the puppy class. She was a consistent Specialty winner and had about 25 Group placements. She was the first Basset bitch to take a Best in Show in Canada, from the classes. When she retired from the show ring, she was bred to Ch. Lyn-Mar Acres Extra Man.

Ch. Santana-Mandeville Rodney, owned by Len and Marge Skolnick, became the top winning dog in the East in 1965.

Barbara Dunning finished Ch. Bar-B Patrick O'Toole and Ch. Bar-B Ringside Gossip. Ch. Bar-B Endless Gossip was bred to Ch. Nancy Evans Double Cross and produced Ch. Bar-B Galloping Gossip.

Walter Brandt and Roger Fredette bred Ch. Ro-Fre la Reine de la Balle to Ch. Lyn-Mar Acres Top Brass. Of the several noteworthy dogs in this litter, Ch. Abbot Run Valley Brassy became the best known. He finished at eleven months with five majors and a Group placing. He produced 79 litters and 478 get. Among these were 48 American champions and several from other countries. He was the top producer for 1966, 1967, and 1968. One of Mrs. Brandt's favorites was Ch. A.R.V. Gabby by Ch. Long View Acres Smokey ex Ch. Driquire of Blue Hill. Bred to A.R.V. Brass Beauty, he sired A.R.V. Dawn, owned by the Joe Lynches, and A.R.V. Gomer, co-owned with Joanne Lynch. After Walter's death, Marge continued with the dogs. She co-owned with several people including Doris Hurry, Barbara Finkelstien Wicklund, Charlotte Larsen, and Dana Knowlton. In time, she had to give up the kennel and her dogs were placed in the kennel of Freda and Jerry Spitz.

In 1966, Sandra Campbell purchased a young show prospect from Paul Saucier's Rockin-Pas kennels in Miami, Florida. Ch. Geronimo of Rockin-Pas (Ch. Maverick of Rockin-Pas ex Ch. Tomo's Hells-A-Poppin) finished easily and went on to establish. an impressive show record from 1967 to 1971. In 1972, he came out of retirement, to be shown in the Veterans' Class at the national Specialty, taking Best of Breed. "Mo" sired Ch. Brigadier's Bumble Bee, Ch. Brigadier's Tiffany, Ch. Liberte Trooper of Craigwood, Ch. Ruggles of Red Gap, Ch. Wal-Bec's Alpha Bravo Sebastion, Ch. Craigwood's Horace Gould, Ch. S. C.'s Balentine Babe. By breeding Balentine Babe to Ch. Sir Tomo of Glenhaven, Sandra emphasized even more strongly the Eleandon blood already present in her line. The Rockin-Pas dogs were heavily line and inbred in this line, down from both Ch. Sir Tomo of Glenhaven and his brother, Ch. Jesse James of Eleandon. In 1971, Sandra acquired Field's Lancer (Ch. Forestbay John Mathias ex Ch. Hiflite's Terianna) who became a top winner during the next two years. He sired Ch. Amazing Grace of Craigwood, Ch. Blackader's Kate of Craigwood, Ch. Lancer's Tally Ho of Craigwood, Ch. Craigwood's Fancy That. The Craigwood prefix was shared by Nancy Taylor after 1973. They obtained Ch. Windamohr's Gamble (Ch. Manor Hill Father James ex Coralwood's Cousin Kate) who finished in nine shows. Among their brood bitches are Ch. P. J. II, Craigwood's Rejoice, Craigwood's Bonhomie Mahalia, and Hiflite's Cher of Switchbark. In 1973, Sandra obtained Hiflite's Kentucky Wonder (Ch. Hiflite's Brumeister ex Hiflite's Caroline) from Carol O'Bryant and Mary Jane Booth. He was shown to his championship and contributed a great deal as a stud.

Paul Mohr finished Ch. Supai's Bashful Payola in 1967, then Ch. Supai's Hermit, and Ch. Supai's Roadblock in 1969. In 1970, it was Ch. Merribea's Buttercup, Ch. Supai's Win'Jammer, and Ch. D'Artagnan Brutusina. He then sold several others who finished. Jim Bruet purchased Ch. Supai's Moonshadow. Nancy Evans and Georgia White owned Ch. Supai's Lead Zeppelin. Ch. Supai's Pete's My Homely Hope was owned by Susan Glady. Diane Malenfant owned Ch. Supai's Sleeping Rainbow.

The Von Skauton kennels of Garry and Dawn Towne began with a puppy that grew up to be Am. & Can. Ch. Schnaps Von Skauton (Long View Acres Ed Too ex Nab-A-Line Sorrowful Ruth). He was entered in his first show in 1964. That year, they also purchased a foundation bitch, Jacq-Scott's Willie Towne (Ch. Margem Hills Sweet William ex Heritage Farms Betsy Ross) from the Jacq-Scott kennels of Jack and Ruby Patterson. In 1966, they purchased another stud, Am. & Can. Ch. Seneca Sambo Leeno (Am. & Can. Ch. Gin Dic's Bit O' Brass ex Ch. Musicland's Poinciana). In the next thirteen years, they took over 225 Best of Breed awards, and placed in the Group over 60 times, in the United States and Canada. Their Am. & Can. Ch. Heine Von Skauton and Ch. Von Skauton's Camillus Clyde won well under breeder-judges at Specialty shows, and their Can. Ch. Kleine Heide Von Skauton was Winners Bitch at the Canadian national Specialty.

John and Margretta Patterson bought their first dog from Herb and Mable Erwin. The dog was bred by the Erwins' daughter, in California, and was sired by Ch. Hubs Kris Kringle, a Lazy Bones son. Then they purchased a Lazy Bones daughter, Ch. Reveilles Moonbeam, from Lloyd Reller. Together with Emily Kultchar they founded the Margem Hill Kennels. Some dogs were purchased from Nancy Evans. This stock went back to Belbay and Santana-Mandeville. Three bitches were bred to Ch. Nancy Evans Double Cross. These were crossed with Lazy Bones breedings and Am. & Bermuda Ch. Sir Tomo of Glenhaven. Tomo, bred by Eleanor Bliss, Eleandon kennels, had been purchased by the Pattersons from Glen Smith. Tomo became a top producing sire, and his get are now known throughout the country.

Ch. BevLee's Emily Bronte, owned by Bev and Lee Stockfelt

Am. and Can. Ch. Seneca Sambo Leeno, owned by Garry and Dawn Towne.
Klein

Ch. Ran-Su's Fanny Farmer, owned, bred and handled by Sue Sutfin, is shown placing Group 4th at the Ashtabula KC under judge Marion Mangrum. Shortly after this win, Fanny annexed a Canadian BIS award.

You will note that the names Eleanor Bliss and Eleandon come forth in many bloodlines. Mrs. Bliss passed away before the most famous dogs were finished. Her breedings left their mark throughout the country. Her dogs were heavy in Lyn-Mar but outcrossed, then linebred. Paul Saucier linebred his Rockin-Pas Bassets from Ch. Sir Tomo of Glenhaven and Ch. Jesse James of Eleandon. Tomo first went to Texas, after Mrs. Bliss' death, then was sold to Margem Hills. Jesse James stayed in Miami. My husband and I were so taken with Jesse that we obtained one of his linebred daughters. Eventually we purchased Ch. Deacon of Rockin-Pas who was bred back to our own bitches down from the Jesse daughter and to outside bitches down from Tomo. The resulting style can be seen in Bassets from many kennels in Northwestern Ohio. Upon our retirement to Florida, Deacon went to John Hackley, in Washington, where such elegance is needed. The same style is evident in the breedings from Hiflite, Glenhaven, Craigwood, Jagersven, and Clowverleaf, where the Eleandon lines were used. Of course, the degree of influence varies with the outcrosses used.

Georgia and Eric White established the Cherry Hills Kennels, in Colorado, in 1967. Their first champion was Ch. Cherry Hills Benadictine. Ch. Glenhi's Bandolero gained a Best in Show from the classes enroute to his championship. Ch. La Z Dee J's Johnny Be Good, co-owned with Nancy Evans, was a multiple Group winner. Ch. Nancy Evans Fair Exchange, also co-owned with Nancy Evans, was a multiple Specialty winner who finished from the novice class in three consecutive days. Mrs. Evans also co-owns Ch. Standpine's Siesta Pancho, a Specialty and Group winner. The lovely, top winning and producing stud, Ch. Tommy's Cousin Geo. O'Glenhaven is co-owned with Thomas Bloomer III.

In 1967, Beverly and Lee Stockfelt obtained their first male, Ch. BevLees Pooh Bear of Willie-O, from Bill Cline. They had previously owned some Basset bitches. He became their first champion, first Specialty winner, Group winner, and placed in the top ten. Willie was bred to a daughter of Ch. Musicland's Bill Bailey and produced Ch. BevLees Hercule Poirot. Jeanne Hills gave them Musicland's Flamenco. When bred to Willie, she produced Ch. BevLees Emily Bronte, Group winner and number one Basset bitch for 1971. They acquired Willie's half-sister, BevLees Forever

Amber, who gave them Ch. BevLees Toonerville Trolley, Ch. BevLees Tale of Two Cities, and Can. Ch. BevLees Madame le Farge. Emily Bronte, bred to Ch. Standpine's Siesta Pancho, produced Ch. BevLees Tom Sawyer, Ch. BevLees Nancy Drew, and Am. & Can. Ch. BevLees Injun Joe who won two Bests in Show in Canada. The Stockfelts linebreed within their own kennel, going out for what they wish to add. They prefer a shorter body than many other breeders do, hoping to avoid disc problems.

Bassets were little known in Montana until the coming of Dr. and Mrs. Byron Wisner and Beartooth Farm. They had met Margretta Patterson and Emily Kultchar when attending Ohio State where Dr. Wisner was a resident in oral surgery. There they purchased their first dogs, Sir Zachary of Margem Hills (Ch. Sir Tomo of Glenhaven ex Cholmondeley D. of Margem Hills) and Margem Hills Madame Phoebe (Ch. Willstone Harvey ex Ch. Margem Hills the Sister). After arriving in Montana, they planned to develop or continue the development of separate and distinct lines. Their Margem Hills breedings extended back to Lyn-Mar and Lazy Bones. Their Santana-Mandeville line was stock from Slippery Hill and Orangepark Kennels. They finished Chs. Beartooth Inez, Fireball, Zephyr, Germaine, Ajax, Wildfire, Lucille, Victor, and Owen.

Joseph and Anne Lynch purchased Ch. Richardson's Padraic of Cuas (Abbot Run Valley Lucius ex Beyer's Minerva) as a companion from Dave Richardson. Helen Boutell encouraged them to show after seeing the dog. Daughter, Joanne, became interested and handled him to a prestigious record of wins that included Best of Winners at Westminster, 1967, followed by Best of Breed there the following year. He also won four BHCA Specialties. Joanne also showed Ch. Abbot Run Valley Gomer, co-owned with Marge Brandt, to a Group placement from the puppy class. He finished easily and was Best of Breed at Westminster in 1971. By 1973 he became a top stud, is the sire of Ch. Custusha's Carlos Santana, another Specialty, Group, and BIS winner.

Ray Wells and Louise Eldridge married and merged the Cape Cod and Great Oak Kennels, moving to North Harwich, Massachusetts. They purchased a puppy, Sobrina of Cape Cod, from Dana Knowlton, and also obtained her sister, Ch. Custusha's Melissa

103

McGee (Ch. Abbot Run Valley Gomer ex Ch. Sara Bayburnhart). Sobrina was bred to Marge Brandt's Ch. Ebenezer of Hampden Meadows producing Handyman of Cape Cod. Ray and Louise continued their interest in field trials and purchased Slippery Hill Orange Julius (Fd. Ch. Dorshire's Sonny ex Ch. Slippery Hill Pimento) from Len Skolnick. They acquired Fd. Ch. Willow's Jennifer and Fd. Ch. Jennifer's Pride (Dual Ch. Double B's Lucky Libertine ex Fd. Ch. Willow's Jennifer) from John Bowman.

In 1967, Het Garwood acquired a pup from the first litter of Ch. Glenhaven's Butcher Boy and Ch. Kazoo's Question Mark, bred by the Robert Booths. She became Am. & Mex. Ch. Hiflite's Jodi. Het obtained Ch. Glenhaven's Lord Jack as a puppy, in 1967, from Alan Turner. Roy Murray handled him to his title but was committed to show another champion, Tom Bloomer's Tomfoolery. Walt Shellenbarger took Lord Jack to California where he accumulated 137 Bests of Breed, 28 Group firsts, 50 other Group placements, five Bests in Shows, and six Specialty BBS. His record made him the top hound in the country in 1971. Het got Ch. Kazoo's Dawn from the Booths in 1968. Her great-grandchildren were brought out in the late 1970s.

Leanore and Ivan Horabin became interested in field trialing in 1970 with help from Elsie Tagg, John and Betts Phillips, and the Lenape BHC members. Their foundation stock came from George Johnston's Sykemoor line, descended from English show and French hunting stock. Many were from members of the famous de l'Ombree pack. They imported Sykemoor Nestor and Sykemoor Neluski (Dalewell Rambler ex Sykemoor Java) in 1968. Nestor's sire was a member of the British BHC pack. In 1972, they imported Sykemoor Tandy and Sykemoor Trinquette (Ch. Wingjays Polygon ex Sykemoor Mirette). From Nestor, they kept Skyline Arlette, Affable, and Ajax out of Fd. Ch. Tagabout's Rolls Royce, and Skyline Candy out of Trinquette. They kept Skyline Bramble from Tandy. The Skyline prefix was adopted. Nestor became a Grand field champion. Tandy, Arlette, Affable, Ajax, and Bramble all gained their field titles.

Dan and Sondra Jones, Marshills Kennels, purchased their first show dog from Nancy Evans. She was Nancy Evans Majestic Queen (Ch. Standpines Johnny Concho ex Evaline's Madam Samantha).

Shortly thereafter, they bought Marischen's Lil' Ladd (Ch. Marischen's Ladd ex Marischen's Miss L) from Paul and Mary Marischen. The Pattersons sold them Margem Hills Fyre Ball (Ch. Margem Hills for the Books ex Margem Hills Pia of Ages Creek). In 1970, they purchased Willstone Harvey (Ch. Orangepark Dexter ex Ch. Margem Hills Ginger Fizz). Bobby Barlow handled Willstone Harvey to his championship in 1971. Harvey sired Ch. Marshills Gollywag, Ch. Margem Hills Bloom'n O' Yankee, Ch. Marshills Wheeler Dealer, Ch. Von Skauton's Camillus Clyde, and Am. & Can. Ch. Heine Von Skauton.

The Joneses purchased Marischen's Sassafras Sara for breeding only. Barbara Borshow sold them Mel-Ann Acres Little Iodine (Gin Dic's Choice ex Kinslow's Clementine) and Kinslow's Bittersweet (Nasa's Color Me Corky ex Beautiful Bouncing Bessie). Others purchased from Margem Hills were: Margem Hills Hotsie-Totsie, Margem Hills Miss So-n-So, Margem Hills Tutti-Frutti, a full sister to Fyre Ball, Margem Hills Maybelline, another sister, and Margem Hills Miss American Pie.

Jerry and Nell Looper bought their first show dog from Jim and Wanda White. He was Ch. Windmaker's Spring Fever. Later that year, 1969, they obtained Hiflite's Suzanne from Bob and Mary Jane Booth. During the first five years, they had difficulty getting bitches to conceive and only managed two litters. They eventually obtained a producing bitch from Pat Lenzen, and by the mid 1970s, their dogs were winning in the Oklahoma area.

Dorothy and Harvey Fullerton owned Hartshead Magnolia who was purchased from Emil and Effie Seitz. Bred to Ch. Barbara's J. P. Morgan Le Clair, she produced Le Clair's Goldie, Cool Hand Luke, Thunder, and Cordelia, beside Le Clair's Merry Madelyn who was purchased as a puppy by Jim and Marge Cook of Azle, Texas. Madelyn finished her championship at the age of two, gained her CD at the age of three, a CDX at four, and her UD at five. Bred to Jocamime's Billy Goat (a Tarzan son) she gave the Cook's Ch. Bugle Bay's Ado Annie, CD. Marge found that she thoroughly enjoyed obedience work and put both a UD and a T on Nancy Evan's Pandora.

Madelyn was bred a second time, this time to Ch. Lanes's Arlo of Castlereagh, owned by Bob Wasley, bred by Bob Arbs. The only

105

puppy in the litter was named Souffle. Always handled by Marge, she finished easily and did well as a champion. Upon gaining her championship, Marge began to train Souffle in obedience. Ch. Bugle Bay's Souffle, UD gained her title easily. Madelyn and Souffle are thought to be the only living champion mother and daughter UD Bassets in the 1970s.

Some of the dogs being run at the trials at this time were: Paul Kulp's Hilawn Repeat; Ken McWilliams' McWilliams' Captain Jaw; E. Robinson's Little Lady Susie; George's Little Girl owned by Bill Germann; Ed Eylander's Ed's Harry; L. LaFollette's Crystal Rock Mountain Dew; Slippery Hill Calvin owned by Len Skolnick; Key Club's Oliver Onslow owned by J. S. Clark; H. Knepp's Rose's Shorty; Navar's Scout owned by Fred Bayless; Germann's Bellows Kay; Holly's April owned by Mike Holly; E. Robinson's Little Lady Susie; J. Phillips' Sandy Oaks Dixie; Coldstream Butterscotch owned by Fred Bayless; P. Bennet's Hi Lawn Roxanne; Bill Siers Sandy Hill Billy Jo; Bellow's Beldean owned by M. Braun; Van's Black Jack owned by Larry Elmore; and Ken McWilliams' Dixie Belle.

Harry and Stella Porter, Bayroc Kennels in Oregon, owned Bassets since 1965 but did not begin to show until 1968. About 1970, they bought Ch. Slippery Hill Nutmeg, Slippery Hill Modesty, and Slippery Hill Ilka from the Skolnicks. They also bought several from Musicland. Ch. Slippery Hill Nutmeg produced Ch. Bayroc's Tom Son. Slippery Hill Modesty gave them Ch. Bayroc's Miss Bea Haven and Ilka produced Ch. Bayroc's Blue Brutus. They made quite a few champions from the Musicland line: Tango, Summertime, Sweet Caroline, and Marie Elena. Ch. Musicland's Sweet Caroline was the dam of Ch. Bayroc's Sweet Sue and Maria Elena produced Ch. Bayroc's Country Gentleman.

In 1969, the Bergishagens added Shadow's Snow White to their Jagersven dogs. She was purchased from her breeders, James and Carol Schadt, and was out of Ch. Gin Dic's Bit O'Brass ex Northwood's Lazy Lizzy. She finished in a few shows under breeder judges. Ch. Margem Hills Mr. Brown was shipped to the Bergishagens for breeding to Snow White, returned to his Texas owner, Bette Williams, then returned to Jagersven on a co-ownership basis, where he gained his Canadian title and was used repeatedly on

Am. and Can. Fld. Ch. Jackson's Samantha Lu,
owned and handled by Sylvia C. Ellingwood.
Ashbey

Ch. Shadow's Snow White, owned by
Finn and Mary Louise Bergishagen.
Gilbert

Snow White. Together they produced a long list of outstanding offspring, such as Ch. Jagersven Blue Ribbon, Ch. Jagersven Blue Banner, and Ch. Jagersven Blueberry Muffin. Ch. J. Bluebonnet went to John Hackley's White Mountain Kennels. A third breeding produced J. Blueprint and J. Blue Jeans who is owned by Lena Wray. Her fourth litter produced J. Blue Tango, J. Blue Angel owned by the Rogers in New York, J. Blue Belle owned by the Wisners, and J. Blue Diamond owned by the Martins. Some of the other title holders from this kennel are Am. & Can. Ch. Stoneybluff Jagersven Marie, Ch. Tason's Molly Brown, CD, Ch. Webbridge Calamity Jane, Ch. Sharlee's Brown Eyed Susan, Ch. Jagersven Headliner, and Jagersven Samson, CD.

By 1970, Joan & Ron Scholz' Ch. Manor Hill Top Spot, bred to Ch. Forestbay Mamie the Minx, produced Ch. Forestbay Joshua who played an important role in the future of the Manor Hill Bassets. By 1975, Manor Hill Moon Bonnet (Ch. Blackie's Bleemer ex Manor Hill Diane) had been bred to Ch. Forestbay Montgomery (Ch. Forestbay Joshua ex Forestbay Manor Hill Mahalia). This union produced Ch. Manor Hill Tooth Fairy who was the top show bitch of 1974 and 1975. Other notable Bassets of Manor Hill that were bred at this time included Ch. Manor Hill Baby Tooth, Ch. Manor Hill Father James, and Ch. Manor Hill Molly-Molly. Ch. Bonnie Ridge Fire-Bird, her son, Ch. Manor Hill Top Spot, his granddaughter, Manor Hill Moon Bonnet. Ch. Manor Hill Tooth Fairy and Ch. Manor Hill Father James are the nucleus of the Scholzes' strain.

Fire struck the Northwoods Kennels of Don and Barbara Martin in 1970. Five generations of stock were destroyed and the Martins had to start all over again. They obtained Galway Theresa from Col. Julian and Elizabeth Dexter's Galway kennels. She had five Specialty wins and was BOS at Westminster in 1973, and was named top winning bitch for 1972. In 1973, they purchased Ch. Tal-E-Ho's Top Banana from the estate of Dr. Frank Blauhut. Banana was bred by Henry Jerman, Tal-E-Ho Kennels, and Mark Dembrow out of Ch. Tal-E-Ho's Prancer ex Tal-E-Ho's Dorinda. He had been handled by Bobby Barlow as a class dog and finished in five shows at the age of nine months. The Martin boys, Peter and Bryan, co-owned him and showed him to thirteen Specialty Bests

Ch. Manor Hill Tooth Fairy, owned by Joan Scholz and handled by Howard Nygood, a consistent Group winner.

Gilbert

Ch. Gin Dic's Bit O'Brass, owned and handled by Virginia Lemeaux. She is shown making a win at the Onondaga KA show under the highly respected breeder-judge Mrs. M. L. Walton.

Shafer

of Breed and two Canadian Bests in Show, making him one of the top winners from 1974 to 1976. He was Best of Breed at Westminster in 1974 and won the BHCA Fall Specialty in 1975 and 1976.

Jean Spaulding purchased Fd. Ch. Trick or Treat and Fd. Ch. Jack O'Lantern from Howard Smith. She became a well-known field trialer on a national level. To fill a need, she began the field trial publication, *The Basset Babbler,* in 1974.

Andy and Sue Shoemaker purchased Duffy of Hahs-C-Enda for their Shoefly Kennels. He was bred by Patricia and Orrie Hahs out of Touloose Lautrec at Hantslot ex Peggy's Jolly Jennifer. He finished by going Best of Winners at the Sacramento Specialty in 1971 and was one of the top ten for 1972, owner-handled. He sired seven champions before his death in 1974.

The Skolnicks' Ch. Slippery Hill Paprika, sired by Ch. Santana-Mandeville Egghead, was bred back to her grandsire, Ch. Santana-Mandeville Rodney, producing Ch. Slippery Hill Katrinka. Katrinka was bred to a Ch. Orangepark Dexter son, Slippery Hill Quixote. Their daughter, Slippery Hill Mocha, was bred to a son of Dexter and Ch. Slippery Hill Lana, an Egghead daughter. This son, Studly von Happy Jack, purchased by the Skolnicks, and Mocha are the sire and dam of Ch. Slippery Hill Hudson. Hudson, owned by Mrs. Alan R. Robson of Glen Moore, Pennsylvania, finished his championship easily and was the top winning Basset in the United States from 1974 to 1977. He was number one of all Hounds in 1975, had over 100 Group firsts, and 30 Bests in Show in his career. He was Best of Breed at the BHCA Specialty in 1974 and Best of Breed at Westminster from 1975 through 1977. He was also Group Second there in 1976 and 1977. The Skolnicks also bred Fd. Ch. Slippery Hill Sophie who took the BHCA field trial the same year that Hudson was BB at the Specialty. Over the years, twenty-six bench champions came from Slippery Hill Kennels. Dual Ch. Slippery Hill Cinnamon, CD was the first Basset to hold an obedience degree in addition to show and field titles. She was also the dam of Ch. Slippery Hill Pimento and Can. Ch. Slippery Hill Portnoy.

The Slippery Hill field breedings were based on a brother and sister mating of Fd. Ch. Beldean's King Kong Gladiator and Fd.

Ch. Slippery Hill Hudson (Studly Von Happy Jack ex Slippery Hill Mocka), owned by Mrs. Alan R. Robson and bred by Leonard Skolnick. Hudson's show record has established him as one of the all-time greats of the Hound Group. He is many times a BIS winner as well as a multiple Specialty and Westminster winner. He is shown winning BIS at the Central Ohio KC under Mrs. Nicholas Demidoff, handler Bobby Barlow.

Booth

Ch. Tal-E-Ho's Top Banana (Ch. Tal-E-Ho's Prancer ex Tal-E-Ho's Dorinda), owned by Peter and Bryan Martin and bred by Henry Jerman and Mark Dembrow, was handled by his owners to numerous good wins in top national competition.

Potter

Ch. Beldean's Slippery Hill Sam (Fd. Ch. Aquino's King Kong ex Fd. Ch. Olson's Samanthe). Fd. Ch. Slippery Hill Calvin was bred to Sam to produce three field champions: S. H. Stub, S. H. Sherman, and S. H. Sophie. Stub and Sophie were among the first Grand field champions. Sophie was the winner of the 1974 BHCA Fall nationals. Her dam, Sam, had won in 1970. Gladiator sired Fd. Ch. Slippery Hill Agnes out of his sister, Sam, and Fd. Ch. Slippery Hill Prudence and Pansy out of his niece, Sophie. Stub, bred to his half-sister, Agnes, produced Fd. Chs. Slippery Hill Ozzie, Otis, and Beldean's Slippery Hill Kong. By 1977, the Skolnicks finished twelve field champions.

From 1970 to 1977, Musicland Kennels produced such dogs as: Ch. Roadrunner (Casey Jones ex Sawyer's Rockyridge Oola); Ch. Sweet Caroline (Pool Shark ex Songbird) owned by Bayroc Kennels; Chs. Morning Glory and Marie Elena (Pool Shark ex Annabel Lee); Ch. Joy (Casey Jones ex Siboney); Chs. Windsong and Willie Jones (Casey Jones ex LuHow's Winnepesaukee); Chs. Summertime, Shaft, Sweet Eloise, and Satin Doll (Pool Shark ex Torch Song); Chs. Goodtime Charlie, Go Go Girl and Molly Bee (Pool Shark ex Windsong); Chs. Belinda and Bugle Boy (Casey Jones ex Windsong; Chs. Honey and Hilda von Mizan (Pool Shark ex Joy) Ch. Misty (Casey Jones ex Windsong); Chs. Rovin' Gambler, Rebel Rouser, Ravishing Ruby, and Rosemarie (Pool Shark ex BevLee's Amy March); all bearing the Musicland prefix. Kennels that were producing from this stock were: Beauregarde, Bowler, Green Acres, Greenbury, Kelmic, Lagniappe, Lazy H, LuHow, Madcap, Ren-Lo-Run, Ro-Barb, Tailgate, and Traak.

Mary Bastable and Fran Gray experimented with their breeding program. In 1972, they obtained Musicland's Satin Doll from Jeanne Hills. After gaining her championship, she was bred to Ch. Belvidere P. Beaureguarde and Ch. Musicland's Casey Jones. From then, they planned to linebreed on this bloodline.

Howard Smith was producing dogs that made an important contribution to field trial bloodlines. Rosie's Road Runner (Rosie's Skipper ex Rosie's Black Satin), mated to Rosie's Bill produced three pups that finished. Bred to Dual Ch. Pettit's Ranger Ric, Road Runner gave Howard three more pups, two of which finished easily. He bred an outstanding litter from Fd. Ch. Rosie's Gentle

(Fd. Ch. Rosie's Bill ex Fd. Ch. Fouse's Cindy Lee) sired by Fd. Ch. Carl's Baby. Six, out of the seven pups, gained their field titles. Fd. Ch. Rosie's Gail was owned by Ray Farmer. She was bred to her sire, Fd. Ch. Carl's Baby, producing Fd. Ch. Ina's Carline. Bred to Carl's Little Fellow, owned by Len Skolnick, Carline produced one of the hottest dogs of the 1976 season, Fd. Ch. Ina's Wimpy.

William and Mary Rider obtained Gail and Rosie's Karl, from the Gentle and Carl's Baby breeding, Howard kept Rosie's Genny, and the Skolnicks took Carl's Little Fellow. Among Howard's other dogs were Grand Fd. Ch. Campbell's Rebel Queen, Fd. Ch. Rosie's Michie, Fd. Ch. Rosie's Sportsman, Rosie's Peggy, and Fd. Ch. Rosie's Gladys.

In 1970, Am. & Can. Ch. Tal-E-Ho's Prancer was whelped out of a litter sired by Tal-E-Ho's George (Ch. Manor Hill Top Spot ex Ch. Talleyrand's Lynette) and Tal-E-Ho's Ka-Ro (Ch. Talleyrand's Keene ex Ch. Talleyrand's Lynette). This male was handled to his championships by his owner, Ann Jerman of West Islip, N.Y., from the bred-by-exhibitor class. Prancer went on to win twelve Specialty shows including the BHCA Specialty in 1971 and, by 1977, produced twenty champions, including the Top Banana dog. Top Banana was bred to his half-sister, Ch. Tal-E-Ho's Scamp in 1976. This mating brought together the original four studs and foundation bitch of the Tal-E-Ho Kennels.

Ch. Richardson's Hello Dolly had been owned by Dr. and Mrs. Lyle Cain, of California, and was a top winning bitch during her career. She was Best of Breed at the BHCA Specialty in 1965. She was sired by Ch. Abbot Run Valley Brassy out of Richardson's Autumn Fire and was bred by Dave Richardson. Rowland Vance bought her in her retirement. Eventually he tried for one litter out of her. She was bred to Tal-E-Ho Pacemaker (Ch. Sir Tomo of Glenhaven ex Ch. Talleyrand's Lynette) and produced Ch. Richardson's Lord Carleton who was brought out in 1973. He had an illustrious career with Jack Patterson handling. In his first four months as a champion, he had four Group firsts, ten other placements, twenty-six Bests of Breed, and a Best in Show. Later on, he was handled by Joanne Lynch. Almaviva is the kennel name of Rowland Vance and his sister, Peg Bowerman. In 1972, their Vance's Almaviva Hello Rachel (Vance's Almaviva Tom Terrific

115

ex Ch. Richardson's Hello Dolly) made her debut in the puppy class at the national Specialty. She, too, gained an easy championship and had a rewarding career.

In 1971 the Halcyon hounds of Lamont and Vickie Steele began with Ch. Tess Von Skauton, CD (Ch. Blackie's Bleemer ex Ch. Sacata Von Skauton) who was obtained, as a puppy, from Garry Towne. She was bred to Ch. Lyn Mar Acres Extra Man (L.M.A. End Man ex Tantivy Demon) twice and to Lyn-Mar Acres Radar (L.M.A. Wing Commander ex L.M.A. Day Dream II). She produced three Specialty winners including Ch. Halcyon Lumberjack, and a Canadian champion and Group winner. Owner-handled, Jacko has won many Bests of Breed and several Group placements. Jacko's littermate, Ch. Halcyon Suffragette, finished breeder-owner-handled with five majors.

The Charles Gillespies bred their Hunting Horn Frederica to Ch. Tal-E-Ho's Prancer twice. This produced Hunting Horn Kingpin and Hunting Horn Kissin Kate who was both shown and field trialed in the late 1970s. Their Fd. Ch. Wynnsom Black Satin was bred by Len Abraham.

Although Pete and Ruth Balladone were interested in showing, most of their dogs did not measure up to their expectations. Therefore, they took to the obedience ring for several years with Pete working Fassett's Friar Tuck, UD and Ruth training Fassett's Fair Oaks Winnie CDX. Their first dog was Manolette de Barranca, bred by Dorothea Fassett out of Ch. Rocky of Long View Acres and Ch. Ducharme's Madam Posette. Then they obtained a young dog who became Ch. Fassett's Giacomino (Ch. Fassett's Blue Louie ex Fassett's Madam Ka-Tee) bred by Dorothea Fassett. This dog was a result of an out-cross. His only line breeding is on the dam's side, down from Ch. Seifenjagenheim Lazy Bones, in the fourth and fifth generation. Giacomino quickly brought the kennel name of Casa Feliche into the spotlight. He gained his first points from the American-bred class and was finished at the age of one year. He went on to be top winner on the West Coast in 1975 and 1976 and rated among the top in the United States. He was handled by Marvin Cates during his career.

Ch. Nasa's Shadrach of Mi-Ber-Sham, CD became the first CD Basset to go Best in Show. This occurred in March of 1974. He

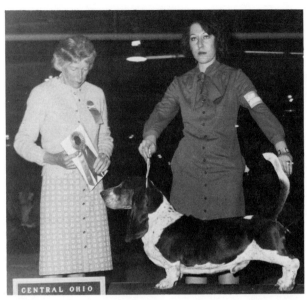

Ch. Richardson's Lord Carleton, owned by Rowland Vance and Eleanor Bowerman, was a well-known campaigner of the 1970s. A BIS winner, he also won many Groups and Specialty shows. He is shown being awarded Hound Group first at the Central Ohio KC under Mrs. W. Potter Wear, handler Joanne Lynch.

Norton of Kent

Ch. Fassett's Giacomino (Ch. Fassett's Blue Louie ex Madam Ka-Tee), owned by Peter and Ruth Balladone and bred by Dorothea Fassett. He is shown finishing at the Longview-Kelso KC under Dr. William Houpt, handler Jeri Cates.

Roberts

was bred by Diane Funk of Houston, Texas, out of Ch. Tyburn Bracco Garibaldi ex Ch. Concho's Senora Felicia. He was co-owned by Mrs. Bert Salyers, her son Mike, and Mrs. Funk. Mike trained him in obedience and gained a title in three straight shows. Jack Potts handled him in conformation.

The Curt Sheehys took a pup from a litter sired by their Ch. Forestbay Montgomery out of Arthur and Susan Vinson's Magnolia Blossom Klutch, and named her Topohil's Blossom Seeley. She gained her championship and was bred to her half-brother, their Ch. Topohil Leader of the Pack. They also bred their Ch. Topohil's Glory Bea to her half-brother, Ch. Manor Hill Father James owned by Joan Scholz.

The NewMyers bred Ch. Rebel's Major Calamity, CD to Ch. Orangepark Dexter. This produced Ch. Rebelglen's Ruffles of Sohigh. Major Calamity was bred several more times but retired from the whelping box because she apparently inherited the reproductive problems of her line. Ch. Rebelglen's Ruffles of Sohigh was co-owned with Jo and Mary Beth Hossler. She finished solely from the bred-by-exhibitor class, but she apparently carried her dam's whelping problems. Ch. Rebelglen's Missy of Rhinelan was bred to Ch. Orangepark Grover. Ch. Priscilla of Rebelglen was also bred to him producing Ch. Rebelglen's Frosty Too who finished with three majors from the bred-by-exhibitor class.

In 1976, Freddie Spitz found that she had to close her kennel and Marge Brandt moved her dogs to Sam Bennett's kennel in Rehoboth, Mass. Barbara Dunning bought the former Houndsville Kennel, in California, and renamed it the Bar-B Dog Corral.

By 1977, the following Basset breeders had become judges: Robert Arbs, Lucille Barton, William Barton, Mary Jane and Robert Booth, Joseph and Mercedes Braun, Barbara Borschow, C. J. Collee, Clare Clowe, Owen Derryberry, Kathryn Ellenberger, Patricia Fellman, Charles Gillespie, Norman Griggs, Hettie Garwood, Keith Haygood, Mrs. Walter Houchin, William Kelly, Joe Lequier, Donald Martin, Philip Markus, Mary Meredith, Frances Messinger, Mary Meyer, Wilton Meyer, Paul Mohr, Carlton Redmond, Hub Robinson, William Russell, Eileen Schroeder, Jeffrey Schwinn, Mrs. Jeffey Schwinn, Ralph and Sylvia Silk, Leonard Skolnick, Helen Smith, Chris Teeter, Ann Thain, Alvin Tiede-

Ch. Nasa's Shadrack of Mi-Ber-Sham, CD, owned by Mrs. Bert Saylers, Mike Saylers and Diane Funk and bred by Mrs. Funk. He is shown being awarded BIS at the Texarkana KC under judge Denis Grivas, handler Jack Potts.

mann, Joan Urban, Eric White, and Jim White. Benj Harris became an obedience judge and Lena Wray was approved to judge Tracking.

It is impossible to include all worthy contributors and their dogs. This has been a survey of only one small portion of the breeders whose bloodlines left a lasting mark on the breed. Among the members of the regional clubs are some of the most dedicated breeders who played such an important part in the progress of the breed in this country. It is regrettable that space does not permit mention of all who offered so much.

BEST OF BREED AT WESTMINSTER

Year	Dog	Owner
1884	Ch. Nemours	Lawrence Timson
1889	Babette	Charles Porter
	Chausseur	Cornelius Stevenson
(1917	Basset recognized and eligible for points)	
1924	Simillante	Erastus Tefft
1925	Musique	Erastus Tefft
1929	Brookmead Mixer	Mrs. G. Sloane
1930	None	
1931	Marvey's Sam	W. H. Attwood
1932	Marvey's Sam	W. H. Attwood
1933	Kilsyth Broker	Gerald Livingston
1934	None	
1935	None	
1936	None	
1937	Kilsyth Frills	Gerald Livingston
1938	Raffer	B. Lippincott
1939	Lady Cinderella	G. Gipolo & C. Straley
1940	None	
1941	Belle Chanson of Neverland	Mrs. E. W. Miles
1942	Upland Fresh	Charles Porter
1943	Ch. Promise of Greenly Hall	Mr. & Mrs. Harold Fogelson

1944	Ch. Promise of Greenly Hall	Mr. & Mrs. Harold Fogelson
1946	Ch. Duchess of Greenly Hall	M. L. Walton
1947	Ch. Braggelonne of Belbay	H. R. Morrison
1948	Hartshead Pepper	Ira Shoop
1949	Ch. Hartshead Pepper	Ira Shoop
1950	Ch. Lyn-Mar's Clown	Mr. & Mrs. M. L. Walton
1951	Ch. Lyn-Mar's Clown	Mr. & Mrs. M. L. Walton
1952	Ch. Lyn-Mar's Clown	Mr. & Mrs. M. L. Walton
1953	Ch. Lyn-Mar's Clown	Mr. & Mrs. M. L. Walton
1954	Ch. Greenore's Joker	Mrs. Michael Hanlon
1955	Ch. Lyn-Mar's Top Brass	Mr. & Mrs. M. L. Walton
1956	Ch. Siefenjagenheim Lazy Bones	Chris G. Teeter
1957	Ch. Look's Choice	Dr. & Mrs. Vincent Nardiello
1958	Ch. Siefenjagenheim Dominoe	Queenie Wickstrom
1959	Ch. Siefenjagenheim Lazy Bones	Chris G. Teeter
1960	Ch. The Ring's Banshee	Chris G. Teeter
1961	Ch. The Ring's Banshee	Chris G. Teeter
1962	Ch. Nancy Evans King Leo la Belle	Nancy Evans & James LaBelle
1963	Ch. The Ring's Ali Baba	Mrs. Frances G. Scaife
1964	Ch. Eleandon's Mr. Pinkerton	Mona Ball
1965	Ch. Richardson's Hello Dolly	David Richardson
1966	Ch. Hunting Horn Noah	Charles & Priscilla Gillespie
1967	Ch. The Chocolate Soldier of Glyn	Ruth Bateman
1968	Ch. Richardson's Padriac of Cuas	Mr. and Mrs. Joseph Lynch
1969	Ch. Governor Chester Klutch	Jean Kraucunas
1970	Ch. Orangepark Roy	Mr. & Mrs. Wilton Meyer
1971	Ch. Abbot Run Valley Gomer	Miss Joanne Lynch & Marjorie Brandt

1972	Ch. Delmas Pinkerton's Cavalier	Patricia Kapplow & C. J. Dawkins
1973	Ch. Sir Raleigh of Bridi	Brian & Judi Kinnear
1974	Ch. Tal-E-Ho's Top Banana	Peter & Bryan Martin
1975	Ch. Slippery Hill Hudson	Mrs. A. R. Robson
1976	Ch. Slippery Hill Hudson	Mrs. A. R. Robson
1977	Ch. Slippery Hill Hudson	Mrs. A. R. Robson
1978	Linpet's Argus	Peter & Linda Weaver
1979	Ch. Strathalbyn Shoot To Kill	J. J. J. McKenna, Jr & Eric F. George

INTERNATIONAL KENNEL CLUB—
BEST OF BREED

Year	Dog	Owner
1941	Nottke's Harvey Prince	Carl Nottke
1942	Ch. Promise of Greenly Hall	Mrs. H. Fogelson
1948	Ch. Belbay Triumph	Belbay Kennels
1949	No entries	
1950	Ch. Belbay Design	Belbay Kennels
1951	Ch. Anthony of St. Hubert	Mark Washbond
1952	Ch. Anthony of St. Hubert	Mark Washbond
1953	Webb's Black Amanda	J. F. Miller
1954	Ch. Slow Poke Hubertus	Chris G. Teeter
1955	Ch. Siefenjagenheim Lazy Bones	Chris G. Teeter
1956	Ch. Siefenjagenheim Lazy Bones	Chris G. Teeter
1957	Ch. Siefenjagenheim Lazy Bones	Chris G. Teeter
1958	Ch. Siefenjagenheim Lazy Bones	Chris G. Teeter
1959	Ch. Bassett's Roustabout	Richard & Evelyn Bassett
1960	Ch. The Ring's Banshee	Chris G. Teeter
1961	Ch. The Ring's Banshee	Chris G. Teeter
1962	Ch. Peppy's Top Serenade of Shadbo	Ray & Beverly Knezevich

1963	Ch. The Ring's Banshee	Chris G. Teeter
1964	Ch. Eleandon's Mr. Pinkerton	Mona Ball
1965	Ch. Richardson's Hello Dolly	Dr. & Mrs. Lyle Cain
1966	Ch. The Chocolate Soldier of Glyn	Ruth Bateman
1967	Ch. Doc Floyd of Manor Hill	Kazoo Kennels & Dr. L. A. Forbes
1968	**Ch. Webbridge Banner Bound**	**Dr. and Mrs. P. L. Fellman**
1969	Ch. Governor Chester Klutch	Jean Kraucunas
1970	Ch. Richardson's Padraic of Cuas	Mrs. Anne & Joanne Lynch
1971	Ch. Governor Chester Klutch	Jean Kraucunas

After the 1971 International, the breed classes were no longer considered the BHCA Specialty.

Ch. Double B's Veronica; handler, Helen Boutell, and Ch. Eleandon's Mr. Pinkerton; handler, Frank Hardy; judge, Col. Julian S. Dexter. Mr. Pinkerton was Best of Breed at Westminster in 1964; Veronica was Best of Opposite Sex.

THE BASSET HOUND CLUB OF AMERICA ANNUAL SPECIALTY

Year	Dog	Owner
1960	Ch. The Ring's Brunhilde	M. L. & Robert Noerr
1961	Ch. Lyn-Mar Acres Top Brass	Lyn-Mar Kennels
1962	Ch. Lyn-Mar Acres Bally Hoo	Lyn-Mar Kennels
1963	Ch. Jesse James of Eleandon	Nicholas & Marcia Polizzi
1964	Ch. Hunting Horn Noah	Charles & Priscilla Gillespie
1965	Ch. Richardson's Hello Dolly	Dr. & Mrs. Lyle Cain
1966	Ch. Kazoo's Galloping Gitch	Kazoo Kennels
1967	Ch. Manor Hill Fringe Benefit	James A. Grinder
1968	Ch. Governor Chester Klutch	Jean Kraucunas
1969	Ch. Richardson's Padraic of Cuas	Mr. & Mrs. Joseph Lynch
1970	Ch. Richardson's Padraic of Cuas	Mrs. Anne & Joanne Lynch
1971	Ch. Tal-E-Ho's Prancer	Henry & Ann Jerman
1972	Ch. Geronimo of Rockin-Pas	Sandra Campbell
1973	Ch. Musicland's Pool Shark	Jeanne Dudley (Hills)
1974	Ch. Slippery Hill Hudson	Mrs. Alan R. Robson
1975	Ch. Tal-E-Ho's Top Banana	Peter & Bryan Martin
1976	Ch. Tal-E-Ho's Top Banana	Peter & Bryan Martin
1977	Ch. De-Alo's March Hare V. Skauton	Ola DeGroat & Garry E. Towne

BASSET HOUND CLUB OF AMERICA SPRING SPECIALTIES

Date	Location	Dog	Owner
March 12, 1972	Detroit, Mich.	Ch. Richardson's Padraic of Cuas	Mrs. Anna & Joanne Lynch
March 25, 1973	Dallas, Tex.	Ch. Reepa's High Fashion	Marianne Paulsson

April 14, 1973	Denver, Colo.	Ch. Dusan's Jason	Robert G. & Mae Schroeder
March 23, 1974	Dallas, Tex.	Lyn-Mar Acres VIP	Margaret S. Walton
March 1, 1975	Mesa, Ariz.	Ch. Tal-E-Ho's Top Banana	Peter & Bryan Martin
May 29, 1976	St. Louis, Mo.	Windamohr's Gamble	Sandra Campbell & Nancy Taylor
June 5, 1976	Colorado Springs, Colo.	Ch. Glenhi's Bandolero	Eric & Georgia White
June 4, 1977	Clayton, Mo.	Ch. Lyn-Mar Acres Extra Man	R. Cromley & J. Walton
March 5, 1978	Scottsdale, Ariz.	Ch. Hooper Knoll's Capt. Fantastic	G. Knollmiller & D. Hoope
March 12, 1978	Detroit, Mich.	Ch. Halcyon Lumberiack	L. F. & V. L. Steedle

A pair of winning Bassets from Joan Scholz's Manor Hill Kennels—Ch. Manor Hill Fringe Benefit (left) and Ch. Manor Hill Michelle. This pair is shown winning BB and BOS respectively at the Pilgrim Basset Hound Club under judge Vance Evans.

Shafer

Dual Ch. Kazoo's Moses the Great, the first to gain the title.

Dual Ch. Tantivy Daisy's Dopey

126

6

The Dual Champions

FANCIERS are justifiably proud of their top winners and producers. However, no award is so rare, nor so coveted, as that of DUAL champion. It indicates that a dog earned a championship *both* on the bench and at the field trials. This is a *real* Basset, the cream of the crop.

Dual Ch. Kazoo's Moses the Great, owned by Pat and Jim Dohr, was the first to gain the title. Moses carried a bench title in both the United States and Canada. He gained both his field title and his Canadian championship in 1963. He was shown to his American bench title by Jerry Rigden, attaining this in 1964. Moses was bred by Ralph and Mary Jo Shields by Ch. Casey of Kazoo ex Ch. Long View Acres Donna.

The first bitch, and second dual, was Dual Ch. Helwal's Desire, whelped August 2, 1960. She was bred and owned by Walter and Helen Smith, and was sired by Ch. Lyn Mar Acres Barrister ex Helwal's Hooligan. She was owner-handled to her victories and finished her bench championship in June of 1963. She was run from 1964 to September 1969 for her field title. There was a lapse of two years, from 1966 to 1968, in her field work. She had been struck by a car while on the trail of a rabbit. It was doubtful if she would ever walk again, having suffered several cracks of the pelvis. Her next time out she placed second. Desire is the dam of Ch. Helwal's Catherine The Great who gained her championship from the bred-by-exhibitor class.

Dual Ch. Braun's Wholly Thursday was the third to gain the honor. She was by Ch. Trojan Echoes Erebus ex Braun's Apjo Mimi, bred by Judy and Arena Hutchinson. Mimi had been purchased as a puppy and was brought back home for breeding. Thursday was a stud puppy. She gained her bench title in 1963, owner-handled by Joseph Braun. She gained her field title in 1970 with a new record of three first places, one having been at the BHCA national trial. She is the granddam of such dogs as Fd. Ch. Dever's Georgie Girl, Fd. Ch. Tomlin's April Fool, Fd. Ch. Tomlin's Little Drooper, and the great-granddam of field champions Carl's Girl and Reynold's Maxie Mae.

Dual Ch. Double B's Lucky Libertine was whelped in 1964, by Ch. Hubertus Playboy ex Ch. Double B's Veronica, bred by Helen Boutell. He remained with Helen while he was exhibited to his championship. When her kennel became overcrowded, she placed this dog with Ray Wells. The dog knew nothing about running a rabbit until Ray trained and ran him to his dual title. Bred to Nancy Evans Valentina, he sired Fd. Ch. Fussbudget of Cape Cod.

The fifth was Dual Ch. Tantivy Daisy's Dopey, bred and owned by Jane Luce, by Dunn's Rusty Dusty Asa ex Barker's Daisy Delle. He gained his bench title in 1967 and his field title in 1971. He was sent out to several areas for his show career and his field competition was at the Eastern trials. He is the only dual who is also a pack dog, part of the Tantivy pack. Bred very sparingly, his descendants have been the backbone of other packs and two granddaughters have finished their bench titles.

Dual Ch. Slippery Hill Cinnamon, CD was the first to hold three titles; bench, field, and obedience. She was whelped in 1966, sired by Ch. Santana-Mandeville Egghead ex Slippery Hill Felice and handled in the field by her breeders, Marge and Len Skolnick. She finished her show title in 1967 and her field title in 1975. She completed her CD in 1976, at the age of 10, trained and handled by Ellen McDaniel. Cinnamon is the dam of Ch. Slippery Hill Pimento and Can. Ch. Slippery Hill Portnoy. She had only two sisters, Nutmeg and Paprika, both show champions.

Dual Ch. Braun's Wholly
Thursday with Joseph Braun.

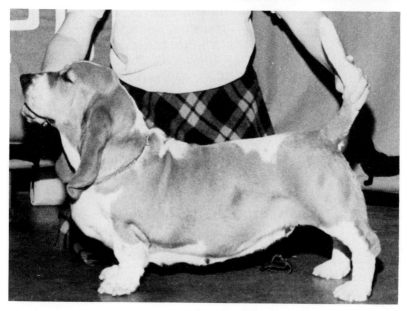

Dual Ch. Slippery Hill Cinnamon, CD

The seventh was Dual Ch. Pettit's Ranger Ric, owned by Tom and Shirley Pettit. He was the first to also hold the title of Grand champion. Ric was whelped March 4, 1972, a product of planned breeding between two individuals who had already proved themselves. His sire, Fd. Ch. Rosie's Jeff, and his dam, Fd. Ch. Dorshires Twiggy are both in the *Top Field Producers Guide.* Jeff's sire, Fd. Ch. Rosie's Bill was another top producer. Twiggy's paternal grandparents were show champions. Ric began field competition in 1973. He finished in six trials, was second in the National Derby Stakes and in Open All Age Dog Stakes in October 1973, at the age of nineteen months. He was campaigned at the shows by handler Jack Patterson. Not quite finished by the 1976 trial season, he returned to the field to gain his Grand champion title with four first places in champion stakes. In the summer of 1977, he and Jack returned to the show ring to gain a championship. Then Tom decided to try for a Canadian championship and a tracking title. Ric was BHCA stud dog of the year in 1975 and has sired 14 field champions and 1 Grand champion from eleven different bitches.

The eighth title was gained by Dual Ch. Jackson's Samantha Lu. She was bred by John M. Foster of Spokane, Washington, out of Meadow Beauty Lucky ex Pinehill's Greta Lynn. She was purchased by Sandi Jackson as pick of the litter, and later came to the attention of Stan and Sylvia Ellingwood. They took co-ownership on her in order to show her. Later they exchanged one of her puppies for full ownership. She gained her bench title in the Fall of 1973. She was then sent to Elsie Tagg for field training. She returned home after gaining her first points at Eastern trials. Her dual title was gained when she took first place at the BHCA trial in Northern California.

7

The Basset Hound Club of America

THE PURPOSE of the Basset Hound Club of America is to guard the interests of purebred Bassets. It is referred to as the Parent Club as is each club which represents a specific breed on a national basis. A Parent Club represents its breed at the American Kennel Club. There are smaller clubs, serving limited areas, which are members of, and under the jurisdiction of, the Parent Club. The Basset Hound Club of America holds Specialty shows, field trials, and an obedience trial in conjunction with the Fall national, plus a tracking test. During the first weekend in October the annual meeting is held. All four forms of competition are offered. There is a dinner, prior to the meeting, plus educational sessions and good-time get togethers. The site is in a different area each year. At one time, the affair was held alternately in the East and the Midwest. In 1977, the first national to be held on the West Coast took place near Sacramento, California, hosted by the Northern California Basset Hound Club.

The Club began in 1933 at a small gathering at the home of William Fritz, in Detroit, Michigan. The records show the following as charter members: Mr. and Mrs. Alfred Bissell, B. F. Chaney, Harold R. Frazee, William Fritz, George C. Gregg, Carmon Klink, Alfred E. Kannowski, W. P. Klapp, Jr., James E. Lee, Ann Levy, Gerald Livingston, Carl Nottke, Effie Seitz, and Lewis Thompson.

In 1934, the Constitution and By-Laws were drawn up and they were adopted in 1935 at the first annual meeting of the Club. The fee to become a member of the American Kennel Club, in those days, was $250, as opposed to the present fee of $25. Raffles were held to raise the money. Field trial rules were drafted in 1936. The Club became an official member of the AKC in 1937. A revision of the Constitution and By-Laws and Incorporation of the Club was executed at a special meeting. Cathryn A. Burton, James Fornary, and George R. Simanek guided the work of incorporation at Racine, Wisconsin.

A Standard for the American Basset was drawn up by Will Judy of the Judy Publishing Company, a well-known dog figure in those days. However, at the annual meeting, in 1940, wtih forty members present, this Standard was rejected. Little is known about the work of the Standard until 1953. A committee consisting of Mrs. Emil Seitz, Jean Look, Mrs. Helen Nelson, Mrs. Frank Hardy, Chris Teeter, and Loren Free presented a proposed Standard at the annual meeting in 1955. This was accepted by a majority vote.

Chicago was the site of the first annual Specialty show. The year was 1955 and there were forty Bassets entered.

Eventually a newsletter was published, prepared by BHCA Secretaries at first. Ethel Ferge was the last to put it out in newsletter form. Ruth Turner was elected Publicity Director and changed it to a magazine-type publication. *Tally-Ho* remains the Club's news bulletin, sent to all members, in magazine form. Mercedes Braun inherited the job from Ruth Turner, by election of the membership, in 1963. Kay Ellenberger took over in 1965. After the new By-Laws went into effect, this duty was by appointment of the Board of Directors. Jean Spaulding, Jeanne Dudley Hills, Eileen Schroeder, Pat Fellman, Beverly Stockfelt, Bob Arbs, and Vickie Steedle all served the Club in this capacity.

In 1961, the membership decided that the Standard should be revised. A committee was appointed headed by Peg Walton. Others on the committee were Dick Bassett, Effie Seitz, and Walter Brandt. The final draft was sent to the Board in 1962. However, this was rejected by AKC. The Board took over the work and it was again presented to the membership in October of 1963. The present Standard was accepted by the AKC in 1964.

Work on revisions to the By-Laws was started, in 1964, by a committee under the chairmanship of Col. Julian Dexter. By October, the 1965 annual meeting was conducted under the new By-Laws. Election was by ballot of the complete membership. Previous elections had been by nomination from the floor and limited to those members who were present at the annual meeting.

Prior to 1960, the Club's Specialty was held at the Chicago International KC all-breed show in the Spring. The first Fall Specialty, to be held in conjunction with the Fall field trial and annual meeting, was held at Lebanon, Pennsylvania, October 7, 1960. There was an entry of 56 dogs. Chris Teeter, who had been instrumental in combining the show with the annual trial was the Show Chairman. For several years, the Club continued to sponsor the classes at International, considering this to be its Spring show. In June 1963, the California clubs hosted the BHCA Spring Specialty at Long Beach. After that, the Spring show moved to different areas by invitation of a local club.

By 1963, interest had grown in obedience. An obedience committee was created, Benjamin Harris, chairman, Bob Noerr, Lena Wray, and Mercedes Braun serving on the committee. At that time, Bassets were required to jump one and a half times their height at the withers for the high jump exercise. The committee undertook to have them included in the few dogs that were only required to jump their height. Eventually, Bassets and a few other breeds were included in this provision, but it had taken quite a while to bring it about. Virginia Jones and Joan Thurlow had joined the committee by that time and worked very hard for the endeavor. It was not until 1968 that the Club offered Obedience classes at the Fall national Specialty.

Until the mid-sixties, the Club was largely under the direction of field trialers. They could forsee the day when it would be possible that the Club would be governed by persons who might be unsympathetic, perhaps even opposed to the sport. Bill Rider proposed that a committee could be formed to look after the interests of the field trialers. The Board appointed him chairman of the Field Trial Rules and Running Order committee. In 1963, the AKC agreed to give Bassets running rules of their own although they are still, largely, run under the same rules as Beagles. By 1969,

133

the committee, as it is known today, came into being. Each trial-giving club has a representative on what is now called the Field Trial Advisory Council. This group reviews proposed changes in regulations, submits needed proposals, oversees the trial schedules, and is in charge of field activities, subject to Board approval. John Eylander succeeded Bill Rider for a short time. Kenneth McWilliams became chairman in 1971 serving until 1977 when Leonard Skolnick took charge.

In 1969, the President, Joseph Braun, realized that many members could not travel to take part in the prestigious Spring or Fall Specialties. If the sport of trialing was to continue to grow, more trials needed to be offered. The sport had already lost a few avid trialers who went to Beagles because they could run more often. For these reasons, he encouraged the Club to hold a regional show or trial, in each of the three sections of the country, if a local club would act as host. The event would carry the prestige of the name of the Parent Club but the profits would remain with the local club. Fanciers could feel more a part of a BHCA event.

The nationals offered the first tracking test, to be held in conjunction with the Fall affair, in 1970. This meant that all four forms of endeavor were represented at the nationals. Few other clubs offer all of this competition during a long weekend.

When a dog gained its field trial championship, there was little more left than placing in the champion stake at a trial entered. Few champions were run after they gained their title. The Club decided to give them more incentive to enter. Grand champion awards were the result, starting in 1972. Dogs accumulate points, depending on their placement, toward this award. When they have compiled a given number of points from the champion stake, they are given the additional title of Grand champion.

By 1974, the need was felt for a revision of the By-Laws. Finn Bergishagen chaired the committee. He withdrew after being elected President and Bob Swanson took over the work. By 1977, the proposed revisions were ready to be presented to the membership.

Local Clubs

It was some time before the breed became popular enough to warrant the formation of smaller groups, or local Specialty clubs.

These serve fanciers in a limited geographic area, offering that personal touch, but are under the jurisdiction of the Parent Club and the AKC. In order to satisfy the AKC that they should be a recognized club, approved to hold licensed events, they have to meet certain requirements. They must, however, have the approval of the BHCA before holding each licensed event. As members, they have a vote in the official business of the BHCA.

The Basset Hound Club of Southern California

In about 1947–48, a few avid fanciers attempted to form a club in California. Much effort was exerted by Bill Morris. It was not until the Fall of 1951 that the BHC of California was actually organized with Mr. Morris as President. Those attending the first meeting were: Mr. and Mrs. Mac Carlisle, Mr. and Mrs. Gill, the Robert Hicks, the Don Loewes, the Bill Morrises, Paul Nelson, Mr. and Mrs. Walter Rowley, and Mrs. Cordelia Jensen Skapinsky. The club was recognized by the AKC and the BHCA in 1953–54. It became known as the BHC of Southern California. It was incorporated in the State of California, as a non-profit social organization, and membership soon reached 100. In the early 1960s, membership climbed to 200. The 1960 Specialty broke all records with 105 entries. By 1977, the BHCSC was donating trophies to 23 all-breed clubs in Los Angeles County. At its Specialty, it offers classes for conformation, sweepstakes, obedience, and Junior Showmanship. Some of its original members were also enthusiastic in obedience. These include such well known people as the Benj Harrises, Ginny Jones, and Joan Thurlow. Ch. Greenacres's Pol Roger, UD, owned by Jim Orton, was the first champion UD Basset. Club members are also interested in tracking work through local all-breed clubs. The early Specialties were held in conjunction with the Harbor Cities KC. In 1966, the club held its first independent Specialty. Each year the club holds a fun day match-picnic. It also supplies a monthly newsletter to its members. This is a very active group of dog people.

The Dal-Tex Basset Hound Club

In August 1954, an organizational meeting was held to form a club in Texas. Exactly who attended this meeting is not known

135

but the earliest membership roster is: Dr. and Mrs. Olen Brown, the James L. Brysons, Mr. and Mrs. Robert Frazier, Robert Gully, Jr., A. C. Puddington, Jr., Claude Savage, Mr. and Mrs. Floyd Smith, the Prentice Yerbys, and William Hughes. At first the club was named the Lone Star BHC. However, the AKC felt that this name was too inclusive geographically, as was the territory it represented. When the club proposed Cen-Tex as a name, AKC frowned upon this too. The name Dal-Tex was finally accepted but the club was required to increase the membership in a smaller area and pull back the fences on some of its earliest members. Meanwhile, some of the original members had moved away or lost interest and the club went through a period of inactivity.

In mid-1958, some dynamic new members joined. A newsletter was published. The club grew to forty-four members, among them Mrs. Laura Crutchfield who owned such well-known champions as Ch. Felix of La Chenil and Dottie Bourke who helped put the club on the obedience map. The club held its first sanctioned match in 1957. In March of 1960, the first Specialty was held in conjunction with the Texas KC show. From 1965 to 1972 the show was held as part of a combined Specialty group. Dal-Tex began to hold a separate Fall show in 1972. When the field trial bug bit Earl Clevenger and Lewis Fox, they undertook to educate the other club members and, by the end of 1975, the club gained approval to hold licensed field trials.

The Susquehanna Basset Hound Club

The Susquehanna Basset Hound Club was started at the home of Norwood Engle on February 6, 1955. The club was started at a meeting of the Norman Buchers, Al Michel, Cy and Dottie Bowers, the LaFollettes, and the Engles. Matches and fun trials were held at the Bernsville, Pennsylvania home of the LaFollettes. Dogs were entered in the fun trial in the morning and shown for conformation in the afternoon. The first sanctioned trial was held on April 15, 1956 at the Pocono Beagle Club grounds. This was the first sanctioned field trial to be held by a regional club. There were nine entries in the derby class, ten in open all-age dogs, and ten open all-age bitches. The next trial was held at the Lykens Valley Beagle Club. That Fall, the trial moved to the Lebanon County Beagle

Club where it has been held ever since. In 1959, the BHCA held its combined national field trial, show, banquet, and annual meeting at this site. It held the event every other year, here, until 1970. Since May 10, 1959, the club has held its Specialty in conjunction with the Lancaster KC show in May. The original officers held their offices from 1955 to 1975. They were: President, Norwood Engle; Vice-President, Norman Bucher; Secretary-Treasurer, Dorothy Bowers.

The Pilgrim Basset Hound Club

In New England, fanciers Walter Brandt, Marge Brandt, Frank Carter, Charles and Priscilla Gillespie, Wallace Balsewicz, Joseph Allen, Dr. Ruth Strong, John and Doris Hurry, the Joseph Kulpers, Isabel Holden, Mrs. Gladys Clement, Frank and Dorothy Hardy, Jeanne Millett, Dr. Pierre Morand, and Janet Yonts formed the Pilgrim Basset Hound Club in 1953. They were later joined by Clip and Helen Boutell, Doug and Jean Knight, the Len Abrahams, Yvonne Ground, and Paul and Kay Gribben, Ken and Louise Eldgridge, Julian and Elizabeth Dexter, Ed Hammond, John Fish, Ray Wells, the Joe Lynches, the Carlton Redmonds, the Willard Woods, Virginia Mash, and Curt and Jean Sheehy. In 1965, the club went to a separate Specialty show. By the end of the 1960s, several members had become interested in field trials and the club went to work to gain approval to hold licensed trials.

The Basset Hound Club of Greater Detroit

Midwest fanciers formed the Basset Hound Club of Greater Detroit at a meeting on November 9, 1954. Chris Teeter chaired the meeting attended by: Ruth Fox, Helen Fox, the Glendon Stevensons, Wilfred and Queenie Wickstrom, Robert Finnerty, Ray and Charlotte King, Milton Stringer, Miss Ligouri Britain, Mrs. Louretta Daly, the Eugene Dembickis, the Robert Schimantowskis, June Schroeder, A. Frank Tuttle, and Mrs. Lester Noel Webb. The club was recognized by the AKC in March 1955 and was incorporated later that year. Two plan "A" matches were held that year and the first Specialty was held in conjunction with the Detroit KC show on March 2–3, 1957. The club has held one or two Specialties

137

annually. Some have been independent shows and others have been in conjunction with the Detroit or Pontiac all-breed shows. Some of the well-known breeders who have been associated with the club during the years are the C. J. Collees, Joe and Erla Lequiere, Mary Jo Shields, the Finn Bergishagens, the Joe Brauns, and the Frank Kovalics. Until he received an honorary lifetime membership, in 1975, Chris Teeter was the only charter member to remain active.

The Rancocas Valley Basset Hound Club

Mrs. Margaret Walton called together several couples to establish the Rancocas Valley Basset Hound Club. Among those present were M. Lynwood Walton, the Samuel Hamlins, John Bodkins, the Truman Smiths, the George Brightenbacks, and the Wendall Crams. Other early members were Bill and Mary Rider, Fred Hoeger, Robert Taber, John and Betts Phillips, Mrs. Charles Creamer, who served as secretary for many years, and Alexander Boyd. By 1957, the club held its first Specialty and in 1960 its first field trial.

The Northern California Basset Hound Club

The Northern California BHC also came into existence in 1955. Early members were Dr. Leo Goldston, Gerry Lee, Dorothea Fassett, Mr. M. Orlick, June Hanns Moiseff, Ruth Turner, Pat and Frances Flevares, the Stanley Bears, the Russell Spensers, the Roy Barriers, and Lucille Barton. The Club's first Specialty show was held in 1958. In 1959, with jackrabbits for quarry, this club held the first field trial for Bassets west of Chicago. In the mid 1970s, interest once again turned to field trialing and in 1975 the club became eligible to hold trials, for the second time.

The Timberline Basset Hound Club

Formation of the Basset Hound Club of Colorado came in 1957 and its name was changed, in 1962, to Timberline BHC Jane Austin, who acted as Nancy Evans' agent in Denver, contacted the people who had purchased pups through her. She asked the McChesneys and Coutchers, both of whom had raised some litters, to do the same. These three, and the Westgaards, were the earliest fanciers in the Denver area. About ten or twelve people attended the inaugural meeting, and after holding several meetings, the club took shape with Arthur Coutcher as President and Jane Austin as Vice-President. The club grew quickly with some very active people joining including the Harry Nichoalds, who owned several dogs out of Lazy Bones, the Allen McLellans, the Slocums, Tripps, William and Elizabeth Sallada, the Lesters, the McCains, McCoys, Sollenbergers, the Lester Nelsons, Claytons, Joseph and Elizabeth Taylor, Ken Lindahl, the Mischlichs, Mr. and Mrs. R. J. Mahaffrey, and Norma Clark. In more recent years, the club was fortunate to have active breeders and exhibitors such as: W. W. Ellis, Rick and Georgia White, the Underhills, and the Fairs. The Timberline club holds Specialties only.

The Western Michigan Basset Hound Club

The Western Michigan Basset Hound Club was set up in 1957 under the direction of John Eylander, his father, Ed, Ralph and Beatrice Seamon, the Harold Campbells, the William Hays, Bruce Beam, Charles Burrell, Peter Waltz, Roy Ingram, Ronald Race, Bonnie Ingram, Arlie Syers, Clark Elliot, James Knight, Tom Barr, Ralph Frein, Aloise and Virginia Michalski, Mike Verwys, and M. Witt. The club became eligible for approval to hold both Specialty shows and licensed field trials. For years, many of the members dreamed of owning their own field trial grounds. Dick and Jack Van Hoven and Robert Oosterbaan were some of the newer, enthusiastic members. The dream became a reality and the club purchased grounds in the mid-1970s. This is only the second club to own such property.

The Kentuckiana Basset Hound Club

The Kentuckiana BHC was organized through the efforts of Joe Miller, John Helm, Clinton Kaelin, Graham Roth, Virginia Brinsteel, Kenneth McWilliams, John Pellerin, Delbert Mullhall, and Alvin Blair, in August 1957. Three charter members, Joe and Mary Miller and McWilliams were still active in 1977. The group met bi-monthly and added members. Soon it was holding sanctioned matches and field trials. In 1960, Bill and Jean Spaulding joined the club. The late Samson Bridges and Ed Foley joined in 1961, Graham and Eddie Tomlin in 1964, Donald Dever and Ralph Travelstead in 1968, and Bill Ashabraner in 1969. In 1967, show interest was strengthened when Patsy Lucas joined, then by Carol O'Bryant, Danny and Sandra Jones, and Charles Kormer. The club's first Plan A trial was held on January 28, 1961 and the first A match on April 8, 1962. The first licensed trial was held in 1962. It was approved for a Specialty which was held in March 1963. Thereafter, the club has held two licensed trials and one show each year. In 1971, it elected to hold its first independent Specialty. Mercedes Braun was invited to judge. The Kentuckiana BHC has held its Specialty prior to the Louisville all-breed show ever since.

The Valley Forge Basset Hound Club

In eastern Pennsylvania, the Valley Forge BHC held its formation meeting at the home of Robert Taber. Attending were Mr. and Mrs. Joseph Navar, Mr. and Mrs. Robert Matthews, Mr. and Mrs. John Nehre, and Joseph Oliviere. The group decided to have a fun trial in December. Another meeting was held in September 1958, Robert Taber was elected President, Robert Matthews, Vice-President, and Pinkie Navar, Secretary-Treasurer. She held this office for the years to come. Others present were the organizers and Robert Swan, Stan Rothenberger, Walter Ozorack, Helen and John Neher, and Elizabeth Streeter. Mrs. Streeter offered her farm as a training area, and the Pennsylvania game warden assisted in getting training permits. The BHCA sponsored the first Spring trial in March of 1963 at Quakertown. Until 1965, the club's trials were held there. It moved to the Pocono Beagle Club grounds in May 1966, and to Stein's Hollow Beagle Club in 1968. The club awards a perpetual trophy to the dog that has the highest number of points each year. The club also gives a perpetual breeder's trophy to the person who does the most for the field trial Basset and produces the most field champions. Joe and Pinkie Navar were awarded the trophy in 1976 for having produced 17 champions in

11 years. Mr. and Mrs. Ronald Grant, Elsie and Scott Tagg, Marylin Yurick, Flo Hudons, Mickie Carter, and Tom O'Conner became some of the more recent, hard-working members.

The Long Island Basset Hound Club

The Long Island BHC was formed in 1955. Charter members were Dr. and Mrs. V. A. Nardiello, Jr., Mr. and Mrs. David Richardson, Mr. and Mrs. Frank Hardy, Mr. and Mrs. Frederick Schulke, Dr. and Mrs. V. S. Altchek, Mr. and Mrs. Lee Friedman, and Mr. William Withers. The first Specialty was held in September 1957 in conjunction with the Westbury KA all-breed show. Twenty years later, the LIBHC was still holding its Specialty in conjunction with Westbury. Among the more active breeders, throughout the years were: Mrs. Nancy Lindsay, Mr. and Mrs. Robert Ellenberger, Mrs. Jeanne Gaitings, Mr. and Mrs. Adam Euler, Henry and Ann Jerman, and Mr. Howard Hunt. Louis Blum, a licensed obedience judge, was at the helm in 1977. Although the membership is small, the club sponsors two AKC sanctioned puppy sweepstakes, a yearly sanctioned match, and sponsored a symposium/workshop in 1977 to encourage an interest in all phases of the sport.

The Fort Dearborn Basset Hound Club

The Fort Dearborn BHC was formed, in the Chicago area, about 1956, by Mrs. Walter Houchin, Donald and Ruth Bateman, and Bestor Coleman. It held its first Specialty in 1957.

The Buckeye Basset Hound Club

The Buckeye BHC formed in the late 1950s. Early members were the Mike Hollys, the Bob Malones, the Eugene Beldeans, Jim Trenarys, Tony and Mary Chirumbolo, Fred Broman, Elmer and Helen Olson, Ned Aquino, the Bob Horsts, and Dick Fouses. The club held its first field trial in 1960. They set about to purchase running grounds near Delroy, not far from Atwood Lake. When they had difficulty obtaining a mortgage, club member Marvin Keeney agreed to hold the mortgage and grounds were purchased in 1960. Eleven years after becoming the first Basset club to own running grounds, the mortgage was burned. This club holds field trials only.

The Potomac Basset Hound Club

In 1959, the Potomac BHC was accepted by AKC after it changed its name from Congressional BHC. It held its first Specialty in 1960. Among early members were Peter Jamerson, the Carl Morrises, Ron Ontko, Joanne Parker, Dr. Eugene Joyce, and Ron McIntosh. Later members were Len and Marge Skolnick, Joan Thurlow, the Ralph Webbs, Mary Jane Fitzpatrick, Larry Phillips, Marsha Titus, Liz Hill, and Ron and Marlene Tokay. The club's first licensed field trial was held in 1972.

The Basset Hound Club of Maryland

The BHC of Maryland was formed about this same period. It held its first Specialty in April 1963. Early members were the Bill Titsworths, Shirley Mueller, Ronald Broyes, Mel and Marie Reidt, Audrey Caslow, Eleanor Stewart, Suzanne Norris, Jon Barton, George Mueller, Joe VanderVeken, and the Carl Kohlhepps.

The Patroon Basset Hound Club

The Patroon BHC held its first organizational meeting on March 11, 1961. Officers elected were: Cliff Warren, President; Mike Maxon, Vice-President; Mary Keller, Secretary; Gertrude Elmore, Treasurer; and John Lennon, Oscar Moser, Robert Keller, Directors. Larry Elmore was the Field Trial Secretary. The first issue of the club's newsletter, the *Bassetroon,* contained a membership list of 39 including some that are still active such as: Clarence Boutell, Larry Elmore, and Joan Elmore. During the first year, the club held two show and field activities at the Neversink Beagle Club grounds. The club had difficulty gaining AKC recognition, but held its first sanctioned trial in 1964 and its first qualifying trial later that year. The second qualifying trial was held in April of 1965. The first licensed trial was in October of 1965. The club membership grew in the next ten years. Ron Grant, Bob and Sandra Quackenbush, and Ed MacGregor also became Patroon members. The club conducts two licensed trials and a mid-summer Basset-Beagle trial each year.

The Gateway Basset Hound Club

Under the guidance of Mr. and Mrs. Robert Lumma, the Lawrence Seilers, the Russell Schroeders, the William Kinslows, and the Kendall Clowes, the Gateway BHC was formed in the St. Louis area. Early members were Jayne Rhees, Gloria Stabler, Ed Maloney, Shirley and Joe Elliot, and Barbara Mathews. By 1965, it held its first licensed Specialty.

The Basset Hound Club of Greater Seattle

In 1963, under the name of the Chinook BHC, the BHC of Greater Seattle was formed. Organizational members were: Pat and Joanne Hanna, Clark and Marie Farmer, Richard and Evelyn Bassett, Earl and Louise Tibbetts, Charles and Janet Tilton, Dana and Marie Conklin, Tom and Hulda Stanfield, Bill and Lorraine Russell, Lois Gregg, and Robert and Barbara Studerus. Thor and Dorothy Sunberg joined in 1965. The club built up its membership by creating interest through matches and training classes. Robert Vickers, Tom and Rose Morgan, John Hackley, Bonnie Thompson, Chuck Tilton, and Jim Eaton soon joined. By 1969, the club gained approval to hold its first Specialty show.

The Valle Del Sol Basset Hound Club

The Valle Del Sol BHC, representing breeders of Phoenix and Tucson, Arizona, began sanctioning efforts in June of 1964, under the name of Rio Salado BHC. The club's first B match was held in May of 1967. An A match was held on April 12, 1970, with Owen Derryberry judging an entry of 35. Tom Harper judged the second A match with an entry of 29 on October 23, 1970. At the first Specialty, in 1971, Douglass Knight gave Best of Breed to Ch. Duffy of Hahs-C-Enda. In 1974, a Sweepstakes was added to the competition. By 1977, the club membership grew to 43, and in 1976, the club began publishing a newsletter called *The Basset Banter*.

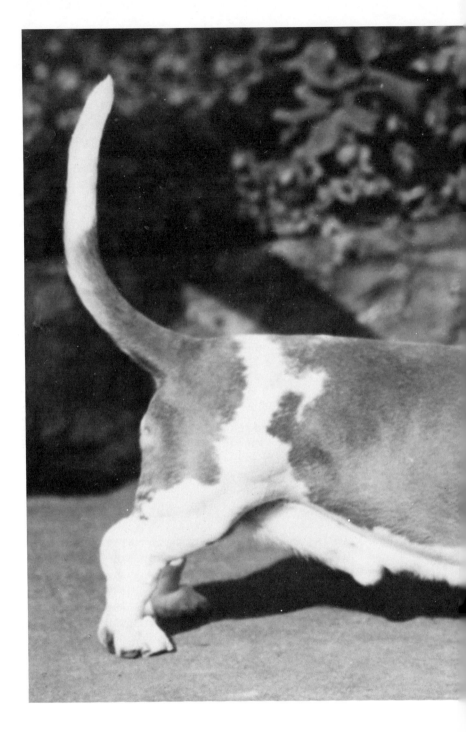

Ch. Richardson's Padraic of Cuas, owned by Anne and Joanne Lynch.
Tauskey

The Basset Hound Club of Sacramento

The BHC of Sacramento was formed in the early 1960s and held its first Specialty in 1966. Early members were: Bud and Diane Rinderneck, Pat and Jack Arnold, Ruth Turner, Neil Bryant, Bill Dunbar, and Harry Miller.

The Basset Hound Club of Greater Houston

The BHC of Greater Houston came into existence in 1970. By 1971 it had 35 members and held its first fun match. Among those associated with this club are Marvin McKenzie, Ben Franklin, Sally Gaudiano, Diane and Bill Funk, Marilyn Riggins, Yvonne Moore, Jane Scott, Pat Willer, Kathy Willer, Winnie McKenzie, and W. E. Schneider. The first fun match was held in January 1971. By October 1974, the club held its first Specialty.

The Basset Hound Club of Portland

The BHC of Portland, Oregon, began as early as 1961 with Denton Burson serving as Secretary. However, it did not hold its second sanctioned A Match until 1974. The club was approved to hold a licensed Specialty in 1975. Associated with this club were: Roy and Doris Butler, Roy and Melody Fair, Pam Wascher, Linda Masson, Harry and Stella Porter, Mary Dretke, and Lee and Peg Bridgeman.

The Berkshire Valley Basset Hound Club

Early members of the Berkshire Valley BHC were: Mickey Carter, Art and Nancy Poehler, Jaime Martinez, Albert Williams, Michael Koricich, Frank Del Mastro, Mrs. Clara Dickson, and Allen Stein. The club was recognized and approved to hold a licensed trial in 1973. It had been in existence since the mid 1960s.

The Lenape Basset Hound Club

In another area of New Jersey, the Lenape BHC was formed in 1968. That same year it held a fun trial in October and a fun match in September. The membership totaled 52 regulars and 9 Juniors. Among the members were: Fred Bayliss, Pat and Marty

Gennet, Carol Robb, the Jack Lewises, Bob and Barb Quackenbush, John and Betts Phillips, the Ewing Carharts, the Fred Atwaters, Les Crelin, Jim Lenahan, Bud Gauss, Don and Lorraine Schwarts, Ola DeGroat, Al Neuberger, Richard Berkman, Barry Jeroloman, Russell Salt, and Dick and Joan Hamlin. The Lenape club held its first licensed trial in November 1972.

The Twin Cities Basset Hound Club

The Twin Cities BHC was first formed under the name of Nokomis BHC to serve Minnesota fanciers. It held its first match in 1971. The present name was adopted in 1972. Bob and Pat Swanson, Bob and Martha Arbs, Denny Neiberger, Dick and Kathy Vlach, Kathy Gilbertson, Marilyn Mongomery, Jeff Jacquart, Nancy and Lloyd Hermes, and Stephanie Swanson are associated with this club. It was approved to hold its first Specialty in 1975.

The Basset Hound Club of Tulsa

The BHC of Tulsa was organized around 1970. Among its members were: E. Wayne and Lura May Nelson, Bob Casper, Hal Haynes, Lucille and Oscar Leopold, Louie and Edith Rockecharlie, Don Bennet, Doris Haynes, Martin Block, Phil Porta, Sam Turner, Peggy Tucker, and Bob Wasley. It held its first Specialty in 1975.

The South Florida Basset Hound Club

The South Florida BHC held its first meeting May 8, 1968. A second meeting was held the following month when temporary officers were elected, the name adopted, and Mary Kronen was appointed head of an advisory committee to write the by-laws. By August, charter membership had closed with 42 on the roll. On May 18, 1969, the club held its first fun match. Another fun match was held in 1970, then two B matches followed in 1971 and 1973. The club's first Specialty and sweepstakes was held in January 1976.

The Basset Hound Club of Corpus Christie

Before 1972, the BHC of Corpus Christie was known as the Tejas BHC. It was founded in 1968 by Knox Williams and Mrs.

Eugene (Joan) Urban. In January, Knox and Joan began publishing a quarterly magazine called the *Hound Crier* in an effort to help gain recognition for the club. Later editors were Bob Arbs, Hettie Garwood, Sally Elkins, Pat Willer, Louisa Myers, Carolyn Ammerman, and Ike Kallus. Unfortunately it was discontinued in 1974 due to publication costs.

In a long, hard effort to gain recognition, the club held nine fun matches, four sanctioned B matches, and two sanctioned A matches. The first Specialty was held on November 29, 1974. Clare Clowe passed judgment on 71 dogs in conformation and two junior handlers. Martha Coody had seven in obedience. John Hackley judged eighteen in Sweepstakes.

The Maumee Valley Basset Hound Club

Northwestern Ohio had need for a club, especially one that would hold field trials. Nine couples from this area met at the home of Joseph and Mercedes Braun to form the Maumee Valley BHC. Both show and field trial fanciers joined together in the undertaking in May 1972. The first fun match was held in January 1973 with the first fun trial following in March. Organizational members were: the Brauns, Rich and Nettie Gargas, Howard and Rosie Smith, Rick Smith, Al and Sue Noller, Irvin and Donna Bowers, Jay and Nancy Peace, Bill and Marty TenEyck, Jim and Pat Dohr, Dale and Lorna Fleming, Bob and Susie Huber, Judy Cowan, and Bill and Betty Hartman. The club gained approval for its first licensed trial by September 1974 and its first Specialty in 1977. The first show was judged by Bob Arbs with a Sweepstakes being done by John Hackley.

The Basset Hound Club of Greater New Orleans

The BHC of Greater New Orleans was formed in the early 1970s. Among its membership was: Earl and Lydia Rose, Evelyn Breaux, Mrs. Fay Walker, Miss Bobbie Stulb, Jerry Walker, Linda Morey, Barbara Steverson, Sharon Pecoraro, Mrs. Gerry Maxsween, Robert Robertson, and Gladys Maddox.

More Clubs on the Horizon

There are a number of clubs that have formed and are still striving to gain the status of a club approved to hold licensed events. Charter Oak BHC is one of these clubs. It has been in existence for many years, serving Western Connecticut. However, the membership covers a larger area than is preferred by AKC so, in 1977, it was still seeking approval to hold point shows. Helen Boutell, before her death, was active in organizing this club. Its membership boasts Curt and Jean Sheehy, Ray and Dorothy Willis, Dave Richardson, Clarence Boutell, Dr. Phillip and Patricia Fellman, Scott Hutchason, Dorothy Siegal, Marilyn Day, Dave Feron, Gail Snead, Rowland Vance, and Kathy Deringer.

Another club that has been organized for several years is the Sun Coast BHC serving the West-Central area of Florida. Among its members are: Lois and Charlie Brining, Howard Hills, Lucian and Roma Reeves, Lee and Carol Richie, Karen Bondaruk, Cookie Martin, Pam Lewis, Pat and Ted Ellis, Paula and Gene Kuhl, and Judi Kinnear.

In September of 1974, fanciers living in the Tarrant County-Greater Fort Worth area of Texas gathered to discuss the formation of a club. Charter members were: Walt and Cathy Auen, Stan and Judy Boganwright, Bubba and Freda Burks, Jim and Marge Cook, Randy and Connie Frederiksen, Danny and Leigh Griffin, Tommy and Aggie Kolinek, Chris and Shirley Landers, Bill and Ann Pope, and Lee and Bev Stockfelt. The club held its first fun match in 1975. By August of 1977 the members were working on the club's third B Match.

Other groups that are forming are the Alamo Area BHC, in the San Antonio area; Capitol District BHC near Rennsselaerville, New York; Dogwood BHC in Richmond, Virginia; BHC of Central California, near Fresno; and Northern Illinois BHC.

Addresses of the local clubs can be had by writing to the Secretary of the Basset Hound Club of America or the American Kennel Club.

THE BASSET HOUND CLUB OF AMERICA OFFICERS 1935 TO 1977

Year	President	Vice-president	Secretary	Treasurer
1935–36	William Fritz	Emil Seitz		Carl Nottke
1937	Emil Seitz	Otto Grigsby		Carl Nottke
1938	Emil Seitz	Harold Fogelson		Carl Nottke
1939	Emil Seitz	Consuelo Ford		Carl Nottke
1940–44	Consuelo Ford	Melvin Freeman		Effie Seitz
1945–50	Roy Smith	Dr. J. P. Honey		Claude Smith
1951	Claude Smith	Harold Fogelson		Roy Smith
1952–53	Claude Smith	Johnny Bose		Roy Smith
1954–55	Johnny Bose	Norwood Engle		Millie Houchin
1956	Leslie Kelly	Chris Teeter		Millie Houchin
1957–58	Johnny Bose	Chris Teeter	Effie Seitz	Donald Bateman
1959–60	Dr. D. Wahl	Norwood Engle	Dorothy Shula	Effie Seitz
1961–62	Paul Kulp	Norwood Engle	Elizabeth Phillips	Julian Dexter
1963–64	John Eylander	Norwood Engle	Darrielyn Oursler	David Feron
1965	John Eylander	Norwood Engle	Mercedes Braun	Donald Bateman
1965–66	Norwood Engle	William Rider	Mercedes Braun	Donald Bateman
1967	Norwood Engle	William Rider	Mercedes Braun	Clare Clowe
1968	Norwood Engle	John Eyelander	Ruth Bateman	Clare Clowe
1969	Joseph Braun	Clifford Warren	Ruth Bateman	Jean Spaulding
1970	Joseph Braun	Clifford Warren	Ruth Bateman	Jean Spaulding
1971	Joseph Braun	Norwood Engle	Ruth Bateman	Jean Spaulding
1972	Donald Martin	Norwood Engle	Eileen Schroeder	Jean Spaulding
1973	Donald Martin	Norwood Engle	Eileen Schroeder	William Kelly
1974	Dodd McDowell	Jean Spaulding	Eileen Schroeder	William Kelly
1975	Joseph Braun	Finn Bergishagen	Jean Sheehy	Jean Spaulding
1976	Finn Bergishagen	William Kelly	Jean Sheehy	John Hackley
1977	Finn Bergishagen	William Kelly	Jean Sheehy	John Hackley
1978	William Kelly	Clare Clowe	Beverly Stockfelt	Pete Weaver

8

The Standard

A Standard is a word picture of the ideal dog in any breed approved by the American Kennel Club. It describes the characteristics that set one breed apart from the other. The goal of the breeder should be to produce dogs as nearly perfect as possible. Judges are duty-bound to use the Standard as their guide in making awards.

The present Standard for Basset Hounds was accepted by the American Kennel Club in early 1964. Revisions had been made, as recommended by the Basset Hound Club of America, to clarify the old Standard and make stronger emphasis on the utility of the breed.

The Basset's versatility has been a threat to his quality since the days when the ladies of the French Court found his medieval quaintness amusing and took him into their chambers. He enjoys his role of an "arm-chair clown." But, lest he be doomed to degeneration by over-emphasis of singular points, the purpose of the breed must forever be kept foremost in mind.

The Basset was bred to be a slow, deliberate trailer, endowed with great physical stamina. The Standard describes such a dog if, and only if, *each* point is carefully considered. Once his loose skin, heavy

HEAD: Medium width, large, well-proportioned; length from occiput to muzzle greater than width at brow; skull well-domed; pronounced occipital protuberance; length of nose to stop approx. from stop to occiput; skull sides flat, free from cheek bumps. Side view: Top lines of muzzle and skull, straight, parallel; skin over entire head loose, distinct wrinkles over brow when head is lowered

EARS extremely long, low-set (far back on head); drawn forward, tips fold over end of nose; velvety; hang in loose folds; ends curling slightly inward

EYES slightly sunken, haw prominent; dark brown preferred (lighter, according to coat acceptable); light or protruding eyes, faults

STOP moderately defined

MUZZLE deep, heavy, free from snipiness; teeth large, sound, regular; scissors or even bite; overshot or undershot a serious fault; lips dark, pendulous, falling squarely in front; loose, hanging flews; dewlap very pronounced

SHOULDERS well-laid-back, powerful; set close against chest

CHEST deep, full; prominent sternum in front of legs; distance from chest to ground not to exceed one-third height at withers of adult

FORELEGS short, powerful; bone heavy; skin wrinkled; elbows set close against sides of chest

TOPLINE straight, level; free from sag or roach

NECK powerful, well-arched, of good length

NOSE dark, black preferred; nostrils large, wide open; liver-colored conforming to head color permissible but not desirable

RIBS well-sprung with adequate room for lungs; heart; rib structure long, smooth, extending well back

PAWS massive, very heavy; pads tough, heavy, well-rounded; feet inclined trifle outward; (down on pasterns, a serious fault); toes, neither pinched nor splayed; dewclaws may be removed

DISQUALIFICATIONS: Height of more than 15" at highest point of shoulder blades; knuckled-over front legs; distinctly long coat

COAT hard, smooth, short; density sufficient for all weather; skin loose, elastic

COLOR: Any recognized hound color

TAIL set in continuation of spine; not to be docked; carriage slight curvature, gay; hair on underside coarse

APPEARANCE: Short-legged, very heavy-boned; movement deliberate but not clumsy; of great endurance; temperament, mild, devoted

HINDQUARTERS very full, well-rounded; approx. equal to shoulder width; a firm stance, no crouching; hind legs straight; rear view, parallel, stifle, well-let-down; hocks turning neither in nor out; hind feet point straight ahead; dewclaws may be removed

SIZE: Desired height not to exceed 14"

Visualization of the Basset Hound Standard, reprinted with permission from *Dog Standards Illustrated*, © 1975, Howell Book House Inc.

bone, long ears, etc., become so exaggerated that they interfere with his work in the field, he is no more Basset-type than his light-boned, leggy counterpart. The fundamental principle, upon which the description of the ideal Basset is based, is the breed's utilitarian value. Also included must be characteristics unique for the breed though many of these are advantageous to him in his work. Let us discuss them point by point. One must remember it is difficult to draw up a Standard that is complete and concise. Lengthy descriptions are frowned upon. Therefore, the picture is not always clear to the novice.

The A.K.C. Standard for the Basset Hound

GENERAL APPEARANCE: The Basset Hound possesses in marked degree those characteristics which equip it admirably to follow a trail over and through difficult terrain. It is a short-legged dog, heavier in bone, size considered, than any other breed of dog, and while its movement is deliberate, it is in no sense clumsy. In temperament it is mild, never sharp or timid.

AUTHOR'S COMMENT: There's not much elaboration necessary here. Heavy bone, followed by "in no sense clumsy," should rule out the slobs that cannot make it around the show ring, let alone spend a day in the field. As for temperament, perhaps *"should* never be sharp or timid" would have been better. There are several bloodlines that have produced many timid dogs. There is always an excuse why this one or that one has been "ruined." But when we see too many relatives with the same shy tendencies, it is hard to close our eyes and say it is not inherited. I am not referring to the young dog making his initial public appearances and finding himself a bit unsure in all the new occurrences. These dogs usually warm up to a few people who are strangers even though they seem a bit wary of some.

HEAD: The head is large and well proportioned. Its length from occiput to muzzle is greater than the width at the brow. In over-all appearance the head is of medium width. The skull is well domed, showing a pronounced occipital protuberance. A broad flat skull is a fault. The length from nose to stop is approximately the length from stop to occiput. The sides are flat and free from cheek bumps. Viewed in profile the top lines of the muzzle and skull are straight

153

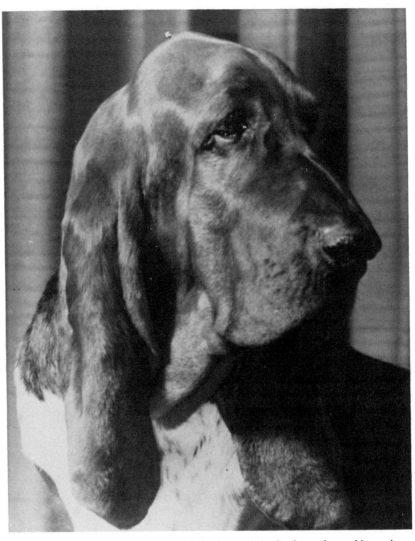
A beautiful, masculine head. Note especially the good depth of muzzle on this specimen.

and lie in parallel planes, with a moderately defined stop. The skin over the whole of the head is loose, falling in distinct wrinkles over the brow when the head is lowered. A dry head and tight skin are faults.

AUTHOR'S COMMENT: Since many, apparently, never read beyond the description of the head, perhaps one of the most important revisions for the new Standard was made in the first paragraph. The old Standard described the skull as being narrow. What was meant was that the skull was narrow in proportion to its length. The tendency grew to breed for wind-splitting appendages that reminded one of an inverted ice-cream cone, and certainly not in balance with the desired broad body. It is amusing to refer to pictures of the Bassets from the era when the original Standards were worded. It would be difficult to find an American Basset that is quite so dry or has such a shallow muzzle, though they were described as having an abundance of loose skin and wrinkles, great depth of muzzle. One must conclude that these words were used to depict the Basset as opposed to other dogs of that time. We continue to use the same terms though our visualization of their meaning is different. Elasticity and wrinkle prevent punctures of the skin in dense undergrowth and, supposedly, abet the scenting organs. Does it necessarily follow that the "dog with enough loose skin for two" is the better Basset? At least, "dryness" is not listed as a *serious* fault.

The muzzle is deep, heavy, and free from snipiness. The nose is darkly pigmented, preferably black, with large wide-open nostrils. A deep liver-colored nose conforming to the coloring of the head is permissible but not desirable.

AUTHOR'S COMMENT: You will ask, if a light nose is not desirable, why is it allowed? Many breeders want a Standard to fit *their* dogs. In order to gain acceptance of more important points, a few minor ones were conceded.

The teeth are large, sound, and regular, meeting in either a scissors or even bite. A bite either overshot or undershot is a serious fault.

AUTHOR'S COMMENT: A close fitting of the front teeth of the upper jaw over the front teeth of the lower jaw is a scissors bite. The upper teeth protrude over the lower in an overshot bite, and when the lower teeth extend beyond the upper, the bite is referred to as undershot. It is common knowledge that dentistry can be used, in some instances, to alter the set of the teeth, creating an illusion of a scissors bite. However, by carefully checking the set of the jaw-bone, such an alteration can be detected. Structure of the jaw is an inherited factor and should be considered as such in breeding. We are to be plagued with bad bites. Stonehenge, in 1887, referred to the works of De Fouilloux, describing the Basset d'Artois as having double rows of teeth like wolves. In this same period, the Comte le Couteulx de Canteleu wrote that "some of them have more teeth than dogs usually have, and many have the 'bec de lievre' or the lower jaw a little shorter than the upper." Two of the best bitches in his pack had such a formation of jaw. The early Standard of the Basset Club (Great Britain) stated that this was not a fault. The American breeders must be vigilant if we are to rid ourselves of this vexation.

The lips *are darkly pigmented and are pendulous, falling squarely in front and toward the back, in loose hanging flews. The* dewlap *is very pronounced. The* neck *is powerful, of good length, and well arched.*

AUTHOR'S COMMENT: The sentences on lips and dewlap are self-explanatory. What is "good length" in reference to the neck? It is such an important item in the make-up of the Basset, and yet has never been strongly emphasized. The British dog may lack our tremendous rib and depth of brisket, but it has maintained a beautiful, long, well-arched neck, so important to elegant carriage of the head. It should be of sufficient length to allow the dog to drop his nose to the ground without breaking gait. Unfortunately, the entry that trots around the show ring, looking adoringly at its handler, is a "ringside pleaser." No Basset looks his best when aping a carpet sweeper. However, I firmly contend, part of the evaluation of gait should include a few steps with the nose dropped to the ground. It takes correct length of neck, plus a well-balanced body, to move true in this position, an important feature of Basset "type."

The eyes *are soft, sad, and slightly sunken, showing a prominent haw, and in color are brown, dark brown preferred. A somewhat lighter colored eye conforming to the general coloring of the dog is acceptable but not desirable. Very light or protruding eyes are faults.*

The ears *are extremely long, low set, and when drawn forward,*

This Basset has a lovely head and also shows good depth of forechest, a good front and good feet.

Among other virtues, this Basset shows a good front, topline, neck and depth of muzzle.

fold well over the end of the nose. They are velvety in texture, hanging in loose folds with the ends curling slightly inward. They are set far back on the head at the base of the skull, and, in repose, appear to be set on the neck. A high set or flat ear is a serious fault.

AUTHOR'S COMMENT: A prominent haw is one thing; a scoop-shovel to collect debris is another. The low-set ear is to be long (as opposed to other breeds) enough to wrap around the end of the nose. The longer the better? This author maintains that, though it may be amusing to see the dog trip over his *excessively* long ears, good judgment dictates that this interferes with his work.

FOREQUARTERS: The chest is deep and full with prominent sternum showing clearly in front of the legs. The shoulders and elbows are set close against the sides of the chest. The distance from the deepest point of the chest to the ground, while it must be adequate to allow free movement when working in the field, is not to be more than one-third the total height at the withers of an adult Basset. The shoulders are well laid back and powerful. Steepness in shoulder, fiddle fronts, and elbows that are out, are serious faults.

The forelegs are short, powerful, heavy in bone, with wrinkled skin. Knuckling over of the front legs is a disqualification.

The paw is massive, very heavy with tough heavy pads, well rounded and with both feet inclined equally a trifle outward, balancing the width of the shoulders. Feet down in pastern are a serious fault. The toes are neither pinched together nor splayed, with the weight of the forepart of the body borne evenly on each. The dewclaws may be removed.

AUTHOR'S COMMENT: Approximately two-thirds of a Basset's weight is borne by the frontquarters. This portion of his body is all-important. The shoulders are well muscled, with shoulder blades very long, forming a right angle with the upper arm. The entire assembly should be placed far enough back to cover the lowest point of the breastbone. Most of the faults of feet and legs stem from a too-short shoulder blade. The sternum bone should be felt. It is easy to be deceived by fat that only appears to be a prominent sternum. If the shoulder is placed back far enough, and the chest is broad enough, the upper arm, of necessity, is slightly curved when viewed from the front. It follows the curve of the rib to the lower part of the forearm, with the wrist straight, terminating in a massive, but compact, paw that turns slightly outward. Quality of feet can be

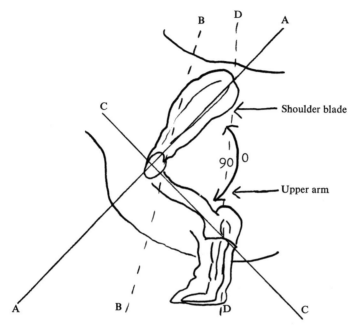

A. Solid line shows 45 degree angle of shoulder blade to ground level, allowing good reach of foreleg.

B. Dotted line shows steep shoulder blade placement and how it limits the reach of front leg. Incorrect.

C. Solid line shows upper arm of correct length, angling back and down to create an angle of 90 degrees between it and shoulder blade.

D. Dotted line shows plumb line from withers to back of heel, the best position to pose front to determine true angulation. Short upper arm would not permit foreleg to stand under withers and cover deepest part of chest, maintaining good balance.

checked by examining how the pads are worn. It is best to evaluate the frontquarters while the dog is "at ease." A smart handler can hamstring them to give the appearance of a good front. On the other hand, a novice dog will often lean into the hand of its handler and distort what may be a good front. Another successful appraisal can be made by requiring the handler to lift the dog under the neck and "drop" it. Much can be seen by the way it gaits.

BODY: The rib structure is long, smooth, and extends well back. The ribs are well sprung, allowing adequate room for heart and lungs. Flatsidedness and flanged ribs are faults. The topline is straight, level, and free from any tendency to sag or roach, which are faults.

AUTHOR'S COMMENT: Most back troubles stem from a short rib-cage. There should be little space from the last rib to the hip, leaving a very few lumbar vertebrae without some support. The rib should be as wide as the shoulder and two-thirds to three-quarters as deep as the height at the withers, which when considered as a unit, add up to powers of endurance. A topline that is level to the last rib, with a very slight rise over the loin, ending in a slightly rounded croup is very different from a roach back. Simple engineering principles tell us that a long topline must have a reasonable amount of arch to take up the shock, lest we doom our breed to slipped discs, etc.

HINDQUARTERS: The hindquarters are very full and well-rounded, and are approximately equal to the shoulders in width. They must not appear slack or light in relation to the over-all depth of the body. The dog stands firmly on its hind legs, showing a well let down stifle with no tendency toward a crouching stance. Viewed from behind the hind legs are parallel, with the hocks turning neither in nor out. Cowhocks or bowed legs are serious faults. The hind feet point straight ahead. Steep, poorly angulated hindquarters are a serious fault. The dewclaws, if any, may be removed.

AUTHOR'S COMMENT: Equally as important as the front, the hindquarter must be correct to propel the heavy body. A Basset is no better than his running gear. The term "well-bent stifle" often bewilders the neophyte. The angulation between the femur and pelvis is approximately 90 degrees. When the hocks are set at a right angle to the floor, viewed from the side, they are well behind the dog and show a distinct curve of the stifle. The distance between

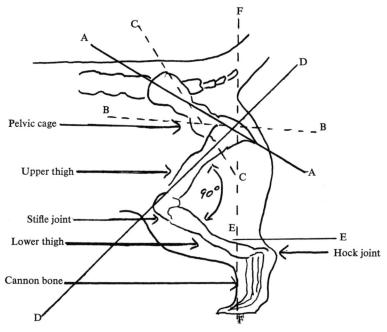

A. Solid line shows pelvic cage angled at 30 degrees to ground.

B. Dotted line shows flat pelvis, which would pull up upper thigh, and result in straight stifle; unless bones are very short, this gives a stiff stilted gait.

C. Dotted line shows steep pelvis, low tail set resulting, and lack of follow-through when moving.

D. Upper thigh of correct length which angles at 45 degrees to ground level, creating a 90 degree angle between it and lower thigh and almost the same between it and pelvis.

E. Correct length of lower thigh. If either thigh were shorter, on the same size dog, they would be straighter in order to meet. This would result in short gait or a straight stifle.

F. Dotted line shows best position to pose the rear to find angulation.

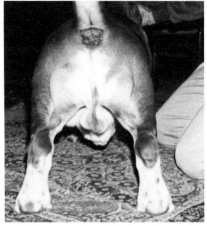

Correct rear. Hocks turning neither in nor out.

Cowhocks.

Spread hocks or bowlegs.

the hock joint and the foot is short. When viewed from the rear, they are to be parallel with each other and almost straight down from the broad, well-muscled rump. The term "crouching stance" should not be applied to obviously inexperienced dogs, especially puppies, that are merely "coming unglued." A good judge will patiently attempt to correctly evaluate the hindquarter while the handler may assist by gently rubbing the undercarriage to encourage the dog to stand. Actually, much can be seen, regarding structure, by the way the dog "sinks."

TAIL: The tail is not to be docked, and is set in continuation of the spine with but slight curvature, and carried gaily in hound fashion. The hair on the underside of the tail is coarse.

AUTHOR'S COMMENT: The tail should be of sufficient length to provide good balance with the length of the dog. It should be very thick at the base tapering to a white tip to be seen in the field. A thin, willowy tail is not in balance with the body, nor is one that is too short. It should not be carried "ring-tail" or "squirrel-tail" fashion, just gaily up, curving slightly forward. The underside is bushy but not silky and feathery.

SIZE: The height should not exceed 14 inches. Height over 15 inches at the highest point of the shoulder blades is a disqualification.

AUTHOR'S COMMENT: The average Basset ranges from 12½ inches to 13½ inches at the withers. A 12½ inch dog would weigh between 55 and 60 pounds. In order to be in correct proportion, a height of 15 inches would require at least 90 pounds of weight. It should be obvious that the best size would be around 13 inches.

GAIT: The Basset Hound moves in a smooth, powerful and effortless manner. Being a scenting dog with short legs, it holds its nose low to the ground. Its gait is absolutely true with perfect coordination between the front and hind legs, and it moves in a straight line with hind feet following in line with the front feet the hocks well bent with no stiffness of action. The front legs do not paddle, weave, or overlap, and the elbows must lie close to the body. Going away the hind legs are parallel.

AUTHOR'S COMMENT: Movement cannot be emphasized too strongly. It is the most important means of true appraisal. With the exception of checking the bite, sternum, rib, and pads, a good judge

A very bad front. Note also the overgrown nails which worsen the already bad picture.

A poor head and front.

A poor, swaybacked topline with a correspondingly steep rear. The same specimen, however, shows a good forechest and shoulder.

A Basset of obvious quality. He displays a good, level topline, good rear angulation, a nicely set neck of correct length and a proper forechest with well-laid shoulders. Compare this hound to the one shown below.

A hound with a poor front, a steep shoulder and lacking forechest.

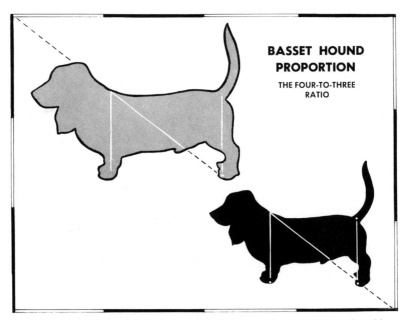

A well-proportioned Basset is built in a four-to-three ratio: the height at the withers is approximately three-fourths of the measurement from withers to tail. The silhouettes illustrate the proportions of a Basset measuring 14 inches at the withers compared to those of a Basset measuring 11 inches.

should know how a dog is "put together" by the manner in which he moves. He can hardly be expected to "flit about like a gazelle;" he's not built like one. His manner should be deliberate, determined, full of drive, and give evidence of exceptional endurance. Though he may have a slight bounce when he really "gets going," he must in no sense be clumsy. A dog with a "hitch" in the hip or shoulder should never be considered for an award. Even though it may be temporary, let him do his winning if, and when, he gets over it.

COAT: The coat is hard, smooth, and short, with sufficient density to be of use in all weather. The skin is loose and elastic. A distinctly long coat is a disqualification.

AUTHOR'S COMMENT: The coat is a most controversial subject. We must keep in mind that it must give protection from the weather. Dogs quartered out of doors in winter often develop a dense, slightly wiry coat. One should not be able to see the skin easily when running one's hand against the fur. But, just how long is a "long coat?" This may be better answered if re-worded to, "What is a long coat?" A long coat is soft, silky, and feathery like a Setter coat, with ear fringes and feathers on the legs and tail. The outer body coat is soft and silky, inclined to waviness. If one keeps the texture in mind, he will not be confused between a "long-coat" and a good winter coat. It would be out of the question to penalize a dog for a coat that is capable of protecting him in severe weather. The clippers will be taken to a few "long-coats" and they will get by, but this will not help when it comes to producing puppies. Mother Nature will give us such coats until all the carriers of these genes are weeded out. The loose and elastic skin will roll rather than puncture in dense cover. However, nothing says that it must be "two sizes big."

COLOR: Any recognized hound color is acceptable and the distribution of color and markings is of no importance.

AUTHOR'S COMMENT: The tyro might inquire what is meant by any recognized hound color. Bassets are black and brown with white undercarriage, paws, tail tip, and possibly around the neck or on the muzzle (tricolor)—or brown and white in the same places. The shade of brown varies in either case from deep mahogany to lemon and is described accordingly, red being the intermediate hue. Open-marked is applied to either tricolors or brown-and-whites when the coat is basically white, on the back, with large patches of color as opposed to solid color. There are varying amounts of white on the muzzle, neck, and legs. Though I have seen it, none is desired on the ears. The distribution of markings is of no importance unless one considers the effect to the eye of the viewer.

DISQUALIFICATIONS: Height of more than 15 inches at the highest point of the shoulder blades.

Knuckled over front legs.

Distinctly long coat.

AUTHOR'S COMMENT: Now, how does all this concern us as lovers of the Basset Hound? With the exception of the purely distinctive breed characteristics, every requirement of the Standard is justifiable on the basis of the Basset's ability to spend a day in the field in slow, determined pursuit of game. You will note, for the most part, the serious faults deal with points that concern his work. We want to improve him, not by exaggerating any of the requirements of the Standard, but by striving for the perfect combination and balance of the characteristics as stated in the Standard. He is not the result of breeders' fads, nor is he the result of whims of judges. A Basset is a working hound, ideally suited for his task which he truly enjoys.

It should be the aim of Basset Hound breeders to avoid such over-emphasis of any point of the Standard as might lead to unbalanced exaggeration.

9

Breeding and Raising
Better Bassets

Too much time, money, and hard work are involved to breed for anything less than the best. Judge the sire by his get when bred to bitches of different bloodlines. Will he be compatible with your bitch? Does he consistently throw certain traits, either good or bad? These are the questions that must be answered before you decide. His winning record is no proof that he will produce quality, though the name might help to sell a few puppies. Often, breeders in the know would not use the current winner if his service were offered free, while they seek a comparatively unknown dog whose bloodlines they value.

There are many excellent books on genetic theory. However since little research has been done with Bassets, a brief resumé of pertinent information may be of help. The term DOMINANT applies to the effect produced by one gene, showing in half the family of a parent having it, and usually appearing in every generation. RECESSIVE traits are commonly overshadowed by DOMINANT. The recessive effect requires two genes, one from each parent, to show, and it usually appears in every second generation.

For this reason, it is important to evaluate the characteristics of the grandparents of a contemplated litter. Though the effect may not show in the sire and dam, it may be transmitted to the offspring if it is in both maternal and paternal grandparents. Some of the foremost characteristics of the Basset are so thoroughly implanted that they show even though they are genetically considered RECESSIVE. Note, however, such items as "long hair" in the following list of RECESSIVE traits. This accounts for the sudden appearance of such a coat in the offspring of apparently "smooth coat" sire and dam whose parents were also apparently "smooth coats." Enough "long coat" genes were transmitted, even though hidden, to show when mutual genetic makeup was used.

We need not concern ourselves as much with the undesirable characteristics that appear listed as DOMINANT. They will be seen if they are being carried. Dominant traits include: normal head, coarse hair, wavy hair, short tail, stub tail, high style hunting, dewlap, short legs, long nose. Recessive traits include: narrow head, fine hair, straight hair, long hair, long tail, low style hunting.

To plan your mating, check carefully into the makeup of your bloodlines, considering brothers, sisters, grandparents and their littermates, as well as the immediate sire and dam. Decide upon the source of the desirable traits and increase the bloodlines carrying them. At the same time, eliminate the carriers of the undesirable. It is best to introduce new genes gradually lest there is a complete hodgepodge caused by too many possible combinations of genes. Line breed until these genes are firmly established. Always select sound animals for breeding stock. Never breed one with a glaring fault. It may not appear in the immediate offspring, but it will be around to plague your stock at some later date.

Bassets are, genetically, a deviation from normal structure. Nature tends toward the normal and punishes overemphasis of abnormalities by producing monstrosities, thus extreme care must be exercised. Breeding a good Basset is a challenge, second only to establishing a good Basset bloodline.

Count the days to establish the proper time for mating. It is more successful to breed when the color of the menses begins to lighten. Better still, mate when the stud and bitch indicate they are ready. Then continue mating every other day until the bitch's desire is gone. This will vary with individuals.

The actual mechanics of mating may be a bit more difficult. In fact, it can be downright backbreaking. The following method is quite successful. Two people are required. Place the bitch either across the knees of one person, or across a block that is "belly" high. This person also keeps her from struggling, nipping, or whatever she may decide to do. The second person handles the male. He is allowed to mount her and is then assisted with the "steering," guided from side to side until he hits his mark. At this time, the bitch is grasped by the stifles and held back against him, he is pushed forward, and held until copulation takes place. Often a young male must be encouraged to allow such assistance. After the first few times, he soon learns to expect your help. After copulation is assured, gently remove the support, allow them to get comfortable (usually end to end) and speak reassuringly, especially to a nervous bitch. Continue this until the job is done. It makes for easier work in the future. Copulation may last from ten minutes to over an hour, so do not be alarmed.

Pre-natal care consists only of proper nutrition and adequate exercise. Calcium is added to the bitch's diet during the last three weeks. She will be more comfortable if fed two meals a day. Accustom her to her draft-free whelping box in advance. To be, or not to be with the mother at the time of whelping is always controversial. Most Bassets are less nervous when you are there to reassure them. Many are slow whelpers. If you are with her, you will know if she is just slow or if she is having trouble.

Each puppy will arrive in its own membrane. This must be quickly removed. The cord is cut about two inches from the puppy's navel. Hold it head down and rub with vigor (it will not come out of its skin). When it is dry, and squalling, give it back to mama, unless she has too many to handle. In the event that a puppy appears but cannot be dislodged, grasp it gently but firmly and rotate it until it pops out. Above all, do nothing to upset the dam. She is better off alone than disturbed by a flustered, would-be assistant.

For your own convenience, you will undoubtedly prefer heated quarters in winter. However, an air-tight box equipped with a 100-watt electric bulb enclosed in a fireproof container is sufficiently warm even in very cold weather. You may prefer a heat lamp. If so, be certain it is not too near nor too hot. When puppies are cold, they cry and try to burrow under each other. If they are quiet, except when hungry, they are warm enough.

An ideal size for an indoor whelping box is four feet by four feet. In can easily be built with a plywood or hardboard floor. The sides may be approximately 30 inches high so that you may reach in or step over with ease. Sides may be made of all wood or wood below and wire above. A small gate, perhaps 16 inches wide, may be made in one corner of the front. Should the weather be cold, or the area drafty, an old blanket may be used to cover the open sides and part of the top. A removable top may be made if you prefer. To prevent the bitch from accidentally crushing newborn puppies against the sides of the box, we made a removable protector of four-inch boards, laid flat on legs that were four inches high. This also affords the puppies a dark place to crawl when they first open their eyes. Observation has taught us that they seem to like to do this. Their eyes are quite sensitive when they first open. Several layers of newspaper, topped by shredded paper, makes a satisfactory covering for the floor. When puppies first attempt to get up on their legs, they need something that is not slippery. I suggest old blankets, carpeting, throw rugs, or large bath towels. This is only necessary until they get strength in their shoulders and hips. Whatever, you probably will have to change it several times a day. Use this box for several weeks before the puppies are due so that the dam knows this is her bed and feels at ease in it. Extra heat may be needed. A heating pad, placed underneath, or a heat lamp will serve the purpose. Be careful that the heat lamp does not burn the puppies or the dam. If hung in one corner, the dam can always go to the opposite side if she is too warm.

Continue to feed the dam calcium and nutritional foods until the puppies are weaned. The first food is offered puppies soon after the eyes are open; a mixture of pablum and milk. Thoroughly soaked, softened kibble or meal gradually replaces the pablum. Puppies should be completely weaned at the age of six weeks though they need the companionship of their littermates for another two weeks. Vitamins are very important at an early age if the puppies are to develop good bone. A multiple-vitamin such as is given to babies should be started at three weeks of age. Beef, cottage cheese, and cooked eggs are excellent sources of nutrition in addition to milk and a high-quality kibble. The importance of proper nutrition cannot be stressed too strongly. A Basset requires as much, if not more, bone-making food than any other breed.

Basset puppies at ten days.

Basset puppies at three weeks.

Mi-Lin's Magic Marker

Basset Hounds are vigorous outdoor dogs, so puppies should be introduced to the outdoors at the earliest possible time. This is both advantageous for house training and to stimulate the breed's natural hunting instinct.

10

Selecting a
Basset Puppy

FIRST of all, selection depends partly on why you want a dog. As I pointed out, in Chapter I, there is no end to the versatility of the Basset. In selecting a puppy, many things must be taken into consideration.

Original Environment

Even if you only want a pet, you do wish to select a healthy one. Kennel conditions, and the condition of the dogs in the kennel, should be your first clue to the health of the puppies. A kennel need not be luxurious to be assuring but it should be obvious that the breeder does keep it clean and sanitary. Do remember that there is often that one dog that insists upon eliminating and stomping in it just as soon as his run is cleaned. This can ruin a first impression.

In late Spring or early Summer, depending on the climate of the locality, Bassets are blowing their undercoats. You may see fluffs of hair even though the kennel is cleaned daily. You should be able to tell whether it is fresh "dirt" or if it has been around several days.

How to lift a Basset puppy.

Basset puppy at eight weeks.

176

A kennel owner who loves his dogs will take good care of them. Do their quarters appear comfortable? Are all of the dogs reasonably clean?

Observe coat condition in the adult dogs. A healthy coat will appear shiny if the hand is rubbed down the back even if the dogs are blowing coat. Adults should be in good flesh. There is a big margin of difference between overweight and underweight. Even the field trial dogs in our kennel had a good layer of flesh over their ribs. It did not detract from their running ability or stamina in the field. Notice if the adult dogs have body sores or purulent matter in the eyes. Such things may be a signal that the puppies are not too healthy either. Do not judge too severely if the dam looks like a "bag of bones." Many do not snap back until eight or ten weeks after whelping even though they receive a maximum of care and nutrition.

Male or Female

Now that we have considered the kennel and the adults in it, what about the puppies? Do you want a male or female? I lean toward my boys because they do not cause the twice a year bother.

Seasons can be messy periods if you have a housedog. Some bitches cannot understand why they are suddenly not allowed their usual privileges like sleeping on the sofa. You must guard your bitch diligently against an accidental mating. Even a fenced yard is not a safe place for an unsupervised bitch in season. Unless you are out with her, some neighborhood romeo may well jump or climb over the fence, causing you the headache of an unwanted litter.

If you plan to show your bitch, you may note a personality change during seasons. She may experience false pregnancies and not be in the best of condition twice a year. You can always have her spayed so long as you do not plan to show or compete in field trials with her. Then, why have a female in the first place? I hear old wives tales such as the females are more affectionate or that males are inclined to roam, perhaps act embarrassingly, or are more difficult to housebreak. These pronouncements are untrue! I have experienced no such differences. Most of this behavior depends on their training. Our top stud dogs have also been excellent housedogs. This even applied to those who spent most of their time living in the kennel and came into the house for periodic visits.

Choose whichever sex you prefer but sex alone should not be a deciding factor unless you want a female to breed.

Choosing a Show Prospect

The chapter on the Standard explains what is desired in conformation. Although it is possible for a good leg to go bad, the ribs not spring, etc., rest assured that a bad leg will never get better, nor will a short rib cage lengthen out. So, if you are looking for a show prospect, pick the very best. Remember, the pick of the litter is only a "hopeful" until it is nearly a year old, and the best will be no better than the dogs in its pedigree. Even if the breeder planned the best mating possible for a beautiful sire and dam, there is no guarantee that each puppy will equal them. One can only try one's best and hope the litter meets his expectations. If you are looking for a sure winner, it would be best to select a dog that is nearly a year old. Some will still look like gawky teenagers until they are about two years of age. These are usually the ones that, if they do mature into beauties, are still going strong when they are eligible for the veterans class.

Things to Avoid

Beware of puppies that are narrow in the rib area with big pot bellies. They may well be wormy, have lacked the best of nutrition, or both. Some buyers have a natural, protective instinct to gather up the smallish pup or the one that hangs back in the corner. They should, instead, assume that it is sick or shy. It could be slow for an honest reason. If so, the breeder will prefer keeping it around until it does blossom. Another fallacy is that the runt is the smartest and makes the best pet. Size has nothing to do with intelligence or personality. Such intelligence is the result of the owner's training.

Choosing a Field Trial Dog

If you are interested in a dog that will hunt or field trial, a pup with running dogs in its pedigree will be more likely to carry such inherited tendencies. Hunting is the natural instinct of a Basset. Most will do a reasonably satisfactory job as a personal gun dog if given the opportunity to develop the skill. Field trialing requires that the job be done in a finer manner. Desire, style, and quality of nose, which may be nurtured for good or spoiled for bad field trial work, are inherited traits. The field trial chapters enlarge upon this. However, I suggest picking the puppy that gives evidence of being nosey, chases a piece of paper that blows across the yard or a cat up a tree, checks on new smells and gives other indications of his future as a good trial dog. We thoroughly enjoy watching the difference in personalities within a litter. The mischievous pup is usually the one who becomes outgoing in either the show ring or in the field.

If you are planning to go into a breeding program, select from the best bloodlines. The poorest puppy, from a litter of good breeding, is a wiser choice than the best puppy from a poor line.

Buying from the Small Breeder

Should you purchase from a kennel or is it safe to buy a puppy from a person who only owns one female? That can only be answered by considering other factors. It is not wise to buy from an individual who owns a mediocre female and bred her to a male of the same quality just to have puppies to sell. Even if you are not concerned with quality, it is pretty safe to assume that as little as possible was spent on nutrition and health care. The best foods, vitamins, and veterinary services cost money. You cannot provide for a litter properly and sell cheap puppies for a profit. Very often, however, someone in a city can have only one dog and would enjoy raising a litter. There are times, as well, when a larger breeder encourages at least one litter from a given female. In these cases, the dam will have come from a good bloodline and she will have been bred to a good male. Often the male is from the same kennel that produced her or was selected under the advice of her breeder. The litter will have been raised under the direction of the dam's breeder or the owner of the sire. Either should have cared enough to check on the pups. If all was satisfactory, either should be willing to recommend this individual. These puppies will be a worthwhile investment because they have been given the best.

On the other hand, when a kennel with six bitches has twelve

179

litters each year, are they actually doing more than raising puppies for sale? I know many kennel owners who, like ourselves, only produce one or two litters a year for the sake of carrying on the next generation or because others have asked for a product of a repeat mating.

Personality Development

You can see there is much to be considered when you are planning to buy. After that, how the dog matures is up to you. Considerable stress should be placed on personality. I have already mentioned the "shrinking violet" and the puppy that is full of mischief. Behavior traits may be the result of inherited factors or environmental circumstances. I suggest reading one of the books specifically written about the subject. One of my favorites, mentioned earlier, is *The New Knowledge of Dog Behavior* by Clarence Pfaffenberger (Howell Book House). Unfortunately there are a few Basset bloodlines that have produced some surly dispositions. They should be severely condemned. The tendency toward timidity can more easily be forgiven since the earliest writers mention that Bassets were slightly suspicious of the unfamiliar.

A breeder must carefully consider correct temperament when projecting his breeding programs. He must also make certain that puppies have the proper exposure to develop outgoing personalities. The first twelve weeks of a dog's life are the most important toward his becoming a companionable adult. Puppies will imitate their dam and/or her kennelmates. If the adults rush happily to greet strangers, so will the puppies. If mother woofs, shys off and hides, the puppies will do so, too, although they do not know why. Puppies can be accustomed to strange, loud noises if the breeder will merely add a bit of clamor to feeding and petting time. Children can do wonders in the development of extroverted puppies so long as they do not injure them.

By the time it is three months of age, a puppy should have been taught certain things. A dog that has learned *how* to learn can be later taught anything within reason. Early lessons need not be difficult. The kennel owner should have introduced the words COME, NO, and GOOD BOY or GIRL. The word COME could have been associated with coming for food and affection. It should have been said in a pleasant, coaxing voice. Through habit, the puppies learn to come when the word is used. NO should have been used, said in a scolding manner, when they did something wrong. They soon associate No with their master's displeasure. They learned to stop what they were doing because it brought about disapproval even though they may not have understood what it was that they did wrong. In this way, they learned that certain acts were taboo. GOOD BOY or GOOD GIRL should have been used as praise for doing right, spoken fondly and with a show of affection.

If you are purchasing an eight-week-old puppy, it is safe to say that you can accomplish the early word training mentioned earlier even if the kennel owner taught it nothing. However, by the time the puppy is sixteen weeks old, it must have had exposure to training and new circumstances in order to develop an outgoing personality. If you are buying an adult, or nearly mature dog, you will have to think about its previous exposure and character development. If the dog comes from a large, secluded kennel operated by a couple of quiet adults who do not have children around, and who have not taken the dog places where it could be introduced to the fun of meeting admiring strangers, riding in the car, or learning that the lead means going on pleasurable trips, its reactions could be disappointing. It could well be that the dog will be less than happy if it is taken from its protected kennel life and associates. However, if the dog has already known the enjoyment of "getting out among 'em", it will undoubtedly adapt to its new circumstances and be pleased that it no longer has to take turns with the other dogs.

Taking Delivery

When you have made your choice, ask the breeder to orient you on diet, previous and future health care, and the mode of training to which the dog is accustomed. Good breeders will do this voluntarily because they believe this is best for the dog. You will be more successful if you follow through rather than change these routines too abruptly.

You will find a few items to be useful for the journey home. A suitably-sized cardboard box, lined with shredded newspaper, in which to put the puppy may be helpful. Or, take along an old blanket or large towel if you can hold your charge. Most puppies will upchuck and/or eliminate if the trip is very long so extra newspaper, paper towels, etc. will come in handy. Some breeders will give you a towel or toy bearing the scent of home when you take your puppy. This sometimes eases the change of homes for the new member of the family.

The First Night

Now that you have your precious bundle home, there is a ninety per cent chance that neither of you will get a full night's sleep. The surest way to get your regular sleep for the first few nights after the puppy comes home is to take him to bed with you. This is fine if you intend to allow him to do this when he weighs 70 pounds and the temperature hits 80°. Bassets tend to be more "creatures of habit" than some other breeds. Settle on a place where his future nights will be spent and act accordingly *now*. He just came from a warm, cuddly family life. Sometimes an old, soft blanket, and a clock to mimic mother's heartbeat, will make him feel more at home. If he is not hungry, or in need of relieving himself, ignore his crying. Pick him up and cuddle him only when he is quiet.

Housing Your Basset

Each owner will have to decide on quarters that are best suited to his circumstances. Many Bassets are happily living in apartments and being walked on a lead. They enjoy having something to claim as their own even if they have the run of the house. An old scatter rug may do. Remember that puppies get bored when left alone. This is when they get into mischief. I suggest an area where your puppy can be confined, cannot damage anything, and cannot harm himself. Keep sponges, insecticides and other potentially harmful items out of reach. A crate is a worthwhile investment for the owner of a new puppy. It can serve as the puppy's bed, his confinement area, helps with housebreaking, and can be taken along on trips to serve as his "home away from home."

If you love your dog, you will not let him roam when out of doors. A fenced yard is ideal. If this is not possible, a portable ex-

182

ercise pen is available at pet stores, or, one can be made from a wooden frame covered with wire. If a stake and chain must be your answer, use it only for short periods. Chained dogs become unruly and chronic barkers. It would be better to take your dog out on lead rather than chain him.

If your dog is to be kept out of doors, there are good books to help with the construction of a kennel. Since it is the practice among a number of kennel owners, I would like to mention that I do not agree with putting Bassets up in the air on wire-bottom runs. Leave this for those who would save themselves pick-up work at the expense of the comfort of their dogs. Do plan for an area where the dog may romp each day. Kennel runs, alone, do not provide enough exercise for a Basset.

Training for Good Manners

Nothing is more pleasurable than owning a well-mannered dog. But dogs are not born this way. Someone had to care enough to do the teaching. The trainer, of course, should be smarter than the dog and *want* to train it. The rest comes about with quiet determination, perseverance, patience, and praise. Basic novice obedience lessons are invaluable to any pet, show, hunting, or field trial dog. I strongly disagree with the conjecture that Bassets are difficult to train. Too often the owner blames the dog for lack of intelligence, or stubbornness, when the fault really lies with the owner's attitude. Bassets form habits easily so training must be consistent. They respond greatly to praise and affection. Let your dog know when he pleases you by saying so. Use a harsh NO when the circumstances warrant.

Housebreaking

Puppies are like babies. They seem to do little more than eat, sleep, and "potty." Even tiny puppies will move away from their sleep spot to eliminate. As soon as they are able, they will crawl out of their box to take care of their needs. Plan to spend several days doing little more than watching for signs that the puppy is looking for a spot to eliminate in. Puppies are sure to do this after eating, drinking, or upon awakening from a nap. Take him out of doors and wait until he does as expected. Afterward, praise your puppy highly and return to the house. These steps are important. Should you wish to stay out and play with the puppy, first return him to the house and go out again. It is important that the little one makes the association between going out of doors and performing his natural functions. If you are diligent, the puppy should be going to the door within a few days. Remember, you must still be observant. He cannot open the door. Make a happy fuss that he went to the door. All dogs do not necessarily whine when they want out. Pick up the clues when your dog tries to tell you what he wants.

It will be more difficult to housebreak an older dog that has lived in a kennel but it most certainly can be done. If you encounter a real problem, a crate may be your answer until the dog gets the idea. No self-respecting dog wants to mess his bed.

I am not an advocate of paper-training. It can lead to a problem because the dog may use the paper no matter where it is.

Lead Breaking

Teaching the puppy to walk on lead may be coincidental with housebreaking or be a separate happening. It is usually a simple chore. If the dog balks, remain calm and use a reassuring voice. Coax, with a steady pull, persuade him to move a few steps and continue to speak in an encouraging voice. He will soon get the idea. If an older dog is pulling and tugging, use a slip-chain collar giving short jerks. Give slack between each tug. You will soon have him walking nicely along beside you even though he may need an occasional correction.

Simple, common sense can be the difference between an enjoyable dog and one that is a nuisance. Grooming can be an easy chore if one starts out calmly, during puppyhood, and makes it a pleasant experience for the dog. My dogs love to be primped. Yours will too if you do it right.

11

Health and Care

Dr. THOMAS PETTIT, of Oneonta, New York, kindly consented to write the following. Tom owned his first Basset while a student at the Veterinary College at Cornell University in 1960. He writes, "Sarie was our one and only Basset for my four years at Cornell. We broke her to run rabbits quickly and enjoyed hunting her on both rabbits and pheasants. She was also Shirley's (Mrs. Pettit) companion on those long nights when I was studying. She was a watchdog over our apartment and equally important, she became my anatomy specimen. No matter what organ, muscle, or bone, I found it on the willing Sarie."

Since starting with Bassets, Tom and Shirley Pettit have become well known for their thoughtful breedings of top running dogs. One of their Grand Field Champions, Petit's Ranger Ric, needs only a few points, at this writing, to become a dual champion, as well as being the top field trial stud in the country.

Care of the Skin and Hair Coat

How many times have we heard that a healthy dog will have a healthy hair coat? This statement is true. It is also true that a

185

healthy, active dog can have a dirty, unkempt hair coat! It is the healthy Basset with the poor hair coat that these remarks are directed at.

Bassets shed hair the year 'round and seem to be worse during the late Spring months. Females often shed within two months after whelping. It is thought that the rigors of delivery and raising a large litter contribute heavily to this hair loss.

Abnormal hair loss or baldness can also occur due to hormonal disturbance, to a variety of allergic ailments and to parasites. Certainly any major hair loss and roughened, red skin should be brought to your veterinarian's attention quickly. Also, if your Basset has a great deal of hair loss and itching, the problem must be dealt with quickly to prevent serious problems.

For control of normal hair loss, the owner is advised to brush the dog daily. The ideal hair brush is one with natural fibers. This prevents static electricity and possible hair damage. The use of a gloved hand or light towel is excellent for the Basset and its skin. The loose and dead hair should be removed to keep the whole hair coat clean and luxurious.

When bathing, use warm water and a dog shampoo because its Ph is balanced for a dog's skin and hair. Always protect your dog's eyes from the soap. A bland opthalmic ointment will do nicely. Protect your Basset's internal ear. Large pieces of cotton, inserted into the ears, will be sufficient protection. Dry the coat thoroughly. A hand operated dryer works better and quicker than towels.

To maintain a healthy coat and skin, the Basset needs a well-balanced diet including essential fatty acids. All these ingredients are present in dry, commercial dog foods. These essentials will oxidize (be rendered useless) if left open to the air. The key to preventing this are the antioxidents already added to dry food and keeping the food fresh and airtight while it is being used.

Adding animal fat, such as bacon, sausage, meat drippings, or suet, will ensure good hair coat. The average adult Basset needs one to two tablespoons added daily. It must be daily. It will take a month before any results can be observed. There are commercial products available to the dog owner whose pet has a shedding problem but they are expensive and usually unnecessary if the owner feeds a balanced diet.

Heat Cyles, Seasons and False Pregnancy

Bassets tend to mature slowly. It is true that some females are in their first seasons at six months of age, but the majority do not cycle until eight months of age or older. Breeding a female prior to her first year of age is not recommended. It is better to wait and let her gain maturity before she is bred.

There is no trouble recognizing an estrus (heat season). The vulva swells a good deal. There are drops of bloody discharge and male dogs are attracted to the female and her rear quarters.

The estrus is divided into three rather equal parts. During the first seven to ten days, the female will attract males but will not accept their advances. During the second seven to ten days, she will accept all males that are brought to her. This is her fertile time. During the last seven to ten days, the female will attract but not accept a male. During this entire period, there will be a discharge. It will gradually decline. The vulva swelling will also disappear. The female may make attempts to escape her confines and often will not obey commands.

A high percentage of Bassets, especially the older females, will experience *pseudocysis* (false pregnancy) following a heat without being pregnant. False pregnancy can occur with or without a breeding. Even though the female is not pregnant, she will show definite changes during the sixty-three days following the heat. Her nipples will enlarge in the last month. Her appetite will increase and she will gain weight, especially in the first month. If she has been bred, the false pregnancy can confuse the owner into believing their dog will have pups. She develops a large abdomen, her teats enlarge, and she may even have milk. Occasionally the female will nest and even bring toys or other objects into the nest. There have been occasions when she will defend her nesting area.

Normally, Bassets have two estrus cycles a year, six months apart. Generally those whose cycles are longer than six months apart are eight years or older. Often the old females will not have a true season. Instead, it is very short, averaging one week instead of three weeks. Those who consistently cycle less than six months apart should be examined by a veterinarian. There could be problems of a serious nature.

Sometimes the owner is worried because the bitch has not yet

Basset Breeding Box

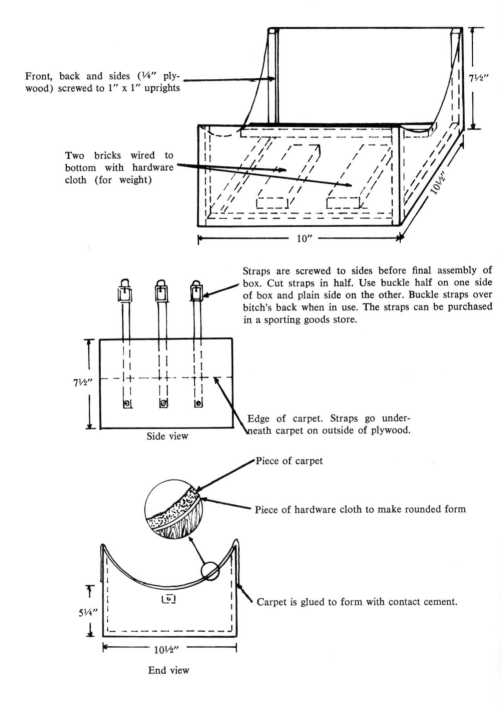

Front, back and sides (¼" plywood) screwed to 1" x 1" uprights

Two bricks wired to bottom with hardware cloth (for weight)

7½"

10½"

10"

Straps are screwed to sides before final assembly of box. Cut straps in half. Use buckle half on one side of box and plain side on the other. Buckle straps over bitch's back when in use. The straps can be purchased in a sporting goods store.

7½"

Side view

Edge of carpet. Straps go underneath carpet on outside of plywood.

Piece of carpet

Piece of hardware cloth to make rounded form

Carpet is glued to form with contact cement.

5¼"

10½"

End view

come in season or because they wish to breed at a specific time. They inquire about hormones. I do not believe in using hormones to bring a bitch in season. Hormonal use is not perfected in dogs and the reactions are often varied and contrary to the desired effect.

If you wish to have a bitch cycle, there is a natural method that is usually successful. Kennel her with another bitch that is in season. Almost without fail, your bitch will cycle and can be bred with a greater degree of assurance of pregnancy than with a hormone injection.

Breeding the Female

Every owner who wishes to breed his Basset dreams of a lovely litter with the average of eight puppies. Most of the time, with effort and perseverance, this will happen. However, it is wise to remember that not only can you lose the pups, you can lose the female as well. Breeding and whelping is, therefore, a calculated risk.

The actual breeding can be a frustrating experience. For the novice, consider taking your female to a knowledgable breeder with an experienced stud. It is advisable and better for all concerned.

The female usually accepts a male on or about the tenth day after the onset of staining. Acceptance is shown by her actions. The female will show her prospective mate that she is willing by raising her tail as he inspects her rear quarters. This is termed "flagging".

It is wise to have control of both dogs with collar and lead. More than one good stud dog has been bitten, perhaps temporarily losing his desire, because the female was not ready.

Once the acceptance has been established, the actual breeding can begin. It is not recommended that the partners be left alone. They will undoubtedly need assistance anyway. Bassets *are* difficult to breed and help is usually needed.

The breeding box has been indispensable in handling Basset matings. This homemade aid will save the participants a great deal of time and effort. The dimensions given are intended for a Basset. The female's rear quarters can be raised as needed by placing towels under her.

The bitch must be held by the collar, preferably by the owner, who will talk to her and calm her during the breeding. The male should have good footing and be helped by someone he knows and

Two of the author's young hopefuls.

A fine litter of newborn Bassets lining up for one of many meals they will take from their doting dam until they are independent of her. This thriving family is owned by Michael Sosne.

trusts. After several mountings, the male will usually require some help in guiding the penis into the vagina. This is accomplished by cupping the hand under the vulva and gently directing the penis to the lips. The male's natural action will do the rest.

Once breeding has occurred, the male's penis will enlarge and the female's muscles will contract. At this point the partners are said to be "tied" or copulated. The male can then be turned with his back end toward the female. When done gently, this will not injure the dogs. The dogs will remain in this position for from ten to 45 minutes or longer. They will come apart naturally. Both dogs should be held and kept calm during copulation. The "natural tie" is important as it creates pressure changes within the reproductive tract and aids the sperm in its travels and ultimate fertilization.

In the Basset, breeding frequently results in a "hand" or "outside tie." This term refers to a breeding where the swelling action of the male causes him to be forced out of the female genital tract. The outside tie is only maintained by actually holding both partners together. This method will only allow a few minutes of actual male penetration. The percentage of conceptions with an outside tie is not as high as with a natural tie.

On occasion, I have been asked to artificially breed dogs, including Bassets. There are many varied reasons for artificially breeding. The most common is when the female has a very small reproductive tract. Sometimes artificial breeding is indicated with inexperienced males or those with physical problems such as arthritis or bad hearts. Artificial breeding can be done if the male is calm enough for the sperm to be collected and if the female is in season. A veterinarian can determine if she is ready. He can perform the service with results that are nearly as successful as a natural tie.

Care and Feeding of the Bred Basset

Feeding should be kept simple with no changes for the first five weeks. The owner should resist the temptation to add food and nutrients. Mother Nature will succeed in putting weight on the female by utilizing her intake to provide for the unborn puppies.

The owner should attempt diet changes during the last four weeks. The female should gradually have her food intake increased to double her previous intake. Because of her increased size and resulting smaller stomach capacity, this should be given in two or three feedings. I am a great believer in dry, cereal foods. The major companies have developed a food that is better balanced nutritionally than our own. Water or broth can be added. Canned food should be given only as a supplement in order to encourage the consumption of the dry food. During this last month, add the following on a three-day rotating basis: cottage cheese, one day, 1 cup liver the next, and 1 cup raw meat on the third. I do not believe in giving milk. It will give the majority of Bassets diarrhea because of the high lactose and low butterfat. Table scraps are fine as long as highly spiced meats and sauces are not used. Spices will cause diarrhea and intestinal inflammation in dogs. Sugars are not digested well and are essentially wasted. Calcium, bone meal and similar supplements are not necessary if she is fed commercial dry dog food. There is hard evidence that the addition of excessive quantities or mineral supplements may cause more harm than good. Vitamins are frequently added and do no harm.

A bitch in whelp should put on weight at a slow, consistent level. This is accomplished by exercise along with feeding. Allow her to exercise to her heart's content. Most Bassets will limit themselves while pregnant, but a few will continue to exercise as if nothing had changed. When she is obviously heavy in whelp, during the sixth week on, discourage jumping and hard running but exercise her regularly under supervision. The female needs to be in decent shape to successfully deliver her litter. Many whelping problems occur because the female is soft, out of shape, and cannot withstand the rigors of prolonged and difficult whelping.

As she gets farther into pregnancy, feed her several times daily to keep her comfortable. Provide plenty of fresh, clean water. The added weight of pups, on the bladder, and the increased number of feedings will create the need for her to eliminate more often.

Whelping

Bassets normally give birth 58 to 64 days following a successful breeding. My experience is that the majority whelp at 62 days.

I feel the best place for a Basset to whelp is in the house. Most prefer the company of the adult family. Only a few seem to resent children observing the proceedings or the handling of the puppies. I like to see my pregnant bitches in the whelping box at least a week prior to the due date. This allows them plenty of time to adjust to the box and the surroundings. As birth approaches, the bitch will nest by ripping up the papers in her box. She will commence to pant and her lips will become dry. She will refuse food and may even attempt to bury her food in the box, presumably for later consumption. She will need to eliminate often and her stools will become soft as she clears every ounce of feces from her intestine. This will give her pelvic area every inch of room necessary for delivery.

A clear discharge will appear from the vagina, as she readies herself for birth. The temperature will drop below 100°F. At this point the owner can expect puppies within 24 hours.

The puppies usually arrive with very little noise on the part of the dam. She usually has several hard contractions while standing. She will then lie down, or sit, lick and examine the vulva. A discharge will appear as the "water sac" breaks, then a bulge appears first at the vagina and then the exterior to the vulva. This bulge is the puppy itself. Another contraction and the entire pup appears, encased in a fluid sac. This often breaks at the moment of birth or shortly before as the mother hurriedly cleans and licks the newborn. The pup is usually born head first but rear presentation is also considered normal.

The female may appear to be rough with her pups but she generally is not. She will lick away the sac and chew the umbilical cord from the pups. She will then eat the sac and the resulting green-black placenta which follows birth. This is normal and necessary for her to do.

The attendant should be ready with towels to rub the puppy after the mother has finished with the umbilical cord. This dries the puppy quickly. Many times the umbilical cord is long (over an inch) and should be trimmed with a scissors. Rarely, will the cord bleed. It should be tied with ordinary sewing thread one-half inch from the abdomen if bleeding does occur.

There may be times when the attendant cannot see a newborn breathing. Pick the pup up and rub it vigorously with a towel. You cannot hurt this newborn pup and roughness may stimulate it to breathe. Immersing the pup's body, all but the head, in very warm water will often shock the puppy into better respiration. A pup may appear to have fluid in its mouth and nose. Clear the fluid by holding the pup firmly by its chest and head, tail toward you. Bring it quickly from a position over your head to a position near the floor. Do it several times. This will usually clear the air passage. Don't give up too quickly on a pup who isn't breathing. If you can feel a heartbeat through the chest, keep trying.

Once the birth process starts, the female will continue to produce pups at a regular schedule. Usually the Basset will have pups in pairs, fifteen minutes apart. She will then rest, care for the pups and deliver more. As a veterinarian, I become concerned when the Basset goes over three hours between pups. At that time, the dog needs to be examined and its condition evaluated.

The Basset female is generally reluctant to leave her newborn pups during the first 24 hours. New mother or old, they prefer to stay with the pups and must be coaxed out of the whelping box for exercise and elimination. You will find they are most anxious to return to the pups. After three days, they will spend more time away from them.

Bassets will not eat until after delivery is completed and then eat only sparingly. In a few days, the dam's appetite is ravenous and she will need food three or more times a day. The dam and her litter should be examined by a veterinarian within 24 hours of the birth of the last pup. The doctor will check each pup and search for any obvious malformities. He will examine the dam and palpate for any retained puppies, retained afterbirths, or an enlarged uterus. The doctor will examine each teat and mammary gland. He will take your dog's temperature, examine the membranes for anemia and listen to her heart and lungs. He may even prescribe an injection of antibiotics and/or a drug to contract the uterus.

In summary: whelping can be a long session for a Basset and its owner. Prepare yourself and the bitch well in advance of the due date. The owner should understand the early stages of labor and be able to recognize them. The whelping area should be kept quiet but an attendant should be nearby during birth. If three hours have elapsed from the onset of initial hard labor or between puppies, contact your veterinarian and follow the advice given. Finally, have the dam and her pups examined by your veterinarian within 24 hours of the last birth.

The Newborn Pups

Fortunately, Basset females tend to be excellent mothers and rarely is anything needed from the owner in the way of help. Occasionally, she will need aid in removing the sac during birth and drying off the newborn, especially if the births are occurring one right after another. There may be need to tie off a bleeding umbilical cord. However, it is the best policy to inactively observe birth and help only if needed. Too many helpers, too much noise, too much attention will sometimes upset the dam causing her to move around and be careless with her pups.

If umbilical cords appear too long ($\frac{1}{2}$ inch is enough), the excess may be removed with sharp scissors. Iodine is an excellent drug to apply to the ends of the cords. This disinfects and dries the ends preventing any bacteria from ascending into the pups' bodies.

The pups should be checked for extra rear toes. Four are normal. Some fanciers routinely remove front dewclaws. This should be done by a veterinarian within three to five days if the breeder wishes.

A word about puppy mortality. Puppies will die in nearly all litters. Some are just not strong enough to survive the ordeal of birth. Others become chilled or are crushed by the dam. I feel that any dead puppy should be frozen in the event that more puppies should die. A frozen pup allows the veterinarian a chance to autopsy and find the cause of death quickly. This could save the rest of the litter.

At ten days of age, the eyes will open. The ears will be open a day or so later. Your pups should be up on their hind legs by 15 days. I like to have the pups eating semi-solid food by 21 days. The pups should be routinely wormed for ascarids (roundworms) at three weeks of age, with their dam, and the stool examined by your doctor shortly thereafter.

The pups should be weaned at five to six weeks of age. This is mostly for the mother's benefit. She needs the rest and the majority of dams no longer produce enough milk for the growing pups at this point. The puppies will now gain weight better away from their mother.

We first start with a very sloppy Pablum mixture, then gradually add dry dog food which has been soaked to a mushy consistency. As the puppies will allow, we gradually thicken the mixture until it is similar to the adult ration. We give cottage cheese and raw hamburger daily along with a vitamin product.

At six to eight weeks, the pups should obtain their first vaccinations. The mother gives them immunity that will last a varied amount of time, depending on the mother's antibody level. Each doctor has his own favorite vaccine and schedule. Follow his recommendations.

Puppies' Eyes

The eyes of your new pups will open at approximately the tenth day after birth. With a small percentage, the lids will become stuck during their first days. In Basset pups, this is not uncommon. The attendant should use a 1% solution of boric acid and tapwater, washing the lids with cotton dipped in the solution. This should be done three times daily for three days. If the problem persists longer, consult your veterinarian.

Umbilical and Inguinal Hernias

A hernia is a bulging of organs or body tissues through an abnormal opening. They are classified according to type and location. A reducible hernia is one that can be returned to the abdominal area with ease. An irreducible hernia cannot be returned without surgery. A strangulated hernia is one where the pressure of the hernia ring causes pooling of blood and eventual gangrene. This condition results in a very hot, painful swelling. Immediate surgery is necessary.

An umbilical hernia occurs in the middle of the abdomen. They are often seen in Bassets and are thought to be congenital and inherited, but the inheritance factor has not been definitely established. An umbilical hernia can also be acquired, occurring during birth if the mother chews the cord too close or lifts the pup by the umbilical cord. Many small umbilical hernias are firm and irreducible. Except for the obvious blemish, they are of no consequence and can be left alone. A large one should be corrected.

The inguinal hernia also occurs in the Basset, and is also thought to be hereditary. This hernia occurs in the groin area next to the abdominal wall. It can follow accidents or injuries. Usually the intestines fill the hernia sac and surgery is necessary to prevent damage to the affected animal.

Consult your doctor as soon as you are aware of a hernia.

The Stud Dog

Essentially the feeding of the male Basset, used for breeding, will not vary from a normal diet. We do not want him overweight lest his interest be diminished, his stamina reduced, and his effectiveness lessened. If breedings are anticipated, add vitamins daily, keeping his weight consistent with his build.

He should be clean and free from parasites, both internal and external. His vaccinations should be up to date. The owner of the female has the right to assume the bitch will not contract any parasites or communicable diseases while she is being bred.

Canine Infectious Brucellosis

A male used for breeding should be tested negative for brucellosis. This contagious disease can spread by breeding. A veterinarian can administer the test.

This disease is relatively new to the dog world. It was discovered by Dr. Leland Carmichael, at Cornell Veterinary College, in 1966. It is very common in some breeds (Beagles) but has not been reported, in large numbers, in the Basset. This disease is being included because of its devastating potential and has been found in at least 38 states.

Brucellosis is caused by a rod-shaped bacteria. It causes abortion and infertility in the female, sterility in the male. The female will abort her puppies during the last two weeks of pregnancy. She will be very sick, have swollen glands and a heavy vaginal discharge. Bred again, she will abort future litters. The male, affected with Brucellosis, will have enlarged lymph glands and a heavy discharge from his penis. Occasionally, the testes will enlarge greatly during the initial part of the disease. Gradually one or both testicles will shrink in size or actually disappear. The male will retain his ability to breed but will be sterile. The disease is transmitted from one dog to another by breeding. In addition, the handling or ingestion of infected semen, urine, vaginal discharge, fetal membranes or even the dam's milk can spread Brucellosis.

Females can survive the disease and may eventually produce live litters. However, such animals remain carriers. They are able to transmit the disease to others. There is *no cure* for Brucellosis. At this time, the recommendation is for euthanasia of affected dogs.

Brucellosis canis has affected humans. Because of our close involvement with the breeding, whelping, and medical care of our pets, the chance of contacting the disease, from a sick dog, is great.

197

The affected human will have a fever, chills, headache, and weight loss. The fact that humans can develop the condition should make dog owners concerned.

Fortunately, Brucellosis is not common in the dog world, especially in the Basset. It can, and has, destroyed entire bloodlines in other breeds. The disease can be detected in a veterinarian's office by the use of an effective blood test. Prevention of the disease is the only approach since there is no cure. To do this, all males should be periodically checked free of the disease. Any female should be tested free prior to breeding.

As the owner of a stud dog, I demand this test of any female brought for breeding. At the same time, it is the right of the female's owner to know the male is free of the disease. Scientists are attempting to develop a vaccine to protect our dogs. It is a difficult job, but some year it may be a reality.

Orchidism

Monorchidism (one testicle in the scrotum) is a congenital problem (existing at or before birth). Usually the left testicle is absent. This condition has occurred in the Basset Hound.

A cryptorchid (retention of the testicle within the abdomen) is more common a condition in the Basset. Normally, the testicle develops within the abdomen and by birth has descended through the inguinal (groin) canal to the scrotal sac. When this descent is arrested for some reason, the dog is said to be a cryptorchid. In my experience, some of these retained testicles will descend by nine months of age. If the testes are not present in the scrotum by one year of age, the odds are that they will not descend except in rare cases. Usually only one testicle is involved with a cryptorchid.

This condition is inherited. It is obviously classified as sex-linked and recessive (hidden and incapable of expression unless both breeding members carry the factor). Females are carriers. This condition can be eliminated from a breed if breeders would recognize the cryptorchid and carriers and not use them for breeding.

For the cryptorchid male, surgical interference other than castration is unwarranted. The American Kennel Club states that changing a dog's appearance by artificial means, with certain exceptions, will result in disqualification from showing.

A retained testicle has an excellent chance to develop into cancer by middle age, presumably due to the higher body temperature of the abdomen compared to the scrotum. Any Basset with only one or no visible testicles should be examined by a veterinarian during a routine visit. Your doctor will advise you as to a course of action to follow.

Sebaceous Cysts (Epidermoid)

Bassets, as all breeds, can develop multiple skin growths. Some are serious and some are not. Whenever an abnormal enlargement is discovered, the growth should be noted as to the location and size. Weekly checking should be carried out to monitor the growth. If the growth stays approximately the same size, it should be examined by your veterinarian at a routine visit. If the enlargement develops rapidly, have it checked as soon as possible.

The most common skin enlargement in the Basset is the epidermoid cyst. They are usually solitary and only occasionally multiply grouped. They start out pea size and can quickly enlarge to acorn size. The cyst is round and will fluctuate when pressure is applied to it. It is most often found in the skin but can also be found movable just under the skin.

The cyst develops due to change in a hair follicle. This can be a degenerative change, an injury, or a cystic change. It is most common in older Bassets. Once one occurs, more tend to develop. In my experience, monthly bathing with a medicated shampoo appears to prevent further cysts.

The cyst can ulcerate. When it does, a gray-white, cheese-like debris exudes from the center. The only treatment for these cysts is surgical removal. Your veterinarian can decide if and when surgery is warranted.

Curvature of the Radius

The radius is a bone of the fore limb between the elbow and the paw. A drastic outward curving of the bone is unnatural. I have seen more Bassets with this condition than all other breeds combined.

This condition is congenital and is due to a disturbance in the distal part of the bone. Because of the number of times I have seen it, and because it is common in certain strains of Bassets, there is strong suspicion to call it a hereditary problem in the breed.

It is not painful. It usually often affects but one forelimb, always before a year of age. It can develop rather quickly and is a disfigurement. It prevents maximum use of the dog. Affected individuals tire more quickly than normal dogs and may limp after extreme exercise.

There have been many causes listed, in other breeds, including hormonal disturbances, traumatic (injuries), nutritional, and possibly a hereditary problem. There are surgical procedures for correcting the defect if attempted before the dog matures. They can be drastic and are not always successful. The owner must decide if such heroic ordeals are warranted.

Ruptured Knee Ligaments or Trick Knee

This condition occurs all too often in the Basset. It presents some special problems to the owner because the symptoms of ligament rupture are also common signs of other problems. The onset is acute. One second your dog is normal. The next, it has a severe rear leg lameness. When the owner has an occasion to observe the actual rupture, the dog will cry out or show signs of extreme pain, which lasts for less than a minute.

An affected dog will initially carry the rear leg. Gradually, it will place the leg and limp around on it. Most owners think of the obvious . . . a muscle pull or tear. Failure to elicit any pain from the dog allows the owner a few hours of relief. However, after a day or two, the dog will still not walk without a pronounced limp and can only run by holding the affected leg off the ground. Close scrutiny of both knees will show a definite or suspected enlargement of the affected area. After 24 to 48 hours of no progress, and possibly knee enlargement, it is time to consult your doctor.

In most cases, the diagnosis of knee ligament ruptures must be done under short-acting anesthesia. Occasionally radiographs will also be done to determine joint changes. If the diagnosis is knee ligament rupture, then surgery is the only recourse. The surgery is highly successful in returning your dog to normalcy and regular use. Without it, your Basset will develop serious arthritis and may damage its other rear leg. The recuperative stage will last several months.

The causes of the problem include jumping from a high object to a low one with poor footing, a blow to the leg while bearing weight, and sudden starts or stops while playing. The veterinarian must decide on a number of possible reasons for the lameness. Included are muscle tears or pulls, fractures, and dislocated joints.

Teeth

The adult dog has 42 permanent teeth. Your puppy starts out with 28 temporary teeth which appear at three weeks of age. By fourteen weeks, these teeth are being replaced. The permanent teeth have all developed by eight months of age. The pup tends to chew during this time. Supply it with rubber toys or large beef bones. The most common problem with Bassets is a large tartar buildup. Tartar is a combination of calcium salts, food debris, and bacteria. It is hard and brown in color. This tartar will work up the tooth and under the gums causing inflammation and irritation. Dog biscuits or large bones enable the dog to keep buildup to a minimum.

The usual treatment is the removal of tartar under sedation by the veterinarian. Occasionally, extractions must be carried out because of abscessed teeth or roots. If the tartar build-up is minor, the owner may be able to remove it with the fingernail.

Any bad breath should mean the teeth and gums should be examined. The appearance of tartar, red and inflamed gums should be cause for action by the owner. Some puppies will have yellow-colored teeth. The administration of some antibiotics to pups will cause the discoloration to the temporary teeth. The permanent teeth will be normal.

The care of your Basset's teeth and gums are important if the dog is to retain all the permanent teeth. Your veterinarian can be of great assistance to you and may offer advice on dental hygiene during a routine visit.

Eyes

The eyes of any dog are important. Several conditions of the eyes and lids are common in the Basset. Some are thought to be inherited defects and a few are known to be due to heredity.

The eye is a sensitive and complex organ. Because of this and its

201

importance to the dog, a correct diagnosis and expert treatment is necessary. There are very few home remedies that could or should be used. Most problems of the eye require veterinary care.

The symptoms of eye trouble can be readily seen by the owner:

Tearing. Excessive tears are due to an irritation and results in an accumulation and wetness in the inside corner of the eye.

Photophobia or fear of light. When the cornea (surface of the eye) is irritated or the conjunctiva (lining of the lids) are inflamed the dog will keep his eye closed to avoid bright sun or light.

Rubbing. Frequently a foreign body will cause the Basset to paw at his eye or to rub his head on the floor.

Redness of the sclera (white part of the eye). Normally only three blood vessels are readily visible in the eye. When problems develop, the blood vessels increase in the white part of the eye. The owner will frequently complain that the dog has a "bloodshot" eye.

Third eyelid protrusion. The dog has three eyelids, an upper, a lower, and a third lid originating at the inside, or nasal, corner. This third eyelid is called the nictitating membrane. Normally this eyelid is nearly invisible in the corner of the eye. With irritation or inflammation, the third eyelid moves across the eye as a protective hood. Many owners will observe a "covering over the eye." It is often their first awareness of a third eyelid.

Swollen or painful globe. When viewing the Basset, the eyeball itself will appear large. The eyeball, to the touch, will be hard and painful to the dog.

Discoloration or hazy color. This sign may be serious. Hepatitis will cause a bluing. Jaundice will cause a yellowing. It should be promptly examined by a veterinarian.

With these symptoms in mind, we will begin a discussion of eye problems most common in the Basset.

Entropion is the turning in of the eyelid. Facial hairs rub on the sensitive cornea. This is painful and results in a great deal of tearing. The dog often shows a third eyelid partially across the eye, tearing, photosensitation, and accumulated matter in the corner of the eye. If left alone, this will result in an ulcer of the cornea and possible permanent eye damage. Entropion is thought to be hereditary although it sometimes follows an eyelid injury. Veterinarians attribute this to the selective breeding of a "diamond shaped" eye. The upper lid tucks in developing a kink in the lower lid, turning outward. The turning out is called *Ectropion*. Because it is hereditary, care should be taken when selecting breeding mates. It can also occur following injury and commonly affects the lower lid. The owner should seek professional veterinary assistance in either case. Home remedies will not help.

Conjunctivitis of the third eyelid or hypertrophy of glandular tissue can be caused by dust, seeds, pollen, etc. Naturally, the Basset, because of his anatomical development and field habits, can collect material near the eyes and cause the tissue to swell. These problems are not an emergency but they will not go away by themselves. Seek veterinary advice.

Glaucoma is a disease of the eye marked by an intense intra-ocular pressure. The result of this pressure is a hardness of the eye, a shrinking of the retina, and developing blindness.

Looking at the eye one would see a greatly enlarged, bulgy eyeball. Both eyes can be affected. The cornea is hazy and without its characteristic transparency. The vessels of the white portion are congested and the pupil is widely dilated.

The Cocker, the Basset, and a number of other breeds *appear* to have a hereditary tendency to develop primary glaucoma. However, only the Beagle has exhibited a glaucoma that can be transmitted from one generation to another. To date, the Basset has not been able to exhibit a reproducible genetically-induced glaucoma. However, as many breeders have suggested, there appears to be a hereditary tendency.

The treatment is medical, surgical or a combination of both. The determination of the treatment is most important and should be left in the hands of a veterinary specialist. Treatment, either surgical or medical, is aimed at decreasing aqueous humor production or increasing the efficiency of its removal.

Cataracts are a condition, common in the Basset, involving the lens of the dog's eye. A cataract is an opacity of the lens and results in a hazy blue, white, or gray color and partial or complete blindness. Most owners detect the discoloration in the eye but are unaware of the reason. Cataracts can be caused by old age, eye disease, injuries, chemicals and by inheritance. There is some hard evidence to support the theory that some cataracts, in the Basset, are inherited. They are common from ten years of age on.

Many dogs have been medically treated with B-vitamins, Selenium, and Vitamin E. I do recommend these drugs in an effort to slow the cataracts. Surgery can be performed but complete sight cannot be restored. Rarely is surgery necessary. Housepets tolerate cataracts very well as long as their food and water dishes are full. Problems arise if they are allowed to roam without supervision because of their limited sight.

Anal Sacs (Glands)

The anal sacs are located under the tail in the area of the anus. The sacs are formed by the turning in of the external skin. Each sac lies between the sphincter muscles of the anus. The sacs contain glands and a duct opening to the outside. The glands are active and produce an offensive, brown liquid.

Normally, the glands secrete this material into the sac. Upon defecation, the sacs are emptied by the action of the sphincter muscles. During extreme exercise, as in fighting, or during extreme fright, such as a car accident, the sacs are also emptied. Wild dogs use the glandular secretion of the sacs to identify their territorial borders. Such actions have been photographed among hyenas and dingos. Domestication has eliminated much of the function of the anal sacs but created the problem of impaction.

This impaction is a common occurrence at a veterinary clinic. The dog will scrub its rear quarters on the ground or floor and makes efforts to chew at the rear. The uninformed owner usually feels the dog has worms. However, the discomfort exhibited by the dog, in the rear area, is due to an impaction and filling of the anal sacs. The debris from the glands has become great and/or the duct opening has become plugged resulting in terrific pressure within the sac. The Basset's only choice is to attempt relief with chewing or scrubbing the area. The attempts are nearly 100% futile.

Digital pressure with the thumb and forefinger on either side of an impacted sac will often eliminate the problem. Place cotton in the palm of the hand to collect the foul smelling secretion. Excessive pressure is to be avoided. It will damage the gland and surrounding tissue. Restrain the head as the removal of impacted debris may be painful. Usually, the impaction is so great that a gloved hand must be used. The hand and fingers are lubricated and the forefinger inserted into the rectum. When the gland is located, pressure is exerted against the gland on the inside with the forefinger and on the outside with the thumb. If this procedure is necessary, most owners will allow their veterinarian to do it. Your dog needs veterinary care if the impaction has been of long enough duration that an abscess has formed.

Bloody Urine

Bloody urine has many causes but there are three most common categories. The main areas to consider are bladder infection, bladder stones, and bladder tumors. There are other less common causes.

The typical, affected Basset will not appear extremely ill but will have a great desire to urinate frequently. The owner's observation will indicate that the dog urinates but a few drops at a time. It may even appear to strain. Your dog will run a mild fever. The condition requires veterinary assistance. Though not an emergency, it should be attended to promptly.

Cystitis is by far the most common cause of bloody urine. The infection is bacterial in origin and if allowed to linger will become chronic and resistant to treatment.

Your doctor may ask for a urine sample. This should not present a problem to the owner. By walking the dog and using plastic cups or aluminum pans, and being patient, the chore can be accomplished easily. The urine should be transported in clean glassware and not be over a few hours old. Antibiotics are usually prescribed.

Bladder stones occur on occasion. The veterinarian can often feel the stones by palpation. Many times the doctor will be suspicious of bladder stones because of the urinalysis, the patient's history, or the physical examination. He may recommend radiographs. If stones are present, your dog will have to undergo surgery. It is major abdominal surgery and the stones are removed through an opening made in the bladder wall.

Bladder tumors are rare. They usually occur in older dogs. They are frequently polyps and non-malignant tumors which require a removal of the growth and a piece of the bladder wall. Surgery is the only answer.

Pyometra

The condition of pyometra, or uterine infection, is common in the Basset Hound. It is very serious and requires quick, expert care by the veterinarian to save your dog's life.

The infection is most commonly seen in middle-aged Bassets, seven years and older, who have never been bred or who have had only one litter, early in life. The condition becomes evident four to eight weeks following a heat period.

The owner will see this typical scene. Their Basset has just nicely finished her heat period. She may or may not have been bred. She is seven years old and never whelped any puppies. For the last week, she has reduced her food intake and increased her water consumption. Last night and today she has refused all food, even choice morsels from the table. She has continued to drink water in large amounts and this morning vomited after drinking. She likes to lie in the cool part of the house and does not respond to her name or commands.

On close examination, the owner would find a fever of 104° (101° is normal). Her gums have a pale color and there is a discharge, usually white and with an odor, from the vulva. This dog has pyometra.

The only solution to the problem is the surgical removal of the uterus. Because the dog is sick, the risks are increased. However, the dog will die if surgery is not attempted. In order to prevent pyometra and possible death of the dog, many owners have considered spaying as an alternative to an episode of pyometra. Once an owner decides a bitch will no longer be having pups, spaying is a rational way to prevent pyometra. The spay surgery is done on a healthy dog with excellent results.

Vomition and Diarrhea

Vomition and diarrhea often happen at the same time. When it persists for over twelve hours, it becomes of concern to the Basset owner. There are home remedies that are used initially, including "Pepto-Bismol" and "Kaopectate." These products do no harm and may clear up the non-specific cases of vomiting and/or diarrhea. With vomition, many owners will allow their dog plenty of water in an effort to prevent dehydration. The dog will then vomit even more. It is more prudent to supply water in the form of ice cubes, up to 4 per hour. This allows your pet to consume the water slowly and will not stimulate more vomiting.

Vomiting and diarrhea can often be classified into one of three large groupings. Nearly always they are a result of dietary changes, parasites, or infection. Veterinary aid is needed in most cases to correct and diagnose the problem.

Dietary changes include the leftover table foods. Dogs cannot tolerate many of the spices and herbs used in cooking and this will often lead to trouble. Excessive fatty meats or spoiled food will result in problems. Bones, especially any that can be splintered or old dirty bones that may have been buried cause many problems. With the Basset, one cannot eliminate the possibility of garbage eating. For most Bassets, this is a dietary change.

There are many parasites in the dog which can cause digestive upsets including the roundworm, tapeworm, hookworm, whipworm, and coccidia. Seldom does the owner see the worm itself. Most often it is detected in fecal examination by the doctor. When you are taking your pet in for digestive upsets, remember to take a fecal sample with you. Usually a teaspoonful is enough. Package it in glass or plastic. Paper napkins and tissue are not wanted.

The third major cause of vomiting and diarrhea is infection. This can be of viral origin, but usually is caused by a bacteria. With this, your Basset is ill. It looks and acts poorly and does have a fever. Bacterial infection will always follow a stomach or intestinal upset if enough time lapses. Veterinary care and antibiotics are necessary.

There are many other causes of vomiting and diarrhea. The owner should evaluate the seriousness of any vomiting and diarrhea that occurs. Many times, because of the amount, character, or number of accidents, the owner will decide not to wait 24 hours and will immediately consult the veterinarian.

Aging or Geriatrics

The aging process is a gradual, but always progressive, condition. It is inescapable and always irreversible. There is no fountain of youth for the Basset. This natural phenomenon, called aging, appears to overtake the Basset with alarming speed.

Our dogs age gradually. The process continues ever so slowly in our breed until ten years of age. It appears, to me, that at that age the Basset ages and deteriorates as fast as ice in the summer sun.

The telltale signs of aging begin with a graying or whitening of the muzzle. The bounce and vitality of puppyhood appear only occasionally. The older Basset will be less tolerant of younger, more playful dogs. Our older dogs will sleep longer and, it seems, deeper.

They will arise with some difficulty and may have temporary lapses of bowel control. These signs will be observable by the owner.

More noticeable will be the development of cataracts in one or both eyes. The blue cast appears to be inevitable in the dog. Also, the hair coat will lose some of its luster, despite all of your efforts to maintain it. Our dog's appetite will diminish and become more selective. As a result, there will be a weight loss, especially in the rear quarters.

In the normal aging process, our Basset will develop a degree of senility. The dog will start to bark for no apparent reason. It will take more serious commands from the owner to control the dog and have it respond favorably. Soon the Basset will be but a shadow of itself.

In the field Bassets, our dogs continue to perform very admirably for long periods of time. High quality work is seen past the age of nine in most cases. But just as the sun rises each morning, there comes the day when aging takes its toll. In a way, it is sad how quickly the process works. It is as if the water faucet is turned down to a trickle and then completely closed. So is the active life of the Basset. Within a month, the dog goes from super performance to a retired, inactive position.

These golden days can be enjoyable to the owner who understands and who realizes that age has slowed his friend. Providing that the health is good, our Basset can remain in the retired state for a long time. Yearly physicals by your veterinarian are recommended.

The old rule of thumb that says our dog's life is seven times our age is not entirely correct. Our dogs mature much more rapidly than a human. In its first year of life, our Basset must age the equivalent of 20 human years. This rapid aging slows so that at age four, the Basset equals a person in the early thirties. Late in the life of the Basset, the dog will age four years to each of ours. Bassets mature slower but live longer, more productive lives than many breeds.

Providing life's natural problems do not shorten our dog's life, there comes a time when the owner may have to decide his dog's future. When the aging process has become so severe as to make our pet's life one without any dignity, then a peaceful end should be considered. The gift of euthanasia (painless death) can be a welcome thing to a suffering or debilitated animal.

12

The Basset in the
Show Ring

DOG SHOWS are the medium by which comparisons are made, awards bestowed, and the official "go ahead" given on the breeding potential of dogs. The merits of the dogs are judged against the breed Standard. Theoretically, the dog which conforms most closely to the Standard for its breed is awarded the highest honor. The opinion of different judges will vary according to their different interpretations of the Standard. It is a natural, human variation. Judges are not computerized or there would be no need for them. Until the breed is uniform, one cannot expect judging to be uniform, but without dog shows there would be no uniformity at all. Breeder-judges may vary even more in their opinions than do the all-rounders. Each breeder seems to develop his line according to his own taste, purpose, and convictions. Breeder-judges usually judge accordingly. The frequent official public rating provided by the shows, plus the rivalry among breeders seeking acclaim, affords the incentive to breed for continually improved quality.

Before You Start

If you plan to show your dog, first compare it with the Standard to see if it is good enough. Make up your mind that even a "gold plated" dog does not win all the time. You will have to learn to accept your defeats as well as your wins. You must be capable of a sportsmanlike attitude no matter what. Be a graceful winner as well as a polite loser. Offer your hand and congratulations to the winner. Then, if you must, have your fit of disappointment in some far-off corner. At least you will be known publicly as a sportsman.

A beautiful show dog does not just happen. His career begins at the time his mother is bred to the male most consonant with her bloodline. Parents and grandparents were undoubtedly the result of the same kind of selective breeding. The dog is no doubt chosen because his conformation is most akin to that of the ideal dog described by the Standard, though there is no "perfect" dog. His personality also indicated that he would enjoy a career in the ring.

Developing a Show Dog

From then on it is a matter of management. His nutritional needs are met to insure development of good bone, teeth, and coat. His lead training begins at an early age as play. He will probably balk either by sitting, rolling over, jumping straight up in the air, and/or yelping as though he is being beaten, or he may be a natural and trot along nicely. Praise is lavished upon him when he complies.

Gradually he is taught that he must walk nicely alongside his handler. This is done with short tugs of the lead. If he pulls forward, he is jerked back. If he is behind, he is tugged forward. As soon as he is in the proper position, he is reassured with words and a tone that tells him he is doing well. He is then taught to walk on both sides of his handler so that the judge can see him at all times. The handler must avoid getting between the dog and the judge. The judge tries to evaluate the gait of the dog. The dog must walk straight and easily without pulling on the lead. He is taught how to execute a turn to reverse directions. The handler stops, turns toward the dog, switches the lead to the hand that is on the side the dog is also on, at the same time turns the dog around, and they

210

Am. and Ber. Ch. Sir Tomo of Glenhaven, owned by Margem Hills Kennels, was an influential sire who stamped many of his get with an elegance much appreciated in the breed today.

Ch. Tommy's Cousin Geo. O'Glenhaven, owned by Tom Bloomer, with his handler Roy Murray.

are off again. Time after time this procedure is repeated until they can make the maneuver with graceful coordination. The dog knows that he is to walk on the same side of his handler as the hand that holds the lead.

He is trained to stand when the handler stops. This is not easy. Teaching the "stand-stay" obedience exercise is the best method. The dog learns to stand while the handler circles him so that he is not obstructing the judge's view. He has also learned to stay posed while the handler stands or kneels at his side and while the judge examines him. He will allow the judge to check his teeth, feel his shoulders, ribs, push upon his back, check his testicles, and perhaps move his legs. He is eager to please because he is praised for his good behavior. He may forget many of these things his first few times in the ring. The handler will merely remind him, reset him or do whatever is required. Experience will make him a polished performer.

Training the Handler

The handler also has a lot to learn and must spend many hours practicing with the dog. It is a dog *show*. The dog and handler should make a beautiful performing *team*. The beginning handler can learn so much by watching others present their dogs especially if they are seasoned exhibitors or professionals. If he is wise, he watches other breeds and observes Group judging. He notes that the front legs of a Basset are placed so that they are well under the chest, viewed from the side, and straight down from the shoulder. There should be no daylight between the upper legs and chest when viewed from the front. The head is held in such a manner that the arch of the neck is shown with the nose held slightly downward to display expression. The topline is as level as possible. The hind legs are set so that the hocks are perpendicular both from the side and rear view. The tail is held lightly, from behind, to form the proper upward curve. Practice before a mirror helps to see just how dog and handler look to the judge.

Ring Procedure

The handler observes the various ring procedures used by the different judges. Dogs always enter the ring to the right, then are gaited as a group. They go around the ring counter-clockwise. Some judges study the dogs slightly before this first gaiting and some do not. It is always safest to pose your dog immediately after entering the ring, unless you have observed that the judge starts right out gaiting after checking armband numbers. If you are first in line, listen and watch for the judge's instructions. You will be stopped after this first gaiting. Then judging varies depending on the judge's preference in routine. Some will go over each dog first, then individually gait each. Others will bring them up one at a time, examine them, followed by gaiting, before going on to another dog. After each dog is examined, they will all be posed again. Pay attention and do as the judge wishes until the final placings are made. The judge will indicate the placements. At that time, these dogs are to stand in front of the numbers which are placed in the ring for this purpose. I will go more deeply into this in following paragraphs.

Other Essentials

Other beneficial aspects of training for the potential show dog are also good for a pet to know. Teach the dog to enjoy riding in the car. Introduce it to a crate so that crating is not taken as punishment. Take your Basset among strangers so he learns that it is fun to make new friends. He will become a "ham" when he finds that his beauty and good behavior draw pleased glances and words of admiration. Teach him to stand on a table for grooming and to enjoy being groomed. Having been started with this at an early age, he should know what to expect of the clippers and nail trimming tools. He is not born a showman—he is made one.

Write to the American Kennel Club, 51 Madison Ave., New York, N.Y. 10010 for the free booklet, *Rules Applying to Registration and Dog Shows*. It fully describes dog shows and classes and contains all regulations pertaining to them. Familiarize yourself with all rules. Subscribe to *Pure-Bred Dogs—American Kennel Gazette*. This monthly magazine contains all the new rule changes regarding every phase of purebred dog activities which are governed by AKC plus interesting articles and a bimonthly column written on Bassets by the Basset Hound Club of America columnist. Show rules are changed from time to time. The wise exhibitor will keep abreast of this information.

If there is an all-breed or Specialty club in your area, by all means join it. They can both be very helpful to you. The all-breed club may have conformation classes. Take advantage of the opportunity and attend these classes.

Dog Shows and Classes

An all-breed show offers classes for dogs of all AKC-recognized breeds. A Specialty show is for only one breed. A benched show requires that dogs be placed on a numbered bench for certain advertised hours. At an unbenched show, dogs need only be present for their time of judging.

A match is an informal show held for practice. Classes may be offered for dogs as young as two months of age. A fun match is the least formal. Sanctioned matches must comply to certain rules but are still intended for the purpose of training. Entry fees are minimal at matches. There are two kinds of sanctioned matches. A "B" Match may offer classes for dogs two months of age or older. Very often they offer awards for puppies and adults separately. At a Sanctioned "A" Match, the classes are more similar to a licensed show. Six months is the minimum age for dogs entered. These matches are held to help a club practice and qualify for licensed shows. Points toward a championship are awarded only at a *licensed* dog show. The minimum age for entries is six months.

There are six classes from which to choose when making entries. A dog over six months of age, and still under twelve months, may be entered in the puppy class. In large shows, the puppy class may be divided between puppies that are six to nine months of age and those that are nine to twelve months. There is a novice class offered, if one chooses to use it, for dogs that are inexperienced in the show ring but are too old for the puppy class. The American-bred class is for dogs that were bred and born in the United States. Back in the days when there were more imports being shown, this class was used to indicate that dogs entered in it were not foreign bred. Now, however, it is seldom used except when an exhibitor wants to take several dogs to help build a larger entry. The bred-by-exhibitor class is a prestige class where only the breeder-owner can exhibit dogs that he, himself, has bred. In co-ownerships, one of the owners must be the breeder of record in order for dogs to be eligible. With the exception of the puppy and bred-by-exhibitor classes, the most hopeful entries are shown in the open class. Classes are divided by sex. Dog classes are judged first. After each of these dog classes has been judged, first in each of the classes returns to the ring. This is called the winners class. When the judge selects the best, it is awarded Winners Dog and points toward its championship. Then the second in the class from which the Winners Dog was chosen enters the ring, with the remaining first place dogs. The best of these is awarded Reserve Winners Dog. Should the Winners Dog be disqualified for some reason, the Reserve Winners would then be awarded the points. The procedure is then repeated for the bitches. At Specialty shows, classes are usually offered for veterans over six or seven years old, field trial dogs and field trial bitches. Requirements for these classes are printed in the premium list. These are called non-regular classes. The winners do not compete for points but the first in each non-regular class is eligible to compete for Best of Breed. At this point champions enter the ring for Best of Breed competition along with the Winners Dog, Winners Bitch and non-regular class winners, if any. Best of Breed is awarded to the dog or bitch that the judge decides comes closest to the Basset Standard. Then, either the Winners Dog or Winners Bitch is awarded Best of Winners. The judge then selects the entry that is Best of Opposite Sex to the Best of Breed winner. Usually this is the end of the judging for that breed. However, at Specialty Shows, classes will be offered that are called multiple-entry classes. A stud dog is entered with several of his get. The quality of the get is judged to decide the placements in this class. A similar class is offered for brood bitches.

At large shows, even all-breed events, there may be a brace class where two entries that are look alikes, owned by the same person, may compete. Occasionally a team class is offered where four dogs, owned by the same person, compete. Braces and teams are judged on how closely matched they are and how they work together.

Later on in the day, the Best of Breed winner will compete with other Best of Breed hounds in the Hound Group. The winner of the Hound Group will compete with the five other Group winners for Best in Show. Study the AKC booklet, *Rules Applying to Registration and Dog Shows,* for details regarding eligibility.

Entering a Show

A premium list is a printed booklet, prepared by the show-giving club or superintendent and mailed to prospective exhibitors, which contains all the information pertinent to that show. It lists judges, prizes, classes offered, entry fees place and dates of show, when and where entries are to be sent, and entry forms. In order to receive these, write to the various show superintendents in your area. These are organizations that provide equipment, printing, and other services to the show-giving club. Any exhibitor can assist you with finding the names and addresses of the superintendents that service your area. The list is also published in each issue of *Pure-Bred Dogs—American Kennel Gazette* as is information about coming shows. It is necessary to enter a show almost three weeks prior to the show. You enter on the form found in the premium list.

When you enter a show, about a week before the show you will receive an acknowledgement of your entry and a schedule showing the time of judging. This also tells you what ring you will be in. Take the confirmation of entry to the show with you. It is also your admission ticket. On it, you will find a number for your dog. At the show, the dog is "Basset Hound number —."

At the Show

If the show is unbenched, it is best to leave your dog in the car while you find your ring, but be sure he has adequate ventilation. Plan to arrive an hour or so before you are scheduled to be judged. Watch your judge do a class or two. This will give you an idea of what to expect when you go into the ring. You are not always judged as early as the time which appears on your schedule because judging can be running a little late. It may never begin before the advertised time, however. Go to ringside about five minutes before Basset judging is scheduled to begin. At the gate to the ring, you will notice one or two people, called stewards, who are in charge of handing out armbands and ushering classes into the ring. Tell them your breed and the number of your dog which was on your confirmation slip. You will be given an arm band with the corresponding number. Place this on your upper left arm. When the steward so indicates, enter the ring and go to the right of the gate. Allow enough space for the rest of the dogs in your class to follow you.

Ch. Braun's Humpty Dumpty C.D., finished from the Bred-by-Exhibitor Class, winning under judge Herbert Cahoon.

When the judge checks armband numbers, hold your arm so that your number is easily seen. You may now set up your dog (pose it). Do not start moving around the ring until the judge tells you to do so. Follow the judge's orders until placements are made. If your dog is placed, go to where the numbers are displayed and stand in front of the number corresponding to your placement. Again, hold your left arm so that the judge can readily see your number. After all classes of your dog's sex are judged, all first place winners will return to the ring to compete for Winners. After this, Reserve Winners will be judged. So, if you are first or second in your class, do stand by to be available for further judging.

Posing a Basset Hound

How to pose a Basset is a matter of what is easiest for you and most flattering to your dog. I will describe the most common method and that which I have found most successful. Stand at the right side of the dog. Grasp the loose skin under the neck while the dog is standing. Lift it off its feet. Lower the dog slowly watching to see that the feet and legs will be properly placed when the dog again is standing on them. If they are not, grasp the dog by the shoulder and upper leg. Let him lean on the other foot while you rearrange his front. Hold the head by grasping it under the muzzle with your four fingers while the thumb is placed on top of the nose. You can later bring the thumb down to the jaw area so as not to distort the muzzle. Or, you can hold the head in place by holding the lead above the dog's neck. Kneel at his right side. Run your left hand under the belly to reassure your dog. Taking hold of the left stifle, with the dog resting on your left arm from underneath, move the hind leg so that the hock is straight up and down when viewed from the side and the back. Then set the right leg to correspond. With your left hand about midway up the tail, lift it from underneath so that it is curved but erect. Try to hold this pose but repeat whatever is necessary. Only the very well-trained dog will not move. If the class is very large, the dog may become fidgety. It is permissible for you to stand up, make a small turn that does not interfere with the other dogs, and set him up again. Do this when the judge is busy with other dogs.

Gaiting a Basset Hound

Gaiting has been mentioned previously, but a few professional touches help in competition. Find the speed that is best for your dog. Try to gait him on a loose lead as much as possible. A little tug should get him going properly should he err. Always use the pattern indicated by the judge. Do go straight away and return directly toward the judge as he or she directs. Judges vary on how they prefer to evaluate side movement. The judge will tell you what to do. As you return, approaching the judge, stop far enough away so that the judge can easily see the front legs stop naturally. If the first stop is not satisfactory, take a step or two. Should there be insufficient room, make a small circle so that you can get a few steps away again. How the dog stops is very important, so be sure it does look its best. If it should sit, touch it from underneath with your nearest toe.

Show Leads and Other Equipment

There are several types of show leads. Try to purchase one that is not slippery and long enough to be thrown around your neck when you are kneeling to pose the dog. I particularly like a flat, braided nylon Resco. This may be used directly on the dog for a collar. If the dog is an adult and a bit hard to control, I suggest attaching this lead to a chain martingale collar by means of a slip knot. An extra snap can be a bit heavy and clumsy. When you are gaiting, fold the excess lead in your hand. When posing, toss the excess around your neck for a professional look. You will notice that the collar and lead are removed when posing some breeds. This is not done by knowledgable Basset exhibitors.

When attending a show, you will want more equipment than the lead. Take a dish for food and water. If the water will be too different than what the dog is used to, take a container from home. I have mentioned a crate before. I firmly believe that a dog is more comfortable riding in one. Especially in hot weather, if the dog is confined to a crate, all car windows can be left wide open or you can often find a shady spot outside the car. The crate may also be used at a benched show providing it is of wire and the size does not exceed the size of the bench. Basset crates usually measure about 21 x 33. If you do not have a crate, purchase a bench chain at the dog show equipment counter. Fasten one end to the dog's collar and to the ring provided on the bench. A rug for the crate or bench will make the dog more comfortable. Take along some towels, a brush or grooming mitt, dry cleaner, and some white powder to make him his most beautiful.

Grooming

Grooming for a show starts with a bath. Any good shampoo will do. An inexpensive cream rinse, as a final treatment, will do wonders to help remove excess hair and dandruff. When the dog is dry, work your fingers through the hair in the direction opposite to its natural growth. Instead of a brush, one can purchase a wire-bristled mitt or a rake that resembles a hacksaw blade. In fact, a fine hacksaw blade may also be used. Hold the skin taut as you rake from neck to tail. Clean the inside of the ears with oil. Cut nails and clean excess hair from between the pads. Smooth the paws by cutting hair from around them and around the nails. Trim the ragged hairs at the tip of the tail so that it is nicely rounded off, and clean his teeth or have the vet do it for you. Many of these items should be done on a weekly basis so, really, there is little extra to do but the finishing touches to get a Basset ready for the ring. Cut the whiskers and mole hairs so that they are even with the fine hair. I use an electric clipper for this, but a good pair of scissors will also do fine. Learn to manipulate the skin to make the whiskers stand out. For a whiter white, spray lightly with water and rub white chalk, which is available at pet stores, into the moist hair. You can use one of the human medicated powders instead, if you prefer. Johnson's Baby Powder is used by many Basset exhibitors.

Dogs may be very clean when they leave home but they still need a final primping before they go into the ring. There are several cleaners, available from pet suppliers, that will spot clean where necessary. The ear tips are always a last minute requirement. Brush them or use a wire mitt just before ringtime. There are also preparations that will add a final sheen and will remove any accumulated dust. Most flea sprays contain oil and may be used for this. Whatever you do, be sure to remove all cleaning preparations before entering the ring. White powder, especially, is considered a coloring and can result in your dog's disqualification if left in the coat.

Accidents Will Happen

Try to get your dog to move its bowels at home. Give it a chance to eliminate before going to the ring. At indoor shows, a sawdust exercise ring is provided for the purpose. Try to avoid accidents in the ring. If, after doing your best, a misfortune occurs, do not let your embarrassment reflect on your handling. It happens to the most seasoned. Stand still until the dog fully relieves itself. A ring attendant will come in and clean up. Should this happen outside the ring, ask the steward to call the clean-up crew. Try to guard the spot, if you possibly can, so that others do not walk through it before it is cleaned up.

Some sort of tidbit may help to keep the attention of your dog. There is often an abundance of bits of liver and dog biscuits scattered around the ring by thoughtless exhibitors. A hound with a nose is sure to be aware of this, but is more apt to gait unhampered if it knows it will receive its reward from your hand at the proper time.

When you go into that ring *smile!!!* The whole idea is to present a pleasing picture. Poise is a fundamental attribute of a successful handler. Save your nervous breakdown until after the judging. Do, whether you win or lose, be gracious; you'll be back again some day.

Professional Handlers

If you find *you* cannot take it, and your dog is good enough, hire a professional handler. He gets paid for his know-how. He learned how to trim, to groom, to be aware of what certain judges look for in a dog and how they want them presented. If you decide to have a professional handler to show your dog, write or phone the Professional Handlers Association for recommendations. When this book went to press, the President of the PHA was Ted Young, Jr., Rocky Hill, CT 06067, phone 203-529-8641. If no longer President, Mr. Young will refer you to the current PHA Officer to contact.

Remember, the amateur with a good dog can win just as often as the professional if he has taken the time and trouble to school himself. Very few exhibitors are fortunate enough to come from a

Lena Wray has enjoyed good success with her Bassets in a number of fields. Mrs. Wray is especially noted for her tracking dogs and has earned the "T" with 12 of her Bassets. She is shown with five of them here (from left), Ch. Party Doll's Geraldine, Slippery Hill Bonnie Parker, Earnests's Shirley Black Kettie, Ch. Julie of Rockin-Pas and Ch. Bret Mavrik of Rockin-Pas.

Ch. LeClair's Merry Madelyn, UD and Ch. Bugle Bay's Souffle, UD, mother and daughter obedience workers owned by Jim and Marge Cook.

dog show family. Handling dogs is a skill that must be learned. Almost everyone starts out as a novice. The author remembers her own novice days of stumbling around the ring. It takes determination to learn by observation and practice. You CAN do it.

Now, go ahead and enter a show. There is so much enjoyment in winning with your "pride and joy." If you loose, there is always a next time. The show-bug will bite; you will know you are crazy but you will have lots of company.

About Obedience

While at the show, watch the dogs in the obedience ring. Here you can find pride in the accomplishment of having trained your dog. You and your dog will enjoy competing by going through a certain routine of exercises and gaining an obedience title.

Many exhibitors enjoy both conformation and obedience competition with the same dogs. It is gratifying to put an obedience title on a champion. Others just plain prefer obedience work or do it because it is enjoyable competition for dogs that are not quite up to winning in the show ring. Obedience is you and your dog . . . . . working together.

Some of the obedience exercises have been covered in the section on training and lead breaking. There are many good books available on the subject. The American Kennel Club is in charge of obedience trials, and sets forth the rules governing them. Write AKC for the free booklet, *Obedience Regulations.* Your introduction will be in the Novice class where the dogs are required to heel on lead, heel on lead around two persons in a figure-eight pattern, heel off lead, stand for examination of the judge, recall, which is to return to the handler, from a sitting position when called, long sit for one minute in a line with other dogs, and long down, which is laying down in a line with other dogs for three minutes. A dog must do the exercises in a certain manner to pass. If it passes the test, it receives what is called a "leg" toward its title. In order to receive a Companion Dog (CD) degree, it must pass three tests satisfactorily under three different judges.

In order to gain the next plateau, a CDX (Companion Dog Excellent) title, a dog must pass three tests, under three different judges, where it will be required to heel off lead, drop on recall,

223

and retrieve an object thrown when given the command to do so, retrieve over a high jump, do a broad jump, long sit, and long down, both of which are done while the handler is out of sight. This competition takes place in the Open class.

Even more advanced work is done by the dogs in the Utility class. Dogs gaining this title have the initials UD behind their names. They must retrieve an article that has been scented by the handler, selecting it from a group of articles, exactly alike, made of metal and another group made of leather, do directed retrieves and jumps and other exercises by signal.

All competitive obedience takes a lot of hard work and training. Tracking is another form of competition, closely akin, but unlike obedience trials. Tracking tests are held apart from shows. The owner lays a track, for training purposes, and teaches the dog to follow it. At a test, the track is laid by a stranger, under the direction of two judges. This track must be nearly 500 yards long with at least two right angle turns. A leather glove is placed at the end of the track which the dog must find. Without help, the dog must follow the track, on lead and wearing a harness, make the proper turns and indicate that it has found the glove. A dog that passes this test carries a TD title. Should it also have a UD, its full title is then UDT.

Walter and Marjorie Brandt went down in history not only for their beautiful show dogs but for their initiative in earning obedience degrees on Bassets. They were the very first people to have Bassets with obedience degrees in the United States. Their Lulu's Red was the first to earn the CD and Lulu's Patches the second. Patches went on to earn his CDX as well as his championship.

The first UDT Basset was Pierre's Bonne Joie, owned by Benj Harris. Although this was the fourth Basset to have earned the TD, it was the first to have the combination.

Ludwig Von B, owned by Stephen and Anna Sandberg of College Park, Maryland, was the first to gain a TD.

Lena Wray enjoyed tracking work about as much as anyone. She took pride in putting TD degrees on her champions. Her husband, Billy, helped with the training, and Lena put more TDs on Bassets than anyone else. Her successes included Ch. Humphrey Jo, CD, TD; Bee Lee's Pruneface Prudence, UDT; Ch. Sir Tomo's Party Doll, TD; Ch. Party Doll's Geraldine, TD; Bee Lee's Mister Fred,

TD; Bee Lee's Miss Tricia, TD; Ch. Julie of Rockin-Pas, TD; Ch. Bret Mavrik of Rockin-Pas, TD; Bee Lee's Bruiser the Behemoth, TD; Ernest's Shirley Black Kettle, TD; and Slippery Hill Bonnie Parker, TD. Lena's interest resulted in her being approved by AKC as a tracking judge in 1975.

Through Lena's enthusiasm, Wanda White became interested in tracking as well as conformation and obedience. She gained a title on Ch. Windmaker's Great Thunder, TD and Windmaker's Weatherman, TD. Jim and Wanda White bred Ch. Windmaker's Ocean Breeze, CD, owned by Deane Noe and Windmaker's Black Storm, CD, owned by Shirley Hiatt.

Buzz Taylor is well known for his high-scoring dogs at all-breed trials. Joan Thurlow became an ardent enthusiast as did Virginia Jones and Karen Highley. Jim and Marge Cook enjoyed the work in the Texas area. Twenty-nine Bassets gained the CD degree in 1975, a far cry from the situation of earlier years.

Ch. Duffy of Hahs-C-Enda, owned by Andy and Sue Shoemaker and bred by Patricia and Orrie Hahs.

225

Field Ch. Germann's Albertino with owner, Bill Germann.

Field Ch. Newton's Black Jackolyn and owner, Kenneth McWilliams.

13

Basset Hounds
in the Field

THE BASSET has a natural instinct to hunt. It merely takes opportunity and experience to cultivate this desire, though some are more eager than others.

In style, Bassets are slow, careful, and deliberate. If unsure of themselves, they may check back at their starting point and take up the track again. Unless trained otherwise, most prefer to run as individuals although others may be in the field with them. It is not uncommon for them to work Indian file. Often they do not wish to honor another's signal of a find. They prefer to seek their own line, each talking to it in his own particular manner. Early writers often stated that they did not believe the Basset would make a pack dog nor would he work as part of a brace. We have since seen both accomplished through selective breeding and training. For field trials, we have been selective to cultivate a style that WILL honor its bracemate and will work a line with another dog. Both are requirements in field trialing.

In selecting a puppy, the inquisitive one usually matures with more incentive than the lazy pup. To assist in training, scents may be purchased and dragged. An old rabbit skin is full of scent. The best training is right in the field.

A hunting Basset is not limited to rabbit as is the field trial dog. A hunting dog, to be of value, must work to please its master on the game that inhabits the territory and is desired. Given the opportunity and encouragement, a Basset can be trained to seek any small game. They were used on small game and birds in the early days in France.

I would like to recount a tale of one of our first bench champions. He was a mature dog when we purchased him. Being novices in the show ring, we did not know how to show off his better qualities. It took approximately a year to finish him. The following hunting season, we decided to allow him to accompany us in the field. His first time out, while the other dogs were busy in search of a rabbit, he followed on my heels waiting for me to break a path in the weeds. We were disdainful of his field work, but because we loved him, he was allowed to tag along the next day. Soon he was venturing a few yards around me. One day he lifted his head, sniffed the air a few times, made several leaps forward, and put up a pheasant. From then on, this was his style. Although it was highly unorthodox, we valued him highly, and shot many birds over him before his untimely death at the age of five.

The hunting dog, referred to as a "meat dog," may be one and the same as a field trial dog. However, often the finest trial dog would try the patience of a hunter because of requirements described in the next chapter. A meat dog is too "rough" for a trial but may better suit the hunter. The hunter's main desire is to put meat on the table and the dog that most often finds it is most appreciated by him. If he comes to a loss, he will swing wide in search of the line. He will often cut corners instead of sticking closely to the line. Keenness of nose is sometimes inclined to prompt a hound to cold trail or fuss along on an old track. This would set a field trialer to panic. However, it would satisfy the gunman because, when good enough, the hound eventually follows through on a cold line that leads to a sitting rabbit. The scent may all but have evaporated but the dog will probably raise the game, driving it around so that the hunter can get a crack at it. A hunter would consider a dog useless if the hunter must find his game for him. Usually, the trial dogs are kept on lead until game is found. They are then put on that line and are expected to run it. This is largely done to expedite the judging. If two hounds were cast instead, each would search in a different direction which may not be near the handlers and judges. When one opened on a find, the other hound would have to join it, perhaps from a distance, while handlers and judges also raced for the spot. It can be done but it can, also, cause problems. Then there is what is known as the "jump dog." If he loses his line, he pounces far and wide until he jumps another rabbit. This is also frowned upon in field trial circles but the hunter will have no objection so long as he finds game.

Language of the Field

You will probably feel more comfortable if you are familiar with some of the terminology most often used by Basset field trialers. To "babble" is to give tongue (bark) without good reason, when not on a line or while searching for the line. A "brace" is two dogs that are running together at a field trial. When a dog "casts" it works back and forth, across the line, trying to find the line. At a check, a hound must not cast too far. A "check" is where the rabbit makes a turn and the dogs must follow. Much field trial scoring is done on how the dogs work a check and which dog finds it first. To "claim" is to bark indicating that a hound has the line. A hound shall only claim when he does have the line. "Open-up" and "give-tongue" also mean barking. A hound that barks too much, especially when not close on a line, is called "mouthy" while one that does not bark is "mute." When a bracemate claims a line, the other hound should go to it, determine if it really has the line, and, if it does have, open up also and work with the bracemate. This is called "honoring" or "harking-in." If the second hound does not honor, it is possible that the first dog is not telling the truth. A hound must not honor if the bracemate is a "liar." A hound is "independent," if it makes sure there is a line before it will honor. A hound "owns" a scent when it is strong enough and he claims it. "Desire" is the appetite for running and surpassing a bracemate. To "lean on" is to depend on the bracemate to do the hard work, pick the checks, and then honor it. A "rough" dog does not stick close to the line, often because it is too fast, and cuts corners. A "liar" barks when it does not have the line. I have seen some beautiful runs made by liars on an imaginary line. "Line" is the trail left by the rabbit. "Nose" is a dog's scenting ability. A rabbit will often "double back" or turn around and run back on the same track. This can be confusing to the dog because it does not want to backtrack. When a rabbit goes into a hole it "holes up" or "goes to ground." A hound will get a "happy tail" (wagging excitedly) when it gets a nose full of rabbit scent but hasn't yet figured out the line. To "potter" is to fuss around needlessly at checks, getting nowhere. A "quitter" or "cold quitter" is a dog that gives up easily when it cannot work out a check. A "jack" is a buck rabbit while the female is called a "doe." A "leveret" is a young rabbit. The classes at a field trial are called "stakes." A "derby" is a young hound. A Basset remains a derby through the calendar year succeeding its birth. "Starters" are all dogs that take a line, and are in competition, at a field trial. It can also mean young dogs that are just beginning to run.

Initial Training

Boldness in puppies can often be cultivated by the breeder when he first takes over from the dam. When he begins to feed the litter, he can develop this trait to a point that will later make hounds more easily broken to gun or put them in a bold, unafraid stance in the show ring.

After the puppies have been weaned for a little time and are in their full stride on pan feeding, start to accustom them gradually to all sorts of noises while they are eating. When approaching with the feed pan, start whistling or singing, bang the pans, and later use a stick to smack the side of the kennel, box, or table. Do this just as they are getting their starving noses into the feed pan. Begin gradually without frightening them too much. They will grow accustomed to the noise and associate it with food.

For the oral part of this training, it is well to adopt some particular call or whistle, something no one else is apt to use and always use this call at feeding time. In this way, puppies can be trained to respond to this call throughout the rest of their lives almost regardless of what might be the temptation for them not to come. I use the same method in teaching the word come. They would have come for food anyway. Without knowing it, they are taught to reenter the kennel run. Later, when the word is used, they come.

Tractability can be instilled into most puppies at this tender age by taking them when quite small, especially on their first trips away from the kennel, into a nearby brush lot or high weeds and trying to lose them. Walk along slowly letting the puppies trail along behind, probably whining now and then and wondering what it is all about. Select a spot where you can stand or sit still for a while in moderately heavy cover. You should be able to see the puppies fairly well but they, with their eyes down close to the ground, cannot see you from any distance. Hounds are guided more by the nose than by the eye. Stand perfectly still and let the puppies figure out that nothing is going to hurt them in their strange surroundings. It probably will not be more than a few minutes before they begin to snoop around. They will gradually become more at ease. Their curiosity will soon lead them to explore all this new strangeness around them. Watch for your opportunity and, when none of them can see you do it, take a few quick steps to one side. Shift your position thirty or forty feet and remain perfectly quiet. One by one, the puppies will come sniffing back to find you. When they fail, there will be some scrambling around and whining as they realize they are lost.

Stand perfectly still in your new location until they become thoroughly worked up. Then give a few soft, low whistles or whatever call you have been teaching in the kennel. Call just loud enough for them to hear. They will stop and listen. Let them listen for a moment before repeating the whistle. Repeat this performance until they finally find you by locating your call. They will be mighty glad to hear you again. Make a big fuss over them and let them know you have saved them from a terrible fate. If you raise a litter, be sure to use this lesson on them when you first take them away from the kennel and while everything around them is so new and strange. If you get a small puppy from a breeder, be sure to use this technique on the puppy while he is still small enough to be frightened when lost.

If this lesson is used on small puppies systematically they will, except for the downright headstrong and unruly ones, grow up to appreciate your companionship afield to the extent of keeping a general line on your whereabouts. They will fall into the good habit of looking you up at the conclusion of a chase. This will save you almost endless work at field trials or on a day's hunt. After all, the dog is supposed to hunt at *your* will. You can develop these little things so that the dog is *where* you want him *when* you want him.

The puppy that is raised running at liberty on a farm, and grows up in a life of self-hunting will too often develop into an uncontrollable wildcat who will try your patience and wear out your nerves (and your muscle) in an effort to avoid losing him. He is impossible to handle to a competitive advantage at a field trial. He will bolt off to anyone who fires a gun. He will hunt to please himself instead of being your assistant. These unfavorable characteristics are given free rein to develop if he is permitted unqualified to follow nature's urge to drive rabbits and eat them. He will lack the leveling influence of human companionship that yard training would provide for him.

Yard Breaking

Yard breaking is a term almost unknown among Basset trainers. I know of a few who do believe in it. It is so exasperating for a handler, at a field trial, or for the hunter, at the end of a day when he can scarcely put one foot in front of the other, to have to run down a wild bolter. Taking the trouble to teach the dog some field manners can make a tremendous difference. It really takes so little effort and time.

The "Come" command has been stressed throughout the book. In case your dog has not already learned it, start now. First, let him wear a collar for several days. Then attach a lead. When he hits the end of the lead, call "Come," and pull him to you. Praise and pet him when he gets there. If he bucks and rears, just continue pulling in slowly, repeating the command occasionally. When he gets to you, rub his ears and make a fuss over him. Make him *want* to come to you. Gradually get him to do this off lead. Never call a hound to you without insisting that he comes. Always reward him for a good response.

"Whoa" or "down" are two more words that can be temper-saving commands. When any well-trained hound is not on game, he can be stopped in his tracks on command if he has been properly

Dover, Ohio, field trial 1951, Dog Stakes. L to R: Bose's Bass Bawl, Engle's Ace, Snowfall Shorty, R.F. Smith's Major, and Trigger Triumph.

Dover, Ohio, field trial 1951, Bitch Stakes. L to R: Queen Elizabeth, Melancholy Baby, Hartshead Jet, Meyer's Black Queen.

233

trained. This is something sorely needed with hundreds of hounds we have seen at the trials. Use a fifty-foot check cord. This should be light enough to handle but strong enough to upset your hound if need be. Walk around with him on the cord. Wait for him to run away from you, or bolt, for some reason. When he has gone twenty-five or thirty feet, command sharply, "Whoa," at the same time stop him gently with the cord. Talk kindly to him while you walk up to where he is, repeating the verbal command. Keep him in place. Rub his ears and tell him he is good. Repeat the lesson. Never check him unless he is really going somewhere. Be sure to give him the command sharply. Do this the instant before you check him and make the checking operation a little more decisive each time. If he does not get the idea, it may be necessary to get a bit rougher and really upset him. You can do this without hurting him yet give him a sharp surprise. He will get the idea sooner or later and stop when the command is given. Many short lessons are better than one lengthy one.

When to Begin Field Training

Field training should never be attempted until your puppy has demonstrated a thorough degree of yard training. He must know you are the boss and yet believes you are such a good guy that he wants to be with you and please you. He should show signs of a little common sense and be reasonably manageable when at liberty.

The starting age is debatable. We hear a vast assortment of answers to the question and many reasons for them. Many say that they have little use for puppies who, given the opportunity, are not doing a job of running rabbits at six months of age. Others contend that it is inviting disaster. Our personal experience shows that most of the best hounds start young but are not encouraged to be competitive until they are at least a year old. Often a terrific derby is a wild dog by the time it is three. It is so heartwarming to watch a youngster full of competitive spirit that we tend to push them too hard. The early starters are usually high-strung and ambitious. If they are permitted to start as young as four to five months, they must be watched closely for the development of bad habits because they are so enthusiastic. The young hound, much like the young boy, will acquire bad habits readily unless properly

234

Field Champions Taber's Solo Sue, Navar's Ears, Navar's Snapper, Navar's Jolly, Navar's Heather, Navar's Jill, and Navar's Ginger.

Field Champion Stakes winners at the 1964 Nationals on October 9: l. to r.: Eugene Beldean with Fd. Ch. Aquino's King Kong; John Eylander with Fd. Ch. Max's Blue Echo; Harold Campbell with Fd. Ch. Campbell's Bit-O-Gold; Fd. Ch. Olson's Samanthe, owned by Eugene Beldean, with Al Michalski, handler.

supervised and coached along. Lacking age and experience, they also lack the good judgment that comes with age and experience to keep them close to the straight and narrow path of good deportment.

The pernicious backtracker is an example. An immature puppy, bursting to go places and do things, might drive the finest kind of line until he encounters a difficult, bothersome check. He just does not have the patience to drill away at that check and work it to a proper conclusion as an older, more experienced hound would do. In his frantic flying around, he encounters the line back of the check and smells. He happens to hit it going in the wrong direction but has no time to be bothered with such details. It smells so good that he just has to run it as fast and as far as he can. Run it he will unless he has a good trainer. The trainer had better well be at the check and take corrective measures if he starts to backtrack.

Another bad habit that is picked up is running catch-up. When running with experienced dogs, the puppy often is left behind at the check. He has learned that the other dogs have the track. Instead of working out his own line, he merely joins the other hounds to find the track again. Or, while they are working out a check, as they should be, he may become so excited that he casts too far from the check in an effort to be first to find it. This may appear to be a smart hound to a novice trialer but it is a mortal sin. However, if the dog should luckily be right, he often gets credit at a trial. Properly, it is better to have a loss, but stay close at the check, than to wander too far even if "a" line is found. If there are enough rabbits on the grounds, a hound is sure to find a rabbit though it may not be the one he was running.

Starting a Puppy

A quiet puppy, inclined to take things easier, will probably be slower to develop. He wants to be so sure of himself. When he does have a line, and comes to a loss, he may circle back and rework the line. This can develop into "pottering" which is just fussing around and not getting anywhere.

When we refer to "starting" a puppy we mean that initial part of his field training from his first trip afield until the time he acquires the ability to run a line by scent for a reasonable distance in a fairly workmanlike way. Specifically, when he can run a line to the extent that he has opened up and can make a few checks, he is considered started. From then on his training must be based on his individual performance.

Like other training, do not keep at the lessons so long that he tires. However, lest he forget, as would a young boy, repeat the lessons often.

There are various opinions as to whether to train a puppy alone, with other puppies, or with an experienced dog or two. It really doesn't matter so long as he is watched and his personal needs are met. Sometimes several puppies will give up and play. Sometimes a youngster will lean too heavily on the older dogs or works alone, anyway, because it cannot keep up. At some stage, before entering trial competition, however, the dog must learn what it is to be around strange hounds and to work with its bracemate. It also has to learn to be put on a line as opposed to finding its own rabbit.

To start your puppy alone, give him a few short trips afield without too much thought of rabbits. Just let him snoop around and get used to all the strange sights and odors. It will require only a few trips until he begins to feel at home in the brush. Should he happen to stumble onto a rabbit on one of these trips, so much the better. Just let him stumble and let him alone. Let him try to catch the rabbit if he takes the notion, or let him nose the line trying to figure out what it's all about if that is what he wants to do. At this point, do not yell at him or call him into the line to try to make him take it. You can, however, walk near the line, if you have seen the rabbit but he has not. Hopefully, he will then get a nose full. Do not be discouraged or rush him. Have patience. If he does try to work the line, praise him.

When he can run a line for a fair distance, follow him. When he comes to a check, do not be too prompt in helping him to pick it even if you know exactly where the rabbit went. Let him form the habit of doing his own work, the hard part of it as well as the easy. If you do too much for him, he will start to look for help. If he has had ample time, and you are *sure* where the correct line is, you may coach him a little to get him back on it. This will help cultivate the idea that rabbits do not disappear into thin air but always go *somewhere* on the ground. We don't want him quitting because he came to a loss.

Pen Training

Some people start puppies in a small, fenced training enclosure that is stocked with rabbits. There should be plenty of cover in it to serve as a hiding place for the rabbits. The puppy, or puppies, play in this pen and are left to stumble onto a rabbit by chance. The pen, if rather small, is only good for a short time until the puppy has the incentive to run a rabbit. Larger areas allow the game to maneuver so that the puppy learns to make checks. However, if the area is large enough for actual work, the trainer must accompany the dog and watch for mistakes so that it does not form bad habits. The biggest problem training in a rabbit pen is likely to create is a lazy field dog due to the abundance of easily found game in the pen. I have seen many dogs, so broken, that would not stay on a difficult check. They have learned it is easier to search a bit and find a new rabbit.

Learning from the Game

We only had two unfenced acres of brush plus neighboring patches. We cut a path down through the center. From the house, we could see a rabbit crossing, or sitting in, the path. They often came up around the yard to munch on the grass. When we saw one, we took a puppy or two out to where it was seen. We usually were able to watch and knew where it went into the brush. We merely walked out to where the rabbit was seen in the clearing, allowing the puppy to sniff around. We knew if it took the line and if it entered the brush on the line. This was a start. When the puppies began to work in the brush, we usually took an older, dependable dog along. It could go to work in the brush and drive the rabbit. We could catch glimpses of it so we knew where the line was. If the pup was trying to work the line, we knew if it was right or wrong. It was a real thrill to watch them take their first line, make their first check, and hear them open up for the first time.

The spark that was bred into our puppies for generations had been fanned into a flame. Do not blame your puppy too much if he gets too excited to use what little common sense he has at this tender age. Watch him carefully. If he is working with a pack, and seems to get rattled by running wild or swinging wild at his checks, remove him from the other dogs. Let him run with those of his own caliber if it seems to work out. A dog must gain confidence in his own ability in order to show independence. He should hark-in to the other dogs but should not lean on them or rely on their being right when they are not.

On Rabbits

While teaching your puppy the ways of the field, you will be surprised what you will learn about how a rabbit runs. Rabbits learn their own area and, since only the smartest survive, it is safe to say that the adult rabbit can give a good hound a real run for his money. If a doe has young ones, she will do her best to lead the hound away from her nest. Very young rabbits do not leave scent. In general, rabbits form habits that conform to the community. In late February and March, the jacks may travel long distances in search of mates but do stay where the young are born.

In due course, the growing leverets follow their mother to her favorite feeding places and imitate her methods of circumventing danger. They learn about danger from watching her reactions. Eventually, they will pass these actions on to their own young. Habits vary according to season.

In dry weather there is little cover and the rabbit must search farther for food. Under a bright moon, scant cover allows the leverets to be more easily seen by predators. So, after such a season, the hare will not rely as much on concealment as on its speed and ability to take flight. They will, therefore, be more familiar with a larger area when protective cover is limited. After a wet summer, the situation is exactly opposite. They have become accustomed to plenty of cover so they usually do not run as far and will squat more often. Rabbits, in their own right, can be very interesting.

Finishing Touches

Now that we have the youngster started, we must work to perfect him. Some successful trialers claim that a good Basset is born,

239

Dual Ch. Double B's Lucky Libertine.
Shafer

241

not made. This may be true from the standpoint of genetic makeup. He does inherit his nose, desire, style, and other hunting traits but they can be nurtured for good or bad. A potentially good dog can be ruined, probably most easily, by developing bad habits. A dog must first be born with good qualities. They must be developed through good training and experience. The younger he is, the more influence training will have upon him. Even the older hound can become what is called "trial wise." They can learn to cheat without notice. They can learn to call a bracemate off the line, then rush back and run it properly, especially if the bracemate is inexperienced enough to allow it to happen. So, one must keep a hound on the straight and narrow. Some are even cursed with the natural tendency to do everything wrong. Do not waste your time with such an individual. Find him a home as a pet before he manages to ruin other good hounds. If you have friends who would like to run their hounds with yours, make sure theirs are not faulty lest yours suffer as a result.

Do not attempt to help your Basset recover a check until he has had plenty of opportunity to do it himself. Then if you do help him, be sure you are certain of the line. Should you fail in getting him to repick the line, it is best to snap a leash on him and take him away from that vicinity rather than let him work unsuccessfully until he becomes disgusted. It isn't good to let him quit nor is it good to let him wander far enough to put up another rabbit. Take him away so that he learns he must find the line or he will be denied the pleasure of further running.

Marking hole is an excellent trait. This action means a rabbit has gone into a hole and the hound indicates it by barking, sometimes digging, but remaining at the hole. Praise him. Help him by digging the rabbit out so that he has the thrill of finding it. He should be encouraged to stay right at the hole should the rabbit go to ground.

Competitive spirit is another desired attribute. However, this can be encouraged too much so that the hound will act improperly just to be in strong competition with another hound. Desire can often be encouraged by keeping the lazy hound on leash while the others are running a rabbit. The "slacker" will usually get excited enough to go to work when he is taken off lead and allowed to join the others.

Brains, or common sense, is another virtue largely inherited. It can be nurtured by close companionship during a hound's youth. Some hounds do not have sense enough to go as slowly as their nose indicates. They are too speedy, overrunning their checks. Run them with a slower hound or alone. Accuracy, or dependability, will demonstrate itself. A dependable hound will run the line as fast as he can and yet make each turn right on the line. He will never give tongue during a temporary loss. He will only open again when he is back on the line. There is nothing finer than a hound that you can always believe. While he is young, work him alone enough so that he relies only on his own good judgement. Do not worry that a bracemate seems to be ahead of your dog. Be proud of the dog that is running behind, who slowly picks his check before the faster one can realize he made a mistake and can get back to picking out the check.

To get a dog used to a gun, start by shooting some distance from him when he is busy eating or playing. The sounds of gunshot should not bother him if he had his early lessons while you made noise in the house or kennel. Then begin shooting up in the air while he is hot on a track. If you shoot a rabbit, leave it alone so that he comes upon it while he is working a line. Give him the pleasure of finding it. This will give him more incentive and he will associate the gunshot with the find.

Keep your hound in good physical condition. Too many Basset trialers believe in the old wives' tales that a hungry hound will run best. They consider lack of proper food, and being wormy, the same as being lean. Did you ever see an olympic champion compete in anything but top physical condition? Does a racehorse have anything but the best? Peak condition is necessary for stamina and endurance. Frankly, poor condition is the only way some trialers can slow down their wild dogs. Do not listen to their snide remarks about those whose meat cover their bones. Fortunately, more of our people are being converted to believe in the importance of good health to the performance of a good working, field trial Basset.

Texas fanciers Tom Bloomer, Don Heironimus and
Marge Cook start off for the field with their Bassets.

14

Field Trials for Basset
Hounds in America

*"A good dog doesn't care where the rabbit IS. He
just wants to know where it went to get there."*

Basset HOUND field trialing is a great and
wholesome sport for both young and old and is growing steadily
in popularity. The first licensed trial in the United States was held
in 1937 by the Basset Hound Club of America soon after its formation. Now trials are either given by the Parent Club or by one
of the local clubs under the approval of the Parent Club. In 1977,
the following clubs were eligible to hold licensed field trials: Berkshire Valley BHC, Rancocas BHC, Lenape BHC, all serving areas
in New Jersey; Potomac BHC (Maryland); Patroon BHC, located
in Northeastern New York; Pilgrim, serving New England; Buckeye, in Eastern Ohio; Maumee Valley, serving Northwestern Ohio;
Western Michigan BHC; Kentuckiana, with headquarters in the
Louisville area; Susquehanna and Valley Forge Clubs which serve
Eastern and Mid-Pennsylvania; Dal-Tex, located in the Dallas area;
and Northern California BHC. One can obtain the addresses of any
of these clubs from the Secretary of the Basset Hound Club of
America or The American Kennel Club. Trial dates are published
in *Pure-Bred Dogs—American Kennel Gazette.*

Types of Trials and Classes

There are various types of field trial competitions to participate in. Dogs gain points toward a field championship only at licensed trials, or member trials, depending on the status of the host club. Only the BHCA is eligible to hold member trials as it is the only Basset club which can be a member club of AKC. Local club trials are called licensed trials. There are also sanctioned or fun trials which are held for practice and/or to give newcomers experience in an informal atmosphere. No points are awarded at these events.

The word "stakes" is used to mean "class" such as Open All-Age Dog Stakes, Open All-Age Bitch Stakes, Champion Stakes, and Derby Stakes. Most trials are run on weekends with Open All-Age Dog Stakes and Champion Stakes usually run on Saturday and Open All-Age Bitch Stakes run on Sunday. Following the running of the Open All-Age Bitch Stakes, usually the first place hounds compete for Best of Winners or Absolute Winner of the whole affair. At some of the larger trials a Derby Stake is offered for hounds whelped on or after July 1 of the second year, and not later than June 30 of the year, preceding the calendar year in which the stake is held. Derby Stakes are usually run prior to the regular stakes. Their purpose is to offer competition for the younger, started dogs that are not yet necessarily ready to run against more experienced dogs. These same dogs may, however, be entered in the Open Stakes. Points toward a championship are only awarded in the Open Stakes.

Field Championships

Championship points are awarded to hounds placing first, second, third or fourth in Open All-Age Stakes, provided there were enough entries. They are awarded on the following basis: one point to the winner of the first place for each Basset Hound actually starting in the stake; one-half point to the winner of second place; one-quarter point to third place; one-eighth point to fourth place. At present, if there are less than 15 starters, one point for each starter is awarded to the first place only. Requirements for attaining a field trial championship are increased as entries warrant. In 1977, a hound must have accumulated 40 points, winning at a minimum of two trials, and placed first at one trial.

Regulations are revised from time to time. For the current rules and requirements write for *Rules Applying to Registration and Field Trials* available free from The American Kennel Club.

Champion Stakes are open to field champions of record. This stake is comparable to the Best of Breed class in the show ring. The honor of the win, or the prize offered, is the incentive. Recently, the BHCA instituted a further award, the title of Grand Champion to hounds accumulating a specific number of points by placing in the Champion Stakes. In an entry of six or more hounds, first place gains 4 points, second place receives 3 points, third place is awarded 2 points, and fourth place gets 1 point. If the entry is five or less, only first place receives points. In 1977, 20 points were needed to have the Grand Champion title bestowed upon a field champion. When entries warrant, requirements are raised. A list of the Grand Champions to date appears at the end of this chapter.

Provisions are made for pack stakes consisting of two, four, or eight couples on hare, though this stake is not usually found at the trials. Additional non-regular stakes may be run if so specified in the premium list and/or entry form.

Mechanics of a Field Trial

A club must apply to The American Kennel Club for permission to hold a field trial. The application must state the day, or days, upon which the club desires to hold the trial. The location must be given as well as the time entries close, drawing time, prizes, and judges. Each club which has held a field trial in any one year has the first right to claim the corresponding date for its succeeding trial the next year. The Basset Hound Club of America has an advisory committee which helps to set up trial schedules so that trials do not conflict with each other. Regional clubs must first apply to the BHCA for permission to hold a trial. When permission is granted by the AKC, the club's Field Trial Chairman and Field Trial Secretary appoint a trial committee of at least five persons and prepare premium lists which are sent to prospective entrants.

The premium list contains information regarding location, trial date, names of judges, cost of entry fee, prizes offered, and entry forms. Entries must be in the hands of the field trial secretary prior

Beating the bush—Texas style.

The gallery at a Basset Hound field trial doing its part of the work.

248

to the closing time stated on the premium list. Usually this immediately precedes the drawing and running of the stake.

At the specified time, the Secretary announces the closing, reads the list of entries, and asks if there are any omissions. Each dog entered is given a number. Running order is then determined by a lottery-type drawing. The first and second number called, corresponding to the name of the dogs, will form the first brace. The third and fourth dogs will be the second brace, and so on, until all dogs have been given their running order. Should there be an odd number of entries, later in the day the judges will name a hound, which has already run, to run as a bracemate, in the last brace, with the odd hound.

There are two judges. Judges are not approved in the same manner as are judges of conformation. However, their names are submitted to AKC and they are approved for the trial as reputable and competent.

Beside the trial chairman and trial secretary, both who handle the arrangements and paper work, there are others involved in the trial. The field trial committee assists with arrangements and must act as a judicial board of review should any complaints be made. The field marshal is in charge of deportment. He must see to it that the next brace is on hand for judging, relay the judges' instructions to the handlers and/or gallery, and keep order in the gallery.

The gallery is another important element of a trial. It consists of the persons not running the current brace. Between runs, they form a line, under the direction of the field marshal, and walk forward in search of a rabbit for the next run. During a run, they enjoy watching the chase or visit with each other but must exercise behavior that will not interfere with the run. Should the rabbit circle through the gallery, or near someone in the gallery, those persons retreat quietly, without crossing the line, so as not to disturb the run.

"Tally-Ho" is the word used when one puts up a rabbit. Even if one does not have a dog to run, Tally-Hoing rabbits can be a sport in itself. The gallery actually becomes quite competitive over who Tally-Hos the greatest number of rabbits. Sometimes prizes are given. When one does put up a rabbit, one must be careful to ascertain the exact spot and watch where the rabbit goes, while calling out "Tally-Ho." It is wise to take a stick to point out the

249

exact spot, when the judges and handlers get near, so that they have the true line.

When "Tally-Ho" is called, the gallery stops and stands quietly. The brace to be run is brought to the line, on lead. When the dogs' actions indicate that they have picked up the scent, the dogs are turned loose and the judging begins. The handlers follow the judges. They may not interfere or assist unless the judges so instruct them. The dogs are expected to follow the path of the rabbit closely and give tongue, but not give tongue falsely.

The dogs are called in (stopped) and put on lead when the judges feel that they have properly evaluated the hounds. At times, the judges call for a second rabbit for the same brace, even a third if circumstances are such that they need it for a good evaluation. Judging may not proceed until the dogs are back on lead. Then the gallery begins searching for a rabbit for the next brace and the procedure is repeated until all hounds have been judged. This is called the "first series."

After first series, the best running dogs are called back to be run again in the second series. They are called back according to whichever hounds the judges felt were best, in that order. They may, however, be changed, in order, as they compete further. Hounds may even be dropped from further competition if their performance becomes poor. A hound cannot move up beyond one that has already defeated it unless that hound is dropped. Usually six or eight hounds are brought back for second series. When the judges are satisfied that they are correct, awards are made.

Though the field trialers take their wins seriously, the trial atmosphere is one of congeniality. Perhaps this is a part of being close to nature or perhaps because trialers are the kind of people who enjoy the little things in life.

The Performance of a Field Trial Hound

What does one look for in performance of a field trial hound? It must take the line on which it is put. When it has the line, it must claim it. Some dogs mouth before they have it while others run a few hundred feet, making very sure, before they open up. Both are undesirable. A hound should bark only when it has the line. Many fast hounds overrun a check. A hound, coming from behind and turning the corner, right on the line, would be considered best. A

A brace of hounds being put on the line.

Part of the gallery during a run.

Two Bassets working out the ground scent before an interested "mini" audience.

hound that is too fast will make more mistakes even though he may still be driving true to the line. There should be no gaps in the line between barks. If a hound loses the line, he should stay near the loss with his work, otherwise he is gambling. If a rabbit holes up, the hound should mark the hole by staying near, barking, even digging. A hound should honor, or hark-in to its bracemate, unless it believes that the bracemate is lying. It should *never* honor if the bracemate is not telling the truth. A hound must not backtrack. It must not quit until told to do so. It sends goosebumps up one's spine to see a dog pursue a rabbit, head down, too busy with the line to see the quarry a short distance ahead out in the open.

The Well-Dressed Field Trialer

How does one dress at a field trial? Anything that is comfortable and protective will be suitable. There is no "uniform" except that field trialers are often referred to as "plaid shirts" because, so often, mens' heavy sport shirts are of that design. The terrain may be through thicket, brambles, thistles, or bogs so clothing of a stout nature will give the most protection. I've tramped on many a weekend that rain gear and hip boots seemed the only logical choice. If you happen to have one, a walking stick comes in handy for beating the bushes.

Food is available at the clubhouse, and often serves as an additional revenue for the trial-giving club. A large breakfast is offered prior to the drawing and a large meal is provided at the noon break.

You may join the gallery while the trial is in progress. Be careful, however, not to interfere with a run. It is always safe to wait, at the kennel area, for someone who is taking a brace to the field to be run. Explain that you are new, that you want to go to the field, but do not wish to interfere with the field, and ask to tag along. Chances are that this person will introduce you to others who are willing to explain what is going on.

Some Famous Families

The following is an interesting study of four bitches that have had tremendous influence on field trialing. They ran rabbits with a certain style and passed their ability along. This is a partial list of their great-grandchildren, who became field champions, as an example of how running traits are handed down.

Field Champion Yoder's Sally Belle: Ingram's Beauty, Jackie Jo Jan, Campbell's Black Jack, Aquino's King Kong, Ray Run Flake, Beldean's King Kong, Aquino's Socrates, Appleton Acres Emmy, Ric Mar's Fenin, Crelin's Shimmy Dancer, Campbell's Bit of Gold, Shellbark's Michi, Oak Shadows Sloppy Joe, Little Boy.

Field Champion Miss Mitzie: McWilliam's Dixie Belle, Carden Duke, Tagg About's Porsche, Christmas Trippe, and Mat's Misty Morning.

Bose's Melicent Hepsy: Fetheroff's Bawl, Little Lady Tammy, Foley's Tammy Baby, Eylanders Blossom, Al's Belle, Paul's Kate, Rosie's Bill, Rosie's Sportsman, Campbell's Black Jill, Belleau-woods' Fancy, Little Sue, Bose's Initiative, Bash's Shag, Bose's Bashette, Bellows' Star, Bash's Spring Fury, Bose's Karen, Shell-barks' Little Mac, Navar's Heather, Navar's Jolly, Navar's Jo Jo, Tabor's Solo Sue, Crelin's Shimmy Dancer, Tulpehocken May, Tulpehocken Nifty, Beacon Tulpen Duke, and Beacon Tick Tock.

Field Champion Eingle's Beckie: Navar's Jill, Rosie's Bill, Rosie's Sportsman, Newton's Black Jackolyn, Matthews Rusty Red, Bash's Black Dahlia and Bash's Sabrena Sue.

Marge and Len Skolnick compile a Top Field Producers Guide for a trial publication called *The Babbler*. The purpose of the Guide is to honor the sires and dams of the consistently good running hounds. Points are accumulated based on the number of dogs in competition with the get at each trial.

Top field producers for 1972 through 1975 were: *Grand Fd. Ch. Pettit's Ranger Ric* (Fd. Ch. Rosie's Jeff ex Fd. Ch. Dohrshire's Twiggy). Bred to Pettit's Priscilla, he produced Pettit's Sundown, Fd. Ch. Pettit's Ricardo, Fd. Ch. Pettit's Southern Comfort, Pettit's Sunshine, and Fd. Ch. Pettit's Meadowlark. Bred back to Fd. Ch. Dohrshire's Twiggy, he produced Fd. Ch. Pettit's Sherlock Holmes, Pettit's Boston Blackie, and Pettit's Ellery Queen. Bred to Pettit's Phyliss, he produced Fd. Ch. Pettit's Cinderella. Bred to Fd. Ch. Dailey's Sad Suzie, he produced Fd. Ch. Sandy Lee's Irish Mist, Sandy Lee's Kelly, and Fd. Ch. Pettit's Irish Spring. Bred to Fd. Ch. Rosie's Road Runner, he produced Rosie's Ric, Fd. Ch. Pettit's Trapper, and Rosie's Peggy. Bred to Pettit's Choconut Valley Jenny,

The beginning of a Basset field trial—Rick Smith and Bill Ten Eyck doing the "drawing."

The end of a Basset field trial with the winners collecting their well-earned rewards. The hounds shown here are Reynold's Big Boy (Tomlin), Happy Hunter's Billy Sunday (Sayers), Sandhill Red Bandit (Lowenower), Willstone's Tamera of Ran-Sue (Patrick) and Tomlin's Little Jet (Tomlin).

he produced Pettit's Jenny R. Bred to Lee's Jody, he produced Buck Hills Duke and bred to Fd. Ch. Choconut Valley Star, he produced Fd. Ch. Choconut Valley Ruffian.

Fd. Ch. Carl's Baby (Fd. Ch. Little Boy ex Fd. Ch. Foley's Tammy Baby) bred to Fd. Ch. Rosie's Gentle, produced Fd. Ch. Rosie's Genny, Fd. Ch. Rosie's Gail, and Fd. Ch. Rosie's Karl. Bred to Fd. Ch. Rosie's Michie, he produced Fd. Ch. Rosie's Red Boy, Fd. Ch. Pettit's Jiminy Cricket, and Fd. Ch. Reynold's Maxie Mae. Bred to Campbell's Rebel Queen, he produced Rosie's Xmas. Bred to Fd. Ch. McWilliams' Dixie Belle, he produced Fd. Ch. McWilliams Ding A Ling. Bred to Rosie's Gail, he produced Fd. Ch. Ina's Carline and bred to Red Acres Clown, he produced Fd. Ch. Red Acres Queen.

Fd. Ch. Rosie's Bill (Hartshead Sportsman ex Rosie's Ed's Miss Mitzie) was bred to Campbell's Cindy Lou producing Fd. Ch. Campbell's Rebel Queen. Bred to Beldean's Gypsy, he produced Fd. Ch. Rosie's Rose and Rosie's Bill, Jr. Bred to Rosie's Road Runner, he produced Rosie's Gladys and bred to Dohrshire's Sassy Sue, he produced Fd. Ch. Dohrshire Rosie.

Fd. Ch. Beldean's Slippery Hill Sam (Fd. Ch. Aquino's King Kong ex Fd. Ch. Olson's Samantha) bred to Fd. Ch. Slippery Hill Calvin, produced Grand Fd. Ch. Slippery Hill Stub and Grand Fd. Ch. Slippery Hill Sophie. Bred to her brother, Fd. Ch. Beldean's King Kong Gladiator, she produced Fd. Ch. Slippery Hill Agnes.

Pettit's Priscilla (Fd. Ch. Rosie's Jeff ex Fd. Ch. Rosie's Phyliss) was bred to Fd. Ch. Pettit's Ranger Ric producing Pettit's Sundown, Fd. Ch. Pettit's Ricardo, Pettit's Sunshine, and Fd. Ch. Pettit's Meadowlark. By Fd. Ch. Pettit's Sportsman, she produced Pettit's Jr. Sportsman.

Fd. Ch. Rosie's Jeff (Fd. Ch. Rosie's Bill ex Rosie's Jet) was bred to Fd. Ch. Dohrshire's Twiggy producing Grand Fd. Ch. Pettit's Ranger Ric and Trefry's Big Tom. Bred to Rosie's Polly, he produced Fd. Ch. Sandy Lee's Applejack.

Fd. Ch. Beldean's King Kong Gladiator (Fd. Ch. Aquino's King Kong ex Fd. Ch. Olson's Samantha). Bred to Fd. Ch. Beldean's Slippery Hill Sam, he produced Fd. Ch. Slippery Hill Agnes. He and Miss Double Rose produced Fd. Ch. Slippery Hill Myra, Slippery Hill Meyer's Mite, Miss Fanny LaBelle, and Solo VI. Bred to Slippery Hill Irma, he produced Fd. Ch. Slippery Hill Agogo and bred to Grand Fd. Ch. Slippery Hill Sophie, he produced Slippery Hill Prudence.

Fd. Ch. Dohrshire's Twiggy (Fd. Ch. Mel Ann Acres Doc Holiday ex Eylander's Josie). Bred to Fd. Ch. Clancy James, she produced Horst's Patty Dee. Bred to Fd. Ch. Pettit's Ranger Ric, she produced Fd. Ch. Pettit's Sherlock Holmes, Pettit's Boston Blackie, and Pettit's Ellery Queen. Bred to Fd. Ch. Rosie's Jeff, she produced Grand Fd. Ch. Pettit's Ranger Ric and Trefry's Big Tom.

Fd. Ch. Slippery Hill Calvin (Tulpehocken Tip Toe ex Slippery Hill Pandora) was bred to Fd. Ch. Beldean's Slippery Hill Sam and produced two Grand champions, Fd. Ch. Slippery Hill Stub and Fd. Ch. Slippery Hill Sophie.

Fd. Ch. Rosie's Gentle (Fd. Ch. Rosie's Bill ex Fd. Ch. Fouse's Cinda Lee) bred to Fd. Ch. Carl's Baby produced Fd. Ch. Rosie's Genny, Rosie's Gail and Fd. Ch. Rosie's Karl.

Grand Fd. Ch. Tagg About Pluto (Sandy Hill Homer ex Fd. Ch. Tagg About Porsche) bred to Grand Fd. Ch. Tagg About Jensen produced Almick's Tagg Me Nova, Brookline's J, and Tagg About Suzuki. Bred to Matt's Satin Sue, he produced Tagg About Peugeot and bred to Brookline's Min, he produced Brookline's Amos.

Fd. Ch. Sborays Caesar (Burch's Big Boy ex Boyer's Amanda Lee) bred to Horst's Patty Dee produced Horst's Trina and bred to Fd. Ch. Miss Fanny II produced Grand Fd. Ch. Keener's Duke and Miss Fanny Starr.

Fd. Ch. Rosie's Sportsman (Hartshead Sportsman ex Rosie's Ed's Miss Mitzie) bred to Grand Fd. Ch. Van's Fantasy produced Fd. Ch. Pettit's Little Fanny and Fd. Ch. Pettit's Sportsman. Bred to Fd. Ch. Hilawn Roxanne, he produced Fd. Ch. Choconut Valley Star. Bred to Grand Fd. Ch. Mickey's At Last, he produced Fd. Ch. Almick's Cactus. Bred to Sarah Plunkett, he produced Tulpehocken Zeke and bred to Sandy Oaks Ritzie, he produced Sandy Oaks April.

Fd. Ch. Ernest T of High Hollow (Tramp ex Anderson's Lady) bred to Grand Fd. Ch. Triple R Patricia produced Triple R Trouble and Rabbit River Ridge Runner.

Fd. Ch. Appleton Acre Issie (Fd. Ch. Ed's Jo Jo ex Fd. Ch. Max's Happy Hunter) bred to Fd. Ch. Foley's Tammy Baby produced Foley's Mary Lou and bred to Maggie XIV produced Appleton Acre Melissa.

Fd. Ch. Dever's Georgie Girl (Fd. Ch. Little Boy ex Eylander's

Grand Fld. Ch. Southern Shots, owned by Richard Gargas, Jr., and shown here with Joseph Braun.

Carhart's Jersey Devil (Hamlin's Adonis ex Fld. Ch. Hamlin's Dolly), owned and bred by Ewing Carhart, Sr. (handling) and Ewing Carhart, Jr. This granddaughter of Fld. Ch. Hamlin's Torpedo was first in a field of 55 bitches at the BHCA national trials.

Thursday) bred to Fd. Ch. Carl's Baby produced Fd. Ch. Carl's Girl and Fd. Ch. Reynold's Maxie Mae.

Eylander's Thursday (Fd. Ch. Ed's Jo Jo ex Dual Ch. Braun's Wholly Thursday) bred to Tomlin's One Spot produced Fd. Ch. Tomlin's Little Drooper and bred to Fd. Ch. Little Boy produced Fd. Ch. Tomlin's April Fool and Fd. Ch. Dever's Georgie Girl.

Grand Fd. Ch. Sykemoor Nestor (Dalewell Rambler ex Sykemoor Java) bred to Tagg About's Rolls Royce produced Tagg About's Austin of Skyline, Fd. Ch. Skyline Arlette, and Fd. Ch. Skyline Affable.

Fd. Ch. Chris's Droopy (Chris Kringle's Caesar ex Dutchess Nancy Lee) bred to Win Pat's Polka Dot produced Dailey's Sad Suzie.

Fd. Ch. Foley's Tammy Baby (Fd. Ch. Ed's Jo Jo ex Fd. Ch. Max's Happy Hunter) bred to Fd. Ch. Appleton Acre Issie produced Fd. Ch. Tomlin's Little Fitz, Foley's Mary Lu, and Fd. Ch. Appleton Acre Miranda. Bred to Fd. Ch. Little Boy, she produced Fd. Ch. Carl's Baby.

Fd. Ch. Little Boy (Bose's Super Speed ex Hidden Hills Sadness) bred to Eylander's Thursday produced Fd. Ch. Dever's Georgie Girl, Red Acres Clown and Fd. Ch. Tomlin's April Fool. Bred to Foley's Tammy Baby, he produced Fd. Ch. Carl's Baby.

Rex of Largo (J. D. Sylvester ex Acona Wren) bred to Norseman's Cleopatra produced Fd. Ch. Candy's Viking and Fd. Ch. Norseman's Bessie.

GRAND FIELD CHAMPIONS
through 1977

1. Hamlin's Dolly   female   Ewing E. Carhart
   (Fd. Ch. Hamlin's Torpedo x Fd. Ch. Irle's Cleopatra)
2. McWilliams Dixie Belle   female   Kenneth McWilliams
   (McWilliams Buccaneer x McWilliams Dixie Peach)
3. Van's Fantasy   female   Thomas Pettit
   (Fd. Ch. Beacon Tick Tock x Crelins Lady Fair)
4. Tagg About's Pluto   male   Elsie & Scott Tagg
   (Sandy Hill Homer x Fd. Ch. Tagabout's Porsche)
5. Slippery Hill Sophie   female   Leonard Skolnick
   (Fd. Ch. Slippery Hill Calvin x Fd. Ch. Beldean's Slippery Hill Sam)

6. Sykemoor Nestor   male   Lenore Horabin
   (Dalewell Rambler x Sykemoor Java)
7. Mickey's At Last   female   Alan Carter
   (Azul Rayo x Crelin's Fancy Dancer)
8. Tagg About's Jensen   female   Elsie & Scott Tagg
   (Fd. Ch. Tagg About's Pluto x Brookline's Minn)
9. Campbells Rebel Queen   female   Howard E. Smith
   (Fd. Ch. Rosie's Bill x Campbells Cindy Lou)
10. Slippery Hill Stub   male   Leonard Skolnick
    (Fd. Ch. Slippery Hill Calvin x Fd. Ch. Beldean's Slippery Hill Sam)
11. Triple R Patricia   female   Robert Oosterbaan &
                                           Richard Gargas)
    (Campbells Troubador x Sues Lucky Lady)
12. Sboray's Caesar   male   Kenneth Harvey
    (Ch. Burch's Big Boy x Boyer's Amanda Lee)
13. Candy's Viking   female   Birger Forseth
    (Rex of Largo x Norseman's Cleopatra)
14. Clancy James   male   Thomas O'Conner
    (Fouses Clancy Lee x Horsts Cricket Blake)
15. Kenner's Duke   male   Eugene Beldean
    (Fd. Ch. Sboray's Caesar x Fd. Ch. Miss Fanny II)
16. Pettit's Ranger Ric (dual)   male   Tom & Shirley Pettit
    (Fd. Ch. Rosie's Jeff x Fd. Ch. Dohrshire's Twiggy)
17. Navar's Slicker   male   Pinkie Navar
    (Fd. Ch. Navar's Zeke x Fd. Ch. Wilson's Mindy Lou)
18. Southern Shots   female   Richard Gargas, Jr.
    (Oak Shadows Sweetie Pie x Lady Cleopatra Amanda)
19. Ina's Wimpy   male   Donald Dever
    (Fd. Ch. Carl's Little Fellow x Fd. Ch. Ina's Carline)
20. Sandy Lee's Irish Mist   female   Robert & Sandra Quacken-
                                           bush
    (Dual Ch. Pettit's Ranger Ric x Fd. Ch. Dail Sad Susie)
21. Daily's Sad Susie   female   Robert & Sandra Quacken-
                                           bush
    (Chris's Droopy x Win-Pat's Polka Dot)
22. Carl's Girl   female   Donald Dever
    (Fd. Ch. Carl's Baby x Fd. Ch. Dever's Georgie Girl)

The Timber Ridge Basset Hound Pack.

The Coldstream Basset Hound Pack.

Louisa Neilson.

15

Packs of Basset
Hounds in America

Hunting a foot pack means the hunting of a
group of Bassets by a Huntsman with a horn, assisted by
Whippers-In. This is the so-called formal manner introduced from
England many years ago. The Whippers-In are less formally referred to as Whips. The Huntsman is responsible for the conduct
of the hounds when they are hunting. He decides what places are
to be checked out, by the pack, to try to locate game on that day.
He aids the pack when they are at fault. The Whips work under
the direction of the Huntsman. They watch for game or warn
him of obstacles in the field ahead. They alert motorists at road
crossings and gather in straying or laggardly hounds. They must
have the physical stamina to run ahead of the pack and turn the
hounds back to the Huntsman if they "riot." Running riot means
that the pack is running game other than the actual quarry. The
organization of the hunt is headed by the Master of Basset Hounds,
or M.B.H., whose word is law. Often the Master is also the Huntsman.

The pack is a highly disciplined unit. Depending on the number of hounds maintained by the particular hunt, the number may vary from five to sixteen or more couples. The pack is trained to such commands as "pack together" which means all hounds must gather about the Huntsman in a tight group. There is control exercised through the use of the horn as well as certain vocal commands. Different notes are blown for casting, packing together, "Tally-Ho" and other commands. The horn is the real secret to control of the pack in the field.

The pack must be composed of individuals that are much alike in size, speed and temperament. This means that they must practically be bred from related strains.

Unity is achieved by training the pack-hound to lead, first, then to be coupled. The youngster is given road work while it is coupled with an older, thoroughly-trained member of the pack. It must be taught basic pack manners. An important part of the training is to teach the dogs to ignore barnyard animals as they pass them in farms and fields.

The Huntsman and Whippers-In carry whips with leather-bound or ash handles to which long leather thongs are attached. A four-inch, colored, twisted cord is attached to the end to make a sharp crack when the whip is used. Whips are rarely used on the dogs. They are merely an additional control measure, and when hunting a large pack, the Master needs discipline.

A collection of good dogs is not enough to make a good pack. There must be teamwork. It takes years before the hounds work as a unit in the ideal manner. It is not too difficult to make a pack of hounds follow the huntsman in close formation. It takes a bit more to get them out in front and working gaily. The pack should work ahead of the Huntsman, changing direction at the Huntsman's will, or returning on command. The pack should run with the line and make the turn as did the quarry. It should fan out at a loss so that the line may more readily be recovered. It requires patience, intelligence, and discernment if this is to be accomplished without intimidation. It is a beautiful sight to see the rapport between the Huntsman and the hounds, the harmony and the gaiety as the hounds move as a unit.

There are at the present time fourteen registered packs of Basset Hounds in the United States. James S. Jones, Joint Master of the

Tewksbury Foot Bassets, Gladstone, N.J., has been kind enough to write the following history of them:

"The first organized hare hunting, by a pack of Bassets in this country, was carried on, I believe, by Mr. Gerald Livingston, who hunted his Kilsyth Bassets in the vicinity of his house at Oyster Bay, Long Island, in the late nineteen-twenties and early thirties. Since there were no indigenous hare on Long Island, Mr. Livingston stocked the country with Jack rabbits brought in from Kansas, and with hare imported from Central Europe. This was a private pack completely supported by the Master. His hounds came mostly from Capt. Godfrey Heseltine's famous Walhampton Pack which was, in its turn, the first pack in England to hunt hare in an active fashion over an extended period of years. (The Walhamptons were active from 1890 to 1914 except for several periods of a few years while their owner was away from England on military service.)

"Mr. Livingston's Kilsyth Bassets made one of their last public

The Tewksbury Foot Basset Hound Pack.

263

appearances at the Eastern Field Trials of the Basset Hound Club of America which were held at Gladstone, N.J. in 1940. On that occasion, three-couple packs were hunted on Jacks in open grazing country. The mounted judge was Josiah Child, Master for many years of the Waldingfield Beagles of South Hamilton, Mass. Pack entries included: Brandywine Bassets, Lenape, Pa., Miss Jane Mather, Master; Kilsyth Bassets, Oyster Bay, L.I., Mr. Gerald Livingston, Master; Bijou Bassets, Old Chatham, N.Y., Mrs. Consuelo U. Ford, Master; Mr. and Mrs. "Pinkie" Thompson's Bassets, Red Bank, N.J.; the Rowe House Bassets of Pottersville, N.J., Percy Chubb & James S. Jones, Joint Masters. From this entry list, you can see that there were several other packs, in addition to Kilsyth, which hunted hare or Jacks in the Eastern States in the period between World War I and World War II.

"Mr. & Mrs. Alfred Bissell had their Stockford Bassets hunting a country outside Wilmington, Delaware. This pack is still in existence.

"Miss Mather's pack hunted cottontail rabbits in the country of her father's Brandywine Foxhounds at Lenape, Chester County, Penna.

"Mrs. Consuelo U. Ford's well-known Bijou pack was descended in part from imports from Dr. Eric Morrison's Westerby Bassets which were kenneled at that time at Great Glen in Leistershire, England. The country around Old Chatham, in New York State, which Mrs. Ford hunted was very rough and hilly with long hard winters. Nevertheless, she very gamely put on regular meets for quite a few years, hunting the local rabbits and some imported Jacks, and with her hunt staff turned out in very smart brown velvet jackets. Mrs. Ford was very largely responsible for the great success of the BHCA 1940 Eastern Trial.

"Mr. & Mrs. Thompson's pack, like all the others of the period before World War II, was privately owned. They started it when they lived near Geneseo in western New York State. Later, when they moved to Rumson, N.J., they were fortunate to be in an area where there were some native European hare. This was the registered country of the Monmouth Co. Harriers. It had formerly been hunted in the twenties, by the Navasink Beagles of which W. Strother Jones and Edward Hurd were Joint Masters. The hare in Monmouth County are descended from those imported from Europe in 1890 or so by Mr. Pierre Lorrillard and released at his nearby Rancocas Stud Farm at Columbus, N.J.

"In the years 1939, 1940, and 1941 Mr. Percy Chubb and the author hunted a small pack, the Rowe House Bassets, in the outer portions of the country of the Vernon-Somerset Beagles in Hunterdon and Somerset Counties in New Jersey, by permission of their Master, Mr. R. V. N. Gambrill. Our hounds consisted of drafts from the Westerby and from Mrs. Ford. We had some good sport and lots of fun hunting native hare and Jacks until the war put a stop to all activities. In 1941 these hounds were given to Mr. Carrol Basset and Mrs. Marion Dupont Scott of Montpelier, Orange County, Virginia.

"The first post-war II pack to become active were the Timber Ridge of which Charles R. Rogers is the founder and first Master. He is still in office. These hounds hunt outside Baltimore, Maryland, in the country of the Green Spring Valley Foxhounds. They are the first publicly supported subscription pack of Bassets in the United States and the first pack to be recognized and registered by the National Beagle Club which is the governing body for the organized packs of Bassets.

"The Timber Ridge have developed a large and enthusiastic following. They have no native hare or Jacks, so they do the best they can hunting rabbits and grey foxes in their very attractive open countryside around Hampstead, Maryland. In 1963, they retired the cup for five-couples of Bassets at the Bryn Mawr Hound Show having won this class five times.

"The next post-war pack to appear on the scene were the Tewksbury Foot Bassets, started by Mr. Harlburton Fales II and myself as a small private pack in 1951. Our foundation stock came from Mrs. Ford, the Westerby, and from Mrs. Walton of Mt. Holly, New Jersey. In 1953, Mr. Richard V. N. Gambrill died and the country he had hunted with his Vernon-Somerset Beagles became vacant. It is an open farming and grazing area lying in Somerset and Hunterdon Counties in New Jersey. Over the years, it had been pretty well stocked with European hare and Kansas Jack rabbits. At Mr. Gambrill's death, the Tewksbury Foot Bassets were reorganized as a publicly supported subscription pack to take over the vacated area. The hounds were "presented to the country" by Mr. Fales and myself and we remained on as Joint Masters. Mr. Louis Starr was the first Chairman of the Hunt Committee. Mrs. James

Casey, Mr. Gambrill's daughter, was elected Secretary and Mrs. Charles B. P. Van Pelt, Treasurer. Mr. Fales and I are still in office as Joint Masters and we were joined in 1959 by Mr. James Cox Brady, Jr. We maintain about thirteen couples of Bassets and try to breed about three litters of puppies every second year. Our season begins the first of August and ends on April 1. We hunt early in the morning until the third week in October which is the start of our "regular season" during which the advertised meets are held on Sunday afternoons. We have some 150 subscribers. Sunday "fields" average about forty people.

"We compete annually at the Bryn Mawr Hound Show held at Malvern, Penna., in June and in the two and four couple Basset division at the National Beagle Club Field Trials held at Aldie, Virginia, in early November. Our T. F. B. Elmer '54, out of Ch. Lyn Mar Clown ex Grim's Unity, was Champion Basset Hound at Bryn Mawr for six consecutive years, and has been quite widely used at stud.

"Among the most pleasant features of our season are the joint meets held from time to time with the various adjacent packs of Beagles or Bassets. For example, on each alternate year we are invited to hunt the country of the Ardrossan (formerly Treweryn) Beagles near Philadelphia and on the off year they visit us. To finish our season, for the past ten years, we have been invited to hunt the brown hare at Thornedale, Millbrook, Duchess County, N.Y., by the invitation of Morgan Wing, Jr., the very active Secretary of the National Beagle.Club, and Master of the Sandanona Beagles. At various other times, we have visited, or been visited by, the Buckram Beagles of Long Island, The Timber Ridge Bassets, the Poona Bassets, and the Little Prospect Beagles. Often, on these occasions, the home pack hunts in the morning and the visiting pack hunts after lunch the same day.

"I've noted above that the National Beagle Club is the governing body for all packs of foot hounds in the U.S. New packs are inspected by a committee and first registered and then, when fully established, they are 'recognized.' A map showing the boundaries of the country is placed on file and the hunt livery and roster of staff are placed on the official list. New packs cannot be started within or near the boundaries of existing packs without sanction from the National Beagle Club Committee.

"In addition to Timber Ridge and Tewksbury, it is nice to note that the following six new packs have been added to the list in the past ten years.

"The Poona; Joint Masters, Kent and the late Adele Leavitt of Fraleigh Hill Farm, Millbrook, Duchess County, New York. This small, but in its time, active family pack is now unfortunately disbanded. In previous years, however, in their old-gold livery, they carried off many ribbons at Bryn Mawr and Aldie. They won the five-couple class for packs at Bryn Mawr in 1958 and the present challenge trophy for this class is presented by Mr. & Mrs. Leavitt in memory of their daughter. Kent Leavitt is currently the 'Basset representative' on the National Beagle Club Committee. He takes an active interest in the field trial grounds at the Institute at Aldie.

"The Bridlespur Bassets are affiliated with the Bridlespur Hunt, run for many years by the Adolph Busch family near St. Louis, Missouri. This is a subscription pack and the joint Master and Huntsman is Mr. Clarkson Carpenter, Jr. They show good sport on cottontail rabbits to an enthusiastic field and compete with success at Aldie each year.

"The Somerset Bassets: At Montpelier Station, Orange County, Virginia, near the famous home of ex-president James Madison, are the kennels of this pack which shows great sport on cottontail rabbits to an enthusiastic following under the leadership of their Master, Mrs. James H. Andrews, Jr., and her genial huntsman, Melvin Poe.

"The Skycastle Bassets: a private pack of partially rough-coated hounds which hunt rabbits and show sport to the neighbors of Mr. John Streeter of Chester Springs, Pennsylvania. Mrs. Elizabeth Streeter takes an active part in the management of this pack. They compete extensively at local field trials.

"Ashland Bassets; Warrenton, Virginia: This very workmanlike private pack is in a sense an offshoot or descendant of some Bassets which Mrs. Amory S. Carhart, the present Master, had in conjunction with the late Mr. "Babe" Gibb in 1941. They hunt rabbits in the country of the Warrenton Hunt and compete successfully at the Aldie Field Trials.

"The Coldstream Bassets: The newest addition to the roster of Basset packs is the Coldstream under the joint Mastership of Mr. & Mrs. Joseph J. McKenna of Media, Pennsylvania. They also hunt rabbits in the former country of the Rose Tree Foxhounds and

267

have, in a very short time, developed a good looking level pack. On their first appearance at the Bryn Mawr Show, in 1964, they accounted for the class for entered dog hounds and followed this up by winning the important five-couple pack class.

"I don't want to conclude this article without mentioning the fact that in the past fifteen years almost all the active hunting packs of Bassets in England have seen fit to use a harrier or beagle outcross in order to obtain a more quickly responsive and active hunting hound. Col. Eric Morrison, founder and now ex-Master of the Westerby, took the lead in this movement and he claims that some thirteen packs are now hunting hounds descended from his Westerby strain which he started cross breeding in 1946. These cross-bred hounds are referred to as 'English Bassets,' the term 'Basset' being reserved for the pure bred variety.

"In April of 1964, I had the pleasure of hunting with a pack of English Bassets, the West Lodge Hare Hounds, in Hertsfordshire. They are a partially rough coated, lemon and white, fifteen inch pack, with only mildly crooked legs. They handle and hunt extremely well and have a very good cry and great drive.

"I quote below part of a letter which I sent in 1959 to the Editor of The Field in London, commenting on this development in England especially as it relates to hunting with Bassets in the U.S.: 'Dear Sir: As joint master of one of the four active packs of Bassets in the United States, I was very interested to read your May 14, 1959 article by Miss Jane Buckland on the subject of the recent crossing of this breed in England with harriers, beagles, etc., and the resultant discussion as to an appropriate name for the cross-bred product.

'In this country the need for such an out-cross has not been felt even with the active hunting packs. I believe the reasons for this include the following:

'a. In the hare hunting countries we do not have frequent fields of deep plough, ditches, stone walls or thick hedges. The fields are grass and the fences are post and rail or three strands of wire which presents no problem to a pack of Bassets.

'b. The central European hare which we hunt, and which are native since about 1925 in our own country in New Jersey, are of considerable stamina and what you, in England, would call a good scenting day comes only once or twice per season! Fortunately it is not expected that we kill very often! With two or three herds of fifty deer or more a common sight on any hunting day, it is a help not to have foot hounds running at too great a pace.

'A pack of the larger cross-bred type—such as the two hounds Doctor (now Col.) Morrison sent us in 1952—would get clean away from us in this relatively wooded deer infested area. Incidentally, these cross-breds were exported to us, unseen, in response to a request for a couple of Bassets similar to a very fine orthodox dog-hound puppy which I'd gotten from Dr. Morrison in 1938. This bears out well the point made by both Miss Keevil and Mrs. Rawle that the name question should be settled to avoid confusion and further misrepresentation! I fully sympathize with the desire to have a smarter more active pack and to kill more hare but we stick to the orthodox type of necessity. Incidentally, they are said to run 'one field in five' slower than a pack of 15-inch Beagles and manage to give most of our good runners a more than adequate workout!

'Lastly, I feel that there has been no tendency in America to look for an out-cross to another breed because the number of Bassets in the country did not have to be cut down drastically during the second war as was done in England. A. K. C. figures show 21,555 Bassets registered in the U.S. during the years 1953–1958 inclusive. The growth has been rapid—from 1,300 in 1953 to 7,000 in 1958. I believe, the English number registered in 1953 was considerably less.'

"The above letter indicates why, in my opinion as of 1964, the American packs will all stick to the 'pure-bred' strain and not find it necessary to attempt any cross-bred experimenting. Even on this basis the breeding of a good hunting level pack is an ambitious undertaking. We all have a good way to go yet before anyone achieves this goal!"

Alfred E. Bissell supplied the following about his Stockford pack, the only pre-war pack which is still active in 1964: "In the early 1930's I started a pack of Beagles and my wife started a pack of Bassets. Being over 60, I had to give up the Beagles as they became too fast for me." Mr. Bissell bought his first Basset from Gerald Livingston. In 1932, the Kilsyth strain of Livingston's was the only pack known to Bissell. The Bissells then imported dogs from the Eastington Park Bassets of Mr. de Lisle Bush in England and Colonel Morrison's Westerby pack. They later imported dogs of the Grims line owned by Miss Peggy Keevil. Mrs. Bissell was the first Master of the Stockford Bassets. She hunted them twice a week and won many prizes at the shows. The pack was given to Mrs. Andrew Porter at the start of the second world war and returned to the Bissells in 1946. For the next ten years they were hunted regularly. It was always a private pack with no dues and by invitation only. Mr. Bissell says, "Now I take them out when I feel like it and have no fixtures. We had volunteer Whips, personal friends, children, and now grandchildren—no horses allowed but I now have golf-carts for the infirm." Jack rabbits are imported from New Mexico each September. These, with the native ones left over from the previous year, usually provide a good hunt.

In 1977, Mrs. Elizabeth Streeter wrote that she became Master of the Skycastle pack after the passing of her husband. Her children, especially her daughter Candida who whips in at Aldie, share her delight with the French infusion into the pack. They showed a conventional pack and a French one at Bryn Mawr in 1977. She recently traveled to visit M. Hubert Desamy, in France, then imported some Griffon Vendeen, which were actually Desamy stock, from Mrs. Wells-Meacham in England. Her former stock was from Kilsyth, Bijou, and a draft from Mr. Colman of England. Her dogs now are a three-way cross between the purebred Basset, the English Basset, and the Griffon Vendeen which makes them ineligible for AKC registration and participation in AKC licensed field trials which Mrs Streeter enjoyed so much.

The staff consists of the Master, or Joint Masters, Secretary, Whippers-in, and Huntsman. The people participating in the hunt are called the Field. Customs observed are: close gates; roll under fences, if possible, or climb near a post; move quietly near stock; stand still when hounds are close by; don't overrun hounds at check; exercise care when smoking in field; stand still and point with cap or handkerchief when quarry is viewed; do not shout. The following is a brief glossary of hunting terms: *drag,* artificially laid scent; *draw,* exploration of likely hiding places of quarry; *field,* those hunting; *full cry,* musical chorus of hounds running their quarry; *hold hard,* stand still; *lift hounds,* moving hounds to new covert; *line,* the line traveled by the quarry; *mark,* the spot quarry was last viewed; *mark to ground,* hounds indicating quarry has gone to ground (technical kill); *pack,* term for the working unit of hounds; *quarry,* animal being hunted; *tail hounds,* hounds running some distance behind the pack; *tally-ho,* the call made when quarry is viewed; *worry,* hounds fighting over quarry killed. Signals are given by horn.

Roster of Basset Packs—1977 (as accepted by the National Beagle Club, the governing body of Masters of Basset and Beagle Packs)

ASHLAND BASSETS: Organized 1960; recognized 1961. A subscription pack. Uniform: green with green collar and scarlet piping. Masters: Mrs. Harcourt Lees and Mrs. James J. Wilson. Location: Elway Hall, Warrenton, Virginia. Hounds: Seven couple Bassets which hunt native cottontails. They meet Sundays, October 19 through March. Visitors always welcome.

COLDSTREAM BASSETS: Organized 1962; recognized 1962. A subscription pack. Uniform: green with oxford gray collar and scarlet piping. Evening dress: green with scarlet facings. Masters: Joseph J. McKenna and Joseph J. McKenna, Jr. Mrs. Eva McKenna was formerly the Joint-Master, before her demise in 1974. Location: Media, Pennsylvania. Hounds: Ten couple Bassets which hunt cottontail. They meet Tuesdays, Saturdays, Sundays, and other days at the convenience of the Masters, from August 1 through April 1.

FLINT HILL BASSETS: Organized 1968; recognized 1970. A private pack. Uniform: green with navy blue collar and gray piping. Masters: Mr. and Mrs. James M. Park. Location: Flint Hill Road, Amenia, New York. Hounds: Six couple English Bassets which hunt cottontail and native brown hare. They meet two days a week from October through March. Visitors welcome.

SKYCASTLE BASSETS: Organized 1948; recognized 1952. A private pack. Uniform: green with crimson collar. Master: Mrs. John W. Streeter. Location: Chester Springs, Pennsylvania. Hounds: Ten couple rough-coated and mixed Bassets. They meet Sundays, holidays, and occasionally on Wednesdays from late October to April 1.

SOMERSET BASSETS: Organized 1957; recognized 1959. A subscription pack. Uniform: green with gold collar and purple piping.

Master: Mrs. James N. Andrews, Jr. Location: Waverley Farm, Somerset, Virginia. Hounds: Seven couple Bassets, hunting cottontails and fox. They meet Sunday afternoons from October through March. Visitors welcome.

SOUTHERN ILLINOIS FOOT BASSETS: Organized 1970; recognized 1972. A subscription pack. Uniform; green with pink collar and black piping. Master: Ralph Bushee and Robert Moran. Location: Chinquapin Oaks, Carbondale, Ill., winter and summer, Deland, Ill. Hounds: Eleven couple Bassets. They meet from October through March on Sunday mornings. Visitors welcome.

SPRING CREEK BASSETS: Organized 1971; recognized 1973. A subscription pack. Uniform; Green with canary collar and green piping. Evening dress; canary collar and facings, black knee breeches and stockings. Master: Frank B. Kenney. Location: Spring Creek Farm, Barrington Hills, Illinois. Hounds: Eight couple tricolored and eight couple black and tan Bassets. They meet September through mid-April, Sundays and by-days. Visitors welcome.

STOCKFORD BASSETS: Organized 1932; recognized 1932. A private pack. Uniform: green with green collar and gold piping. Master: Mrs. Alfred E. Bissel. Location: near Chadds Ford, Pennsylvania. Hounds: Five couple Bassets. They meet at the convenience of the Master.

STRATHALBYN BASSETS: Organized 1966; recognized 1966. A subscription pack owned by the Strathalbyn Farms Club and its members. Uniform: green with gold collar and red piping. Masters: Mrs. Walter L. Moor and Eric George. Location: Strathalbyn Farms Club, R# 4, St. Louis, Missouri. Hounds: Ten couple Bassets which hunt cottontail. They meet Sundays and Wednesdays from October through March. Visitors welcome.

TANTIVY BASSETS: Organized 1965; recognized 1965. A private pack. Uniform: green with black collar and silver piping. Master: W. J. Luce. Location: near Bucyrus, Kansas. Hounds: Ten couple which hunt cottontail. They meet at the convenience of the Master. Visitors welcome.

TEWKSBURY FOOT BASSETS: Organized 1950; recognized 1953. A subscription pack. Uniform: green coat, robin's egg blue collar, black buttons engraved T.F.D., and navy blue stockings Masters: James S. Jones, Joseph B. Wiley, Jr. and John Ike, III. Location: Gladstone, New Jersey. Hounds: Twenty and one-half couple of English Bassets (mixed breeding) which hunt native European hare and jack rabbits. They meet Sundays and holidays from October through March, early morning hunting from August 15. Visitors welcome.

TIMBER RIDGE BASSETS: Organized 1946; recognized 1947. A private pack supported by subscription. Uniform: green with old gold collar and blue piping, white stock and trousers, black velvet cap. Master: Charles R. Rogers. Location: Hampstead, Maryland. Hounds: Ten couple Bassets which hunt hare and fox. They meet one day a week, either Saturday or Sunday, from October through March.

WAYNE DUPAGE FOOT BASSETS: Organized 1973; recognized 1975. A subscription pack. Uniform: green coat, canary yellow collar and red piping. Masters: Mrs. Arthur A. Anderson, Dr. Betsy Kjellstrom and Dr. Ted Kjellstrom. Hounds: Twelve

The Southern Illinois Foot Basset Hound Pack.

273

couple Bassets which hunt cottontail. They meet Sundays and Wednesdays, and desirable bye days.

WINWARD BASSETS. Organized in 1971; recognized 1973. A private pack. Uniform: green with beige collar and yellow piping. Evening dress is green with yellow facings and beige collar. Masters: Mr. and Mrs. Bickford Henchey. Location: Upland Road, Bedford, New York. Hounds: Eight couple Bassets which hunt cottontail and hare. They meet Sundays and occasionally Saturdays and holidays, at the convenience of the Masters, from September 1 through March 31. Visitors welcome.

The locations given are, in most cases, the locations of the kennels. Visitors are welcome, where noted. However, phone ahead to make sure it is convenient for you to visit.

16

The Basset Hound
in Britain

I T is impossible to give a detailed account of the breed's history in the British Isles without taking up the whole book. It is a fascinating history, not surprising in a unique breed, and worthy of closer study. However, space permits only a sketchy outline of the main events and the people involved. Much of the information about the twentieth-century breeders was written by George Johnston of Wigton, Cumberland, England.

Despite the proximity of France, it was not until the late 1800s that the first Basset Hounds were introduced into Great Britain. In 1866 M. LeComte de Tournon presented some to Lord Galway. They had been bred by M. LeComte Couteulx de Canteleu and were the smooth-coated Artois variety. Lord Galway eventually passed them on to Lord Onslow. In 1874 Sir Everett Millais imported Model who was exhibited the following year. Model was the first Basset to appear on the show bench in Britain. He was from the Couteulx kennels. This fine hound attracted much attention which resulted in many more joining the ranks of Basset fanciers.

In a letter to Mr. Croxton-Smith dated 1894, Sir Everett related that, due to a scarcity of the Basset at the time he imported Model, he bred this dog with a good-sized Beagle bitch. In 1877 he showed second generation hounds that were not distinguishable from Bassets. He gave up this strain when the Earl of Onslow imported a couple named Fino and Finette from Couteulx in 1877. Model was bred to Finette giving Millais his first purebred Basset bitch in lieu of a stud fee. She was named Garrenne. Lord Onslow kept her brother Proctor. From then on Millais began breeding in earnest. He was a true amateur and never sold a hound, preferring to give them to interested people. Isabel was produced from a union of Model and Garrenne in 1878. Lord Onslow's Fino was bred to Isabel. George Krehl imported Fino de Paris in 1880. With these the fanciers were able to guarantee the first Basset class in England at Wolverhampton this same year.

During these years Lord Onslow's kennel was under the care and management of Mr. T. Pick. He had been breeding a hound he imported named Juno. Millais referred to her as the most prolific Basset ever in the country though hardly the best. Her union with Proctor produced Cigarette. This hound was made famous through her daughter Medore who was bred to Fino VI producing Champions Forester, Fresco, Merlin, and Flora. Millais had a share in the breeding of Proctor. Cigarette was bred by Lord Onslow, Medore by Herbert Watson, Ch. Bourbon, Fino V, and Fino VI by George Krehl. F. B. Craven was the breeder of Ch. Forester, Fresco, Merlin, and Flora. Fresco died on his way to the Spa show. Merlin died in Melbourne, Australia, in 1892, having been sent there to found the Melbourne Basset Hound Pack. Forester and Flora were in Millais kennels. By 1886 the breed had prospered enough to find an entry of 120 hounds at the Aquarium show in London. The leading breeders had formed the Basset Hound Club two years earlier. Sir Everett later severed connections with the club because he believed it was not advancing kennel interests. Prior to this he had presented Mr. Arthur Croxton-Smith with a couple who were the parents of Champions Welbeck, Wensum, and Wantage.

By 1886 a difference in genetic makeup could be seen in the hounds. Fino de Paris had a pronounced Bloodhound-type head, heavier bone and build, thicker coat, and richer coloring than did George Krehl's four hounds secured from Lord Onslow. The latter were straighter in leg and shorter in ear. Though Model and Fino de Paris were brothers they and their progeny were not similar in type. Model and Fino were not Bloodhound type. The mating of Guinevere and Fino de Paris in 1882 produced Fino V and Bourbon. The problem of the two types of Couteulx hounds was discussed in an earlier chapter. Fino carried the Fino de Paris type. Bourbon took after his dam with lighter color, finer bone, thin skin and coat. This was the only litter Guinevere produced before her death. The best specimens thereafter date back to these two hounds.

In 1894 Sir Everett Millais resolved that twenty years of inbreeding had caused the Basset to deteriorate. The general mass of hounds had become below average in size. There was increasing difficulty in breeding and rearing them. Barrenness was becoming prevalent. When reared they succumbed to distemper in a most alarming manner. It was his opinion that French imports were far inferior to the English strains. Fresh blood from this source would be no benefit, thus a cross breeding was inevitable.

He chose to cross with the Bloodhound because the Basset head should closely resemble it. His experimental work with Beagles had previously proved that the return to Basset formation in legs was only a matter of one or two generations. Only the question of color remained a problem.

The first cross was between the Basset hound Nicolas, a son of Ch. Forester, and the Bloodhound bitch Inoculation. The puppies were produced by the method now known as artificial insemination. Twelve were born. They were nearer the Basset anatomy than the Bloodhound but all took after the dam in color.

The next cross was between Ch. Forester and his half-Basset granddaughter Rickey, a product of the first cross. Six puppies were tricolor, one black and tan, all of Basset anatomy.

Dulcie, one of this ¾ Basset and ¼ Bloodhound litter, was bred to the Basset named Bowman. The next cross was between a Dulcie-Bowman female and the Basset Hound Guignol. Of the six puppies born, four were tricolor, one lemon and white, and one black-and-tan. It was impossible to distinguish them from purebred Bassets.

Millais opined he had attained his purpose. The offspring of the four great sires, Fino de Paris, Fino V, Fino VI, and Forester, for the most part had not equalled the size and bone of the parent. By the use of the Bloodhound cross, both third and fourth generations were comparative in size to Forester.

Int. Ch. Sykemoor Blossom by Sykemoor Garnet (Trumpeter of Reynalton ex Ch. Rossingham Amber) ex Sykemoor Jealousy (Ch. Grims Whirlwind ex Sykemoor Gossip).

The influence in the American bloodline will be seen in the pedigree shown of Walhampton Ferryman, sire of Walhampton Andrew and Alice. From these descended such dogs as Maple Drive Murkey, Walhampton Aaron, Peggy Leach, Maple Drive Jigelo, Field Ch. Hillcrest Peggy, Ch. Westerby Vintage, Chausseur, Hartshead Masked Knight, Smith's Red Bear Tongue, and many more. Ch. Forester appears five times in the sixth generation.

Partial Pedigree of Walhampton Ferryman

		Sandringham Zero
	Walhampton Merryman	
		Mimi
Walhampton Ferryman		
		Walhampton Farmer
	Walhampton Freda	
		Walhampton Maizie

Other leading breeders at this time were Mrs. C. C. Ellis, Mr. Loet, Mr. Krehl, Mr. Kennedy, and Mr. Muirhead. At the turn of the century, the Basset was very strongly positioned and firmly established in Britain. Probably no other imported breed had such a sound foundation and this has surely had a lasting effect on the breed. The first fanciers were people of means and were able to buy the best hounds France had to offer.

In the early 1900s the principal breeders were Croxton-Smith, Mrs. Ellis who owned Chs. Zena, Paris, and Forester, Mrs. Walsh who had Ch. Bowman, and Mrs. Lubbock with her notables Locksley and Maid Marion. Mrs. Mabel Tottie had a strong kennel in Yorkshire that housed rough and smooth Bassets including Ch. Louis le Beau, Solomon, Napoleon II and Chs. Puritan, Priscilla and Pervance, and Tambour. The brothers Godfrey and Geoffrey Heseltine began to breed and hunt the Walhampton pack which became famous for decades. Their convictions were strong regarding the breed. Major Godfrey Heseltine later wrote that his brother,

279

Lt. Col. Christopher Heseltine, O.B.E., and he, joint Masters of the Walhampton Basset Hounds, resigned their membership in the B. H. C. because in spite of a rule passed by the club "that no unsound hound should be awarded a prize," judges continued to be appointed who disregarded this rule by giving top honors to hounds which were unsound and badly built in body and legs. These judges were accused of giving priority to dogs whose heads most closely resembled Bloodhounds', encouraging breeders to produce animals for the sole purpose of obtaining this point. The by-product of such a practice was the alarming weakness of the rest of the breed's conformation.

The Masters of Basset Hounds formed an Association about 1910. These fanciers kept hounds for hunting the hare. Lord North was President, the Hon. W. F. North, his son, compiled a stud book. Only hounds affiliated with the association were permitted to be entered in the stud book. North never completed compilation. In 1926 Major Heseltine produced the first volume.

This period was the crest of the wave for Bassets. H.R.H. Queen Alexandra was a regular exhibitor. Her Sandringham hounds were both rough and smooth. Sandringham Bobs, Babil, Dido, Vero, Vanity, and Weaver were all prominent in the show ring. In 1924 the Brancaster prefix of Miss Adams came to the fore. She based her kennel on Walhampton Zilla. At the same time, Mrs. Foster-Rawlins combined Dandie Dinmont Terriers and Bassets under her Potford prefix. Her Potford Ragout was used as a model for a Danish porcelain statuette of a Basset. Miss Adams bred Rob Roy and Rosabel of Reynalton first shown by Mrs. N. Elms in 1929. She also had a large kennel of Beagles and Bloodhounds and a fine stud of Arab horses. Another horse lover was Mrs. Edith Grew who established her Maybush kennel prior to the 1930s.

From 1900 to 1932 the Walhamptons had been steadily growing stronger. They bred judiciously and brought their pack to perfection for the show bench and for hunting. They believed that no Master should be entirely satisfied if he would continue to improve his pack. Godfrey Heseltine was a regular correspondent with leading French breeders. He made a series of three importations. The last occasion was 1920 when he introduced Meteor and Pampeute. The merging of English and French bloodlines was successful and resulted in a long line of famous hounds: Chs. Walhampton Andrew,

1923, Gratitude, 1925, Ambassador, 1928, and Lynnewood, 1931. Heseltine considered Nightshade to be the best Basset he had ever known. Overseas breeders made use of the fine Walhampton bloodlines. Among those exported to the U.S.A. were Chs. Walhampton Andrew and Linguist, Walhampton Ferryman, Walhampton Alice, Walhampton Abbot, Walhampton Dipper, and Walhampton Lawless. For over thirty years the Heseltines reigned supreme, until their untimely death in 1932 resulting in the dispersal of the pack.

Mrs. Elms and Mrs. Grew purchased some of the dogs at the dispersal sale. From then until the outbreak of World War II their kennels were all powerful. From two of her purchases, Walhampton Nightshade and Walhampton Lynnewood, Mrs. Elms bred the Reynalton hounds Ch. Orpheus and Venus, and from the same strain Chs. Monkshood, Minerva, Narcissus, and Amir whom she exported to the United States. She judged several times and always supported the Basset classes at major shows. At Crufts, in 1935, she entered no fewer than sixty Bassets, Beagles, and Bloodhounds. She had the secret of producing hounds of substance and great bone which continued to be known as the Reynalton influence.

Mrs. Edith Grew had the breed since childhood. Her Maybush hounds were well known. Among the Walhamptons she purchased were Ch. Walhampton Ambassador, the period's top Basset, Walhampton Nicknack, and Walhampton Grazier. These hounds were the ancestors of her Chs. Pigeon, Partridge, Patience, and Plover. Other good hounds bred by her were Maybush Mallard, Martha, Puffin, and Marcus. Marcus was exported to America. Mrs. Grew seemed to be dogged with misfortune in breeding dogs. It was doubly sad when the outbreak of war prevented her campaigning Maybush Musket, her favorite hound, reckoned to be the best she had ever bred.

The war saw the closing of many kennels and severe reductions in every breed. Only thirteen Bassets were registered in 1939, and seven in 1940. Mrs. Grew and Mrs. Elms managed to breed a few hounds during these dark years and the breed still had a nucleus at the cessation of hostilities. Advancing years, however, prevented the two brave old ladies from breeding many dogs so the task of reconstructing the breed fell on the shoulders of Miss Peggy Keevil.

New blood was unobtainable in Britain and the introduction of outcross blood was a prime necessity. Miss Keevil purchased three hounds from France, all tricolors. They were Ulema de Barley, 1946, bred by M. Mallant; Aiglon des Marriettes, 1951, from Mme. Raulin; and Cornemuse de Blendocques bred by M. Leduc. All were fine hounds and accomplished the rejuvenation of the breed. Ulema was a prepotent sire in France. He had the most influence on British Bassets, siring some grand hounds which included littermates Chs. Grims Westward and Whirlwind. Aiglon was litter brother to France's top sire Azur Des Mariettes. He too sired some good hounds. The bitch Cornemuse could not have such an apparent influence as the dogs but nevertheless played her part. These hounds, with those Miss Keevil already had, refounded the breed in Britain. By the early 1950s it was in a healthy, if not numerous, position. The Grims kennel of dual purpose was winning on the bench and hunting successfully. From the kennel have come an impressive list of champions: Chs. Grims Wishful, 1940; Grims Warlock, 1946; Grims Doughnut, 1947; Grims Waterwagtail, 1949; Grims Useful, 1950; Grims Wideawake, 1951; Grims Willow, 1951; Grims Whirlwind, 1954; Grims Westward, 1954; Grims Gracious; and Grims Vapid. Just as the Walhamptons dominated things in their day, the Grims did in the 1950s and 1960s.

In the early 1950s the breed gradually crept out of the shadows. In 1953 Mrs. Angela Hodson was chiefly responsible for forming the Basset Hound Club. The original club had been disbanded in 1921 owing to a split between the show bench and hunting fraternities. Mrs. Hodson had the Rossingham kennels and was first Secretary ,of the reformed club. She was most fortunate in having Ch. Grims Willow in her kennel. This fine bitch bred Champions Rossingham Amber, Rossingham Badger, U.S. Ch. Rossingham Barrister and Rossingham Blessing, India Ch. Rossingham Brocade, and Rossingham Cosy. Amber and Badger in turn produced more champions. The Rossingham line had plenty of size and length, good bone, and quality.

Among the first to support the new club was the old stalwart Mrs. Grew. She was still keen though no longer breeding dogs. It was a sad blow when she passed away January 23, 1963.

Another to join the ranks was George Johnston who had owned some Reynalton hounds in 1939. He and his son, George Jr., disbanded their well-known kennel of Dandie Dinmonts and began breeding their Sykemoor Bassets. Rossingham Amber became a champion in their hands and was behind almost every Sykemoor hound. Mr. Johnston Sr. died in 1958 but his son kept the kennel going and bred Int. Ch. Sykemoor Blossom, Ch. Sykemoor Aimwell and Wiza. He exported many hounds that became champions in other countries. In 1959 he imported a young French hound named Hercule de L'Ombree. The Basset Hound Club purchased Lyn-Mar Acres Dauntless from the U.S.A. These two hounds proved useful outcrosses and produced winning progeny. Another- addition to the already available American lines in Britain was Int. Ch. Bold Turpin of Blackheath imported by Mesdames McArthur-Onslow and Kewley. All three were fused successfully and were a decided advantage to the breed.

One of the last available Reynalton stud hounds was owned by Mrs. Wendy Jagger. With him and the Grims hounds she built up her noted Fochno kennel. Ch. Grims Whirlwind was her popular stud hound. Trumpeter of Reynalton was a valuable link with the past. Whirlwind sired Chs. Fochno Trinket and Trooper. This perfectly matched blue-mottled pair were virtually unbeatable and won many Brace classes. Trooper sired champions in the Grims kennel. Trinket produced winning puppies. Fochno stock founded kennels in Australia, Italy, U.S.A., and India.

The Townsons and their Kelperland prefix were also well known in Bloodhounds. Their Rossingham Badger was the first to attain the high honor of Best of Opposite Sex in Show at Windsor in 1958. He was the pillar of the kennel appearing in the pedigrees of most Kelperland hounds including Chs. Kelperland Artful and Baneful, Kelperland Blazer, and others. Their Bloodhound, Ch. Kelperland Scarcity, was reckoned to be one of the best ever bred up to that time.

Mrs. Hodson relinquished the post of Club Secretary which was filled by Mrs. Margaret Rawle of Minehead. Despite being a busy farmer's wife, she still found time to look after the interests of the club and her Barnspark hounds. She owned two Grims champions, Gracious and Vapid. From these were produced Ch. Barnspark Rakish, Vanity, Rollick, Rustic, Charity, and Teddyboy. Her export, Barnspark Loyalty, was a winner in Scandinavia and Barnspark Rambler gained a championship in the area.

Another great supporter and regular exhibitor was Mr. John Evans and the Stalwart hounds. He also had a celebrated kennel of

Ch. Fochno Trinket, a Crufts winner, with owner,
Mrs. Wendy Jagger. Sire, Ch. Grims Whirlwind;
dam, Sykemoor Gossip.

Ch. Grims Whirlwind, considered one of the top sires in England.

Bulldogs. With Grims blood and American bloodlines he bred Ch. Stalwart Debbie, exported to Italy, Stalwart Anna, Hardy, Hopeful, Blazer, and many others. Keen on the working side, he whipped-in for the Basset Hound Club Working Branch and organized many meets. Mr. Evans also managed West Lodge Hare Hounds for Lionel Woolner. This pack was bred from Bassets, Beagles, and Harriers. A type was established that reproduced itself and proved ideal for fast hunting.

One cannot give a complete resume of all the British kennels. Those mentioned are the oldest. Hounds from them can be found in many pedigrees. Their stock was used to found other kennels in Britain and abroad. It would be only fair to give mention to some of the later kennels which became ardent supporters. In Scotland were the Crochmaid dogs owned by Mrs. McArthur-Onslow and her daughter Mrs. Kewley. Mrs. McKnight had the Chantinghalls. The sole Irish kennel to the time of this book was Ballymaconnell operated by Mrs. Bridgham. The Harraton kennels of Messrs. Frost and Bell, Dalewell belonging to Mrs. Beard, and Robert Varon and Mr. Ghent's Highpeak were in the north and midlands of England. In the southern area were the kennels of Breightmet owned by Mrs. Baynes, Fredwell by Mrs. Wells, Mrs. Hunt and her Hunters-brook hounds, Mrs. Matthews carried the Hardacre prefix, Mrs. Rowett-Johns the Wingjays, and Mrs. Seiffert had the Maycombes. There were the Cornmeade breedings of W. W. Wells and the Appeline hounds of Mr. & Mrs. Douglas Appleton. Mrs. M. Nuttall bred from the Grims line. Stalwart Carol bred to Janvrins Dasher, both descendants from this line, produced Fivefold Chipmunk which was exported to the U.S. and acquired by your author. Gerard Kemp of Surrey became active and adopted the Buzbuz affix. His experience as a reporter for the "Daily Mail" made him the logical editor of the Basset Hound Club newsletter. His young wife, Sheila, took an active interest in the club's Working Branch.

Almost a century after the first Bassets were introduced into Britain, the breed registration for the year exceeded 800. Mrs. Sieffert was the Basset Hound Club Secretary, and the membership exceeded 300.

The Working Branch is the hunting group of the club and is discussed in the next chapter. The Basset Hound Club awards Working Certificates to hounds which prove themselves able hunters.

SIZES OF EARLY BRITISH BASSETS

	Onslow's NESTOR	Onslow's FINO	Millais's MODEL	Millais's GARRENNE	Ch. BOURBON	BLONDIN	BERTILLE	THEO
age	3	4½	7½	2½	4½	2½	3	8½
weight	39	39	46	38	40	35	33	35
height at shoulder	14	13	12	9¼	12	12	11	13
length nose to croup	36	33	32	29	35	33	33	35
girth of chest	24	24	25	24	25	23	22	22
girth of loin	22	23	21	16	19½	19½	19	19½
girth of head	15½	16½	17	13	15	14	14	13
girth of forearm	6½	6	6½	5	6	5½	5½	5
length occiput to tip	9	10	9	8	8½	8½	8½	8
girth of muzzle	9	8½	9½	7	8	8	7	6½
length of tail	12	11	11½	9	11½	12	11½	11
ears tip to tip			19	17	20	19	21	18½
height of forefeet			2½	2½	2½	3½	3	4

Ch. Long View Acres Bonza (Ch. Abbot Run Valley Brassy ex
Ch. Kazoo's Flora Tina) was another American-bred that went to
England. Bred by C. J. Collee, Bonza won well prior to his ex-
patriation. He is shown here with the author just after taking BW
at the Western Michigan Specialty.

Frank

Long View Acres Rioter Braun, an American-bred Basset that was
exported to England to provide a valuable outcross for British
hounds. He is shown here with the author.

To become a bench champion a hound must win three Challenge Certificates under three different judges. Challenge Certificates are offered for competition by the Kennel Club at Championship shows, one for Dogs and one for Bitches. A judge is entitled to withhold any award if he does not feel the quality is good enough. Champions can compete with the other hounds. The winners of the various classes are called back to compete against other class winners of their own sex. Best Dog and Best Bitch receive Challenge Certificates. They then compete against each other for the Best of Breed award. The Best of Breed winner is then eligible to compete for Best Hound, and the Hound Group winner competes for Best in Show as in the United States.

In the late 1960s, Keith Frost and Trevor Howard imported three more dogs from the United States. Ch. Long View Acres Bonza (Ch. Abbot Run Valley Brassy ex Ch. Kazoo's Flora Tina) was sent by Chris Teeter and Joseph Braun. His get were sent to several other countries. Among his daughters were the top winning bitches Ch. Langpool Miss American Pie and Ch. Langpool Carrie Anne, both out of Dr. Elizabeth Andrews' Balleroy Barshaw Caprice. A young bitch out of Ch. Long View Acres Kokomo Joe ex Ch. Double B's Fun and Fancy was sent by the author. Later a young dog named Long View Acres Rioter Braun (Am. & Can. Ch. Long View Acres Kinston ex Long View Acres Bambi, a Banshee daughter) was sent out.

Ch. Dreymin Appeline Coral, daughter of Grims Lager (Lyn-Mar Acres Dauntless ex Grims Glamour) ex Appeline Dawn (Int. Ch. Crochmaid Bold Turpin of Blackheath ex Appeline Serious). Both grandsires were U.S. imports.

17

British Working Meets

THE field activities in Great Britain differ from those in the United States. The Working Meet is the equivalent of our Field Trial. Gerard Kemp, editor of the Basset Hound Club's newsletter in 1964, describes the activities as follows:

"There are only two packs of purebred Basset hounds at present being hunted in Britain. Both of them are built around the Grim's pack of Miss Peggy Keevil, one of the country's foremost breeders who lives in Inkpen, new Newbury, in Berkshire.

"Miss Keevil has loaned a bitch pack to friends in Gloucestershire and, herself, hunts with her main pack which forms the nucleus of the Basset Hound Club pack.

"Both packs hunt hares. The hunt staff in each case consists of a huntsman (responsible for the whole operation) and his 'whippers-in.' These usually number three or four and are the runners that move on the flanks of the hunt to prevent hounds straying or shooting off after distractions or causing trouble. They carry whips, more for cracking than actually striking hounds.

"The people who support the club hunts (also known as meets) travel from all over Britain, some staying overnight in hotels. Each time the hunt is held, it is in a different part of the country.

"The hounds hunt only hares. An average of about thirty people turn out each time to follow across the countryside on foot. Sometimes the followers have been known to cover as much as ten miles.

"The club has recently introduced a hunt uniform: traditional black hunting cap, white stock, with brown hunting jacket and yellow collars, white breeches, and brown knee-length stockings. Footwear is light studded boots. The huntsman carries a small copper hunting horn which he uses during the meet as a signal to hounds, 'whippers-in,' and followers.

"Miss Keevil drives her van to each meet and unloads about six or seven 'couple' of hounds, that is about twelve or fourteen dogs. These hounds are joined by those brought along by club members. The total number of hounds turning out is usually about fifteen to twenty couple. The introduction of a string of individual Bassets, to a pack trained to hunting, means that the hunt is straightaway handicapped. Over half the hounds turning out on a meet may have little idea of going in a hunting pack. The club's hunt staff realizes this only too well. The number of individual Bassets that, in fact, fall in with the Grim's hounds (all old hands at the hunting game) varies from meet to meet. Sometimes the hounds all seem to get the idea from the start; sometimes about half are left behind to hang around their owners, frolick with the other Bassets, or shoot off in other directions after odd rabbits or hares that the pack is not hunting; occasionally the situation arises where the trained Grim's hounds are going full steam after the hare, accompanied only by two or three couple of member's hounds.

"The Working Branch, as this section of the club is called, have weighed the pros and cons of all this and have come to the conclusion that more good is done by persevering with an attempt to encourage *all* the Bassets to do the job they were bred for, rather than taking out only *pack* hounds. After a few meets, the hunt's staff is rewarded by the knowledge that there are Basset Hounds (even ones who live in cities) that will hunt with the best of them.

"Our club chairman, Alex McDonald, who is also the Huntsman with the Working Branch pack, has recently written an appraisal of the practical side of hunting such a mixed bag. This is part of what he had to say, 'I am only too well aware that in trying to hunt a pack of six or seven couple of hounds that know me, and are entered to hare (put to hunt) together, with further hounds that

290

neither know me nor a hare, I am being foolish to a degree. The chances of achieving good hunting under these conditions are minimal. I am astonished at every meet when we have a good run lasting maybe forty-five minutes. Why do I do it? The answer is not easily set out in detail but the main thing is that I believe the Basset should be kept as a working breed. To see a really happy Basset, you have to see him hunting; and I want members of the Club and Basset lovers, generally, to see this for themselves. I maintain that, until you have seen a Basset pack hunting, it is impossible for you to know and understand the Basset hound.

'There is a choice to be made between the club managing a professional pack and continuing with the quaint compromise which we now have of trying to weld together something of a regular pack plus anything else that turns up on the day. The implications of the first choice would be that we tried to stick to one part of the country and concentrated on building up a small, but regular, band of enthusiasts each with perhaps one or two couple of real workers. This would, I am sure, give much better hunting and make for far more kills. If we continue on the general lines of the past two or three seasons, we can only do so if the support we get from members takes a more helpful form.'

"Mr. McDonald's excellent account goes on to give general advice to novices turning out on hunting days. Always allow plenty of room around Miss Keevil's van when her pack hounds are unloaded. This is so that the 'whippers-in' will have a chance to move about. Members who think their hounds will go with the pack are advised to unleash their hounds to mingle with the Grims hounds. However, any signs of skittishness or nervousness and they are advised to clap the hound back on the lead straight away. Should a member's hound suddenly shoot off down the road giving tongue after a cat—and takes the pack with him—then the huntsman is quite definitely not amused.

"He goes on to give this practical advice to newcomers: 'We go into a field and I start to draw (work) with the regular hounds. If yours is a real novice, that has not hunted before, then keep him on a lead. If he is loose he won't know what it is all about and will make the job of the whippers-in far more difficult. Keep quiet and get about twenty yards behind me. Watch the hounds and when one gives tongue and the others go to him, picking up speed

291

as I start trotting, then let yours go. With luck, we shall be away. If the hare scent is stale and we have to draw again, watch your hound carefully. He may come back to you, but, don't rate him (scold him), let him stay and run him up to the pack when they give tongue and are away again. Above all, keep him under control.'

"The worst thing, Mr. McDonald says, is for the hound to start hunting on his own hare independently of the main pack. Followers should do everything possible to avoid this: 'Make no mistake: a large field following behind the pack, particularly over plough, will put up hares very often indeed. Let me know by raising your hand above your head, by all means, but try to keep your hound quiet. At last, the pack is away, hunting fairly well. Your hound will have gone with them, in which case you should keep up as best you can so that, at the first check, you will be able to make sure your own hound is there. But, be careful, don't let him see or hear you. If he does, he may stop working and return to you. On the other hand, if this is your first meet, your hound may not have joined the pack. The only thing you can do is to keep your hound under control and try to be in position to turn him loose when the pack are near and in full cry.

'After about half an hour's run, during which time the hunt may have gone in a complete circle, the pace has dropped. Hounds are casting themselves, that is to say, they are spreading out a little, noses down, some of them feathering. This is the tricky part. I am standing still just inside the field. My whipper-in is just visible, halfway up the hedge, and, on the other side, another whipper-in can be seen streaking for the far corner on the far side of the other hedge. To the novice, it may look dull and boring. Nothing seems to be going on. The novices start to talk. Hounds lift their heads to listen and I am furious. It is, in fact, a critical moment. We all know that we are close to a tiring hare and, with patience and concentration, we shall find and kill. The novices get bored, breaking the concentration. This is the time to keep outside the field where the hounds are and quietly watch them through a gap in the hedge. Study them, see their different styles, watch Melody feather and whimper. See Gaffer go to her and try. Melody gives a funny yelp and they all go to her. Celery confirms the line and they are off again.

'A hunted hare plays a lot of tricks, but Bassets will work out most of them if so allowed. A hare may double back, and if the followers keep too close, the hounds' task becomes nearly impossible. Very often, when hounds are busy, followers will see a hare nearby in the next field. The best thing for them to do is to keep quiet. They should only let me know if they are absolutely certain the hare is the one being hunted.

'There are many times when it is most helpful if the followers join in and do something. For example, if hounds are heading for the road, and a follower is favourably placed, he can stop traffic. Again, if the pack splits up and a solitary hound is seen to slip off alone, a follower can tail it and send it back either by shouting 'Get to him' or slipping a lead around the hound's neck.' "

Mr. Kemp finished his article with another hunting expert's comments on overdoing the "holloaing," the term used when a hare is seen: "Recently I read about a brace of hare jumping up in the first field drawn. Hounds went away in view, but two groups of followers started to 'holloa,' then three more hares got up and more people 'holloaed,' until, each group was 'holloaing' its own particular hare and pandemonium was rife. The kindest thing to say about these particular vocalists is that they were quite inexperienced and that nobody told them anything. It does not require a very prolonged course of this sort of thing before the hounds become very flashy and wild, and, as Frostyface said of Mr. Puffington's hounds, 'always staring about for holloas and assistance.' A truly dreadful state of affairs."

The advice, offered by the authorities on Working Meets, should be carefully considered by the novices who plan to enter into the field work in countries that pattern their Working Branch after the British.

18

The Basset Hound
in France

W E have already established how the Agasaeus and the Segusian spread from the Rhone district throughout the rest of France and other countries. As we study the topography of these countries, we can understand why some areas nurtured the griffons while others preferred the smooth coats.

In areas such as Ardennes, Artois, Saintonge, and Gascony, the smooth coat was a useful little hound. The terrain was grassy; much of it was fields, farmlands, and woods. The breeders in these provinces concentrated on the body structure and coloring that best suited their individual fancy and developed the characteristics that made up the distinctive strains.

The rocky land and thorny growth found in Brittany and Vendee called for a very different coat. Here the Griffon coat was necessary to protect the little dogs from the elements. Again the breeders concentrated on the points which they favored and by selective breeding developed their particular variety.

One thing all Frenchmen agree upon is that the Basset should be more agile than the dogs found in England and America. They prefer a smaller, lighter-boned hound. Throughout many writings on the subject of their use in the field, these dogs were expected to capture the hare. They often ran for hours, even days, in their pursuit, though they were also used to drive the game before the bowman's shaft in the days before gunpowder. Authors of books on sporting dogs have high praise for the work of the Basset.

Even in modern times, his work in the field is a mark of his quality. You will note that the Basset Griffon-Vendeen must pass certain tests before he is enscribed. The breeders of this variety, even now, set his price according to his hunting abilities. The Basset in France remains a useful, unspoiled-by-the-show-ring dog. Beauty, to the Frenchman, is based upon the attributes which best enable the dog to do a good day's work.

As time went on, some of the characteristics that were peculiar to certain varieties were found to be less desirable than those of others. These varieties began to die out while the others became more popular. In the mid-twentieth century, the most popular variety in France was the Basset Griffon-Vendeen. The Artesien-Normand was second in popularity. The Fauve de Bretagne and the Bleu de Gascogne have enough supporters to maintain a club to guard their purity, but they are definitely in a minority group.

Although I have used the term "variety" because it is an expression familiar to the American reader, in reality these are distinctly different breeds of Bassets. Even the Dachshund is often called a Basset by the French.

By 1967, still another breed had gained enough fanciers to form a club. This breed was recognized by the name Basset Hound.

Twentieth Century Developments in France

The French, in general, do not look on hounds as pets. This may seem strange to American and British fanciers. Hounds are common enough in the countryside yet no hound breed is truly high up on the popularity list.

Thanks to "an American in Paris," the following pages may give us a better insight regarding the Basset d'Artois, the Basset Artesien-Normand, and the new Basset Hound. Mr. John Miller refers to himself as "a West Coast dog lover, non-hunter and former Beagle owner, living in Paris since 1960, and the caretaker of a $2\frac{1}{2}$ year old English-bred Basset Hound." Mme. T. A. Peress, Secretary of the Club du Basset Hound, was kind enough to prevail upon him to write. Mr. Miller is a committee member of that club.

The rich French tradition in hounds and hunting differs, in many ways, from the Anglo-Saxon. To appreciate the place of the Basset Hound, in France, one must study both the breeds and the prevailing customs. The Basset Hound is finding acceptance even though the criteria for judging often differs from that of the English-speaking world. This is a tribute to the universal appeal of the breed. Remember, the name Basset Hound, used in this chapter and the next, refers to the newest breed and should not be confused with the Basset d'Artois nor the Basset Artesien-Normand.

In 1930, Standards for French Hounds, prepared jointly by the *Societe de Venerie* and the *Societe Centrale Canine,* listed both the Basset d'Artois and the Basset Artesien-Normand. The Societe de Venerie voiced dissatisfaction in the Basset d'Artois but indicated it would prefer to see the Basset Artesien-Normand lose its mixed characteristics and become a pure Basset Normand by taking on the characteristics of the larger Normand Hound and a Standard was drawn up about 1925. The *Club du Basset Artesien-Normand* felt that they had a perfectly acceptable dog and paid no attention to the Societe de Venerie. They continued in the same lines.

The Basset d'Artois, however, had neither fixed model nor club. In the following years, the dogs became so heterogeneous that, by 1937, it could no longer be considered a single breed. In 1938, the Societe Centrale struck it from the list of recognized breeds. Some breeders remained dedicated and attempts were made to revive the breed. However, during World War II, most of the little remaining stock was lost or dispersed.

There are still dogs, undoubtedly mixtures of the Basset d'Artois and the Basset Artesien-Normand, that are called Basset d'Artois by their owners. They are uniformly big, heavy dogs weighing 70 to 80 pounds. They give the impression that, had the breed continued under favorable circumstances, it would have become the equivalent of the new Basset Hound.

The 1951 Standards noted a tendency for the Basset Artesien-Normand to become smaller and lighter. These Bassets, currently seen in Northwestern France, are small-boned and lively, weighing about 35 pounds. Their heads are somewhat different from those of their ancestors. This breed's Standard never required a marked occiput. It merely said that the occiput was often apparent. The result is that it is now rarely found. However, the ear mania has caught on and ears have now become long and soft. By 1970, the whole general appearance changed considerably from the 1929 study by Busson.

Registration and Shows in France

The French Kennel Club is called the Societe Centrale Canine. It is a federation composed of regional canine societies and Specialty clubs. The Societe Centrale keeps a stud book called the *Livre d'Origine Francais* (LOF). Each breed is numbered separately.

Puppies are declared within a month after birth with their names and noseprints being sent to the Societe Centrale. A provisional entry is made in the LOF and the official birth certificates are sent to the breeder. The first letter of the dog's name must indicate the year of birth (T in 1970, U in 1971). When the dog is a year old, it may be "confirmed," as being a representative of the breed, by an accredited judge. If confirmed, the dog may then be permanently entered in the LOF.

In order to permit development of new breeds, there is also an initial register, called the *Registre Initial* (RI). Unpedigreed dogs may be entered if they are judged at least "good." If the dog breeds true, as shown by three generations accepted in the RI, the fourth generation is transferred to the LOF procedure.

The main function of the regional societies is to organize shows. The annual Paris show is the only one sponsored directly by the Societe Centrale. No regional society may hold a show in Paris. Clubs may organize Specialties in the regional shows and propose the judges for these events.

Shows in France are casual affairs. Mrs. Linda Benabdi, who now resides in the United States, told me that the judging, at the shows she attended, was closed to the public. When the judging was completed, and the prizes handed out, the dogs were returned to their cages before the public was allowed to enter and tour the arena. The judges touched the dogs very little, only to examine the teeth, ears, and eyes closely. Otherwise, great stress was put on movement. According to Mr. Miller, a dog is eligible to participate in shows when it is old enough to be "confirmed" as described previously. It may not receive points, however, before the age of 15 months. Show classes are open, young (12 to 14 months for most breeds), national-bred (foreign breeds from French kennels), working (for dogs holding working certificates), champion, reproducer (dog or bitch and three offspring), couples (two), group (three or more); pack (six or more scent hounds), and breeders (any three from the same kennel). Couples, group, and pack classes require that the entrants are owned by the same person. There is no officially sanctioned competition between sexes or breeds. Dogs, in the ring, are first grouped according to the judge's opinion of their quality and rated "excellent," "very good," "good," "relatively good," or "insufficient." The first four dogs in each group are ranked. The Best of Breed are the open class "First Excellents." The judge may award certificates, counting for beauty honors, to the first place winners, only if he considers them exceptional, worthy dogs. There are two kinds of certificates. In shows held under national auspices, the CAC award counts toward a national championship. A CACIB award is given at shows held under international auspices. It also counts as a CAC. The second place dogs may be awarded "reserve" certificates. These are for much the same purpose as the American Reserve Winners.

In order to become a national beauty champion, a hound is required to earn three CAC awards, under two different judges, with at least one of the CACs from the Paris show, plus a working certificate, called the *brevet de chasse* (BC). Rules governing a meet, for the BC, are described in the chapter on the Basset Griffon-Vendeen. Under recently established rules, a hound must score "excellent" in two meets before it is awarded the title of working champion. To become an international champion, a hound must also gain two CACIBs, in two different countries, under two different judges.

The necessity of gaining a working certificate often excludes otherwise worthy dogs from becoming champions. It has become more difficult, and very expensive, to set up these meets. Many dogs have completed their show requirements but their owners have found it impossible to arrange for their meets. The requirement of a BC, however, does insure that French hounds will not develop such exaggerations as to render them incapable of performing the breed's work. While this system has its merits, it does have its drawbacks. For the French, who place great emphasis on a working hound, this plan apparently works.

19

The "New" Basset Hound

THE INTERNATIONAL Canine Federation, of which France was one of the founding members, considers the Basset Hound, as we know it, as an American breed and entirely distinct from the four other remaining native French Bassets. In France, the Basset Hound is simply one of 41 officially recognized scent hound breeds. In spite of the common origin, the Basset Hound is different from the livelier, faster, more highly strung Basset Artesien-Normand, which Mr. Miller compares with the American 13″ Beagle. The Standard for the Basset Hound, which was adopted by the International Canine Federation, is the same as that of the American Kennel Club.

It is felt that the first dogs, to make their homes in France, were American, taken there and left by their owners. They first appeared in the late 1950s. The first to be registered in the LOF was Mascot von Hertzogtum, a German-bred dog, of Anglo-French production, by Agile des Mariettes ex Merit of Kimblewick. This dog was imported by Mr. Douglas Walker-Macran in 1958.

The first to be born, and eventually registered, in France was

Seulement dit Soliman LOF 4, bred by Mr. Clayton Fasker, in April 1957, by Warwick Fernando ex Sabrina Fair. In 1961, Count D'Andlau, in Strassburg, acquired and registered Warwick Fernando (Sheira of Lyn Mar Acres ex Lyn Mar Acres Lustre), Sabrina Fair (Ch. Meyer's Kasko Kid ex Delanter's Marsh Run Ruby), and Seulement. Count d'Andlau did not use his dogs for breeding. None of these first four played a part in the subsequent development of the breed in France.

In 1961, five English hounds were imported. Mr. Walker-Macran acquired Breightmet Weaver. Grims Vintage and Grims Viscompte went to Danny Robin. M. de Keguelin de Rozieres imported Grims Vocal and Barnspark Chorister. With these he founded the first Basset Hound kennel in France, under the name of Gue Pean. The first registered litter was produced by Mr. Walker-Macran from a mating of his Breightmet Weaver to M. de Rozieres' Barnspark Chorister in 1962.

M. Paul Liot, who was unfamiliar with the breed, had an opportunity to hunt with two bitches, Nathalie and Olympe, from M. de Keguelin's kennel. He then purchased them because he was so captivated by their work. With the aid of M. de Keguelin, he was able to find a suitable stud dog, William the Marquis. With these he founded his Doucigny Kennel, in 1966.

At about the same time, Mr. Anthony Burstall, who was well acquainted with the breed in England, imported three of the Langstone hounds: Idol, Jupiter and Maxwell. He founded his Rocheneuve Kennel with these dogs.

Until recently, these three kennels formed the backbone of Basset Hound breeding in France. The dogs mentioned before are to be found in most French pedigrees today.

Progress, in breeding, was slow. The quarantine in England made it impossible to use English stud dogs. The currency restrictions, in France, made it difficult to import dogs. In spite of this, there was a gradual renovation in breeding stock. Three new kennels had been founded by 1971. Substance was gained through the use of Lyn-Mar Acres Sir Profumo who was owned by M. Baudoin in Belgium. High hopes were placed in Houndsville Delayed Edition who was imported by Mme. Peress and was eligible for stud service in April 1971.

It soon became apparent that the breed could not prosper, in an orderly fashion, unless a club was formed. The judges, for instance, rarely had the opportunity to see the Standard. M. Liot, who had become interested in the Basset Hound because of its hunting ability, recognized the difficulties. Together with M. de Keguelin de Rozieres and Mme. Thelma Peress, agreed to assist in forming the *Club du Basset Hound.* A provisional executive committee was formed with M. Liot, President; M. de Keguelin de Rozieres and Mr. Burstall, Vice-presidents; and M. Albert Peress, Executive Secretary. The club was registered with the Societe Centrale in June of 1967. The first general assembly was held in November. At this time, M. de Keguelin de Rozieres felt that he lacked the time necessary to continue in his position. He was replaced by M. Lamberteaux. The other officers were confirmed in their functions. They remained in these offices for many years to come. The membership grew from eighty, in 1968, to approximately 150, in 1971. Mme. Thelma Peress, who served as Corresponding Secretary, is largely accredited with the success of the club. By 1971, the club was producing one bulletin and four newsletters a year. It patronizes at least three shows each year and holds a meeting in June, near Paris, for members, friends, families and hounds.

In spite of these efforts, up to this writing there have been no Basset Hound champions in France. The fanciers have not been able to set up a meet so that the hounds could qualify for their working certificates. There were, however, three dogs qualified in conformation that showed marked hunting ability.

At one time Bassets have been the laughing stock of the crowd when a hound would accompany a group of hunters setting out in the morning. By the end of the hunt, it was usually the most admired of the hounds participating. The general feeling is that Bassets prove very useful in the somewhat wooded country where the game they push has sufficient cover to move in rather restricted circles. There is a scarcity of hunting rights in parts of France and the fee for their use is high. Using Basset Hounds offers the hunter the advantage of keeping both the hounds, and the game, in a smaller area. Bassets have been used in France for roebuck and boar as well as hare and rabbit. M. Liot's dogs also performed well on stag.

The chief priority of the club is the education of the public, the judges, and the breeders. A considerable amount of effort was directed towards getting owners to register and show their dogs. The club was fortunate in having the enthusiasm and cooperation of its members. The Basset Hound rapidly became the most frequently shown of the hunting breeds in France, in terms of percent of total registrations. By 1977, there were about 2000 registered Basset Hounds in France and the club membership had grown to 200. Twelve hounds qualified for their brevet de chasse during the 1977 season.

Only one champion of each sex can be made in each year because one of the requirements is a win at the annual Paris show. As of 1977, there were only six French Basset Hound champions due to this regulation, until International Ch. Tarza Beau Monde, owned by the Bergs, Americans residing in Belgium, won the honor.

Houndsville Delayed Edition, another American dog, who was owned by Mme. Peress, was one of the finest dogs in the country. He never gained a championship due to the brevet de chasse requirement. He sired only one litter, but the offspring had an excellent effect on the breed by producing heavy bone in their puppies.

Two other American imports were Jagersven Angelique and Jagersven Lafayette, both out of Ch. Glenhi's Tom Tom of Glenhaven ex Jagersven's Empress, sent by Finn and Mary Lou Bergishagen.

20

The Basset of Saint Hubert or the Ardennais

THE Basset of Saint Hubert is a very old variety. It was preserved for a long time in the Ardennes but has now vanished. Its disappearance was probably largely due to its color which could be confused with the quarry in dense cover. These dogs were either shiny black-and-tan or uniformly red copper. Lacking in white, they were more difficult to see in heavy brush.

They were named in honor of the patron saint of the Abbey of St. Hubert in the province of Ardennes. It is your author's opinion that they descended from the hounds brought to the abbey when St. Hubert established it. He selected hounds from the Rhone district where the smooth-coat Agasaeus was known to have been. Undoubtedly, by selective breeding, he developed the type known as the Basset of St. Hubert, from the Agasaeus which was described as being a sorry-shaped, smooth-coated, low, slow-moving brute.

The Basset of St. Hubert was noted for its tremendous endurance.

It was able to hunt for several days without tiring. Its disposition was simple. It was used for hare hunting and was evidently first-class on roe. The Marquis de Fourdras praised the variety highly in his hunting tales.

Compared to the other very early varieties of Bassets, the St. Hubert's head was extremely large and the muzzle square. Its body was much heavier. The ear was set low, but not quite so low as the Gascogne. The voice was very strong, though the tone was slightly dull.

Description of the Basset of St. Hubert

GENERAL APPEARANCE—a strong dog very much of the Saint Hubert in miniature.

QUALITIES—straight on the track, fairly fast, very demanding, an excellent dog for hare and roe.

HEAD—well developed, large, but not wide.

SKULL—high and narrow, the occipital bone well developed.

MUZZLE—well developed, straight forehead.

EYES—brown, eyelids very loose.

NOSE—black, nostrils very open.

FLEWS—hanging and prominent.

EARS—long, soft, well set and pendant.

NECK—powerful, always with dewlaps.

SHOULDERS—sloping and dry.

BODY—strong (full), back wide, chest deep, abdomen slightly tucked up, quarters very muscular.

FORELEGS—half-crooked.

FEET—strong and closed (clenched), very sturdy.

TAIL—well set and carried with elegance.

COAT—short and dense on the body, finer on the skull.

COLOR—black-and-tan or reddish.

HEIGHT—about 14 inches.

ORIGIN—the Ardennes.

21

The Basset
Saintongeois

THIS is another of the French smooth coat varieties that has all but entirely vanished. At one time, it was popular in the province for which it was named, Saintonge, located on the western coast of France between Vendee and Gascony. The Saintongeois closely resembled the Bleu de Gascogne. Its smooth coat was black-and-white-mottled, though the ticking was not as profuse as that of the Gascogne, nor the black patches on the cloak as large. It was more vivid in color. The eye was brighter. The voice was loud and clear, high-pitched, rising to a howl when excited. The Saintongeois was slightly larger in size than the Gascogne.

This little hound was eager and industrious and fast on the track. In temperament, however, it was more delicate than other varieties and often lacked courage. This may be the chief reason for its disappearance.

Alain Bourbon favored these colorful hounds and bred them, as well as the Gascogne and the Artois, at his Villa of St. Hubert in Mayenne. A cross between the Saintongeois and the Gascogne proved a successful combination of the qualities of type and those of the hunt.

The present French Standard for the Artesian-Normand (formerly known as the Basset of Artois) disqualifies any ticking on the body that resembles blue-mottling. It is quite possible that this extremely impressive type of marking, seen in the American Basset, may have resulted from Bourbon's crosses between the Saintongeois, the Bleu de Gascogne, and the Artois, and was carried by imports from his bloodlines.

Description of the Basset Saintongeois

GENERAL APPEARANCE—pretty dog, a little lighter than the other varieties.
APTITUDES—powerful voice, very good on the track.
HEAD—very dry.
SKULL—narrow.
EYES—brown, dark, may sometimes be lighter.
NOSE—black, nostrils open.
FLEWS—well developed.
EARS—attached low, pendant, shorter than the Gascogne.
VOICE—high and clear, very noisy.
NECK—long and thin with less dewlap than the Gascogne.
SHOULDER—dry.
CHEST—deep but not very wide.
BACK—sufficiently long and firm.
BELLY—tucked up.
THIGH—massive and muscular.
BODY—long but not exaggerated.
FORELEGS—half-crooked.
FEET—harefoot.
COAT—fine and dense.
COLOR—black-and-tan, without cloak, will have some tan spots in undercoat.
HEIGHT—12 to 14 inches.
ORIGIN—Saintogne.

22

The Basset
Bleu de Gascogne

THESE very striking little smooth coat hounds were, like others, named for the region in which they became popular. Gascony is a province located along the southern west coast of France. The terrain is suited to a smooth coat variety.

The Gascogne is somewhat smaller than the Artois. Though the latter is sometimes slightly mottled, the two are very different in type. The Gascogne always has a black head, black ears, and shows tan points over the eyes and on the cheeks. The body is always blue-mottled bearing large black spots. They are lighter in build than the Artois. The muzzle is snipier, a marked distinction.

The breed was almost extinct when M. Alain Bourbon, some time in the early 1900s, set to work to revive it. To accomplish this, he crossed Artois dogs with Gascogne bitches. Through many generations of selective breeding, he worked back toward the Gascogne type which has become well-fixed and very uniform.

The breed's coloring is seen in the American Basset, leading one to believe that this variety is in the background of our bloodlines. The Gascogne is noted for its particularly musical cry, and is very agile in the field.

307

Though the Gascogne is not the most abundant smooth coat in France, it is, in your author's opinion, the most eye-catching. It is one of the few varieties still pure in that country. The principal guardians of the variety belong to the Club du Bleu de Gascogne of which M. Boulous is the president.

Description of the Basset Bleu de Gascogne

GENERAL APPEARANCE—a strong and massive dog in relation to its size.

HEAD—rather long and well developed; skull high and narrow, peak well developed; stop slightly defined; muzzle well developed; nasal bone rather convex; lips not too pendulous.

EYES—dark brown; eye-lids not too closed.

NOSE—black, strong and long; nostrils well open.

EARS—folded, very long and nicely set on behind the line of the eye.

BODY—long; neck long and light, with dewlaps; shoulders lean and sloping; chest broad and deep; back rather long, belly drawn up.

LEGS—fore-legs half-crooked; hind-legs muscular; thighs not beefy but well-muscled.

FEET—rather long, toes rather arched; pads hard.

STERN—fine, set on low and carried upwards.

COAT—short and dense.

COLOR—tricolor, so-called trout-color, blue-mottled, white with black-and-tan spots above the eyes.

HEIGHT—at shoulder, from 13 to 15 inches.

WEIGHT—from 50 to 58 pounds.

23

The Basset
Artesien-Normand

THIRTY years ago, the Artesien-Normand was known as the Basset of Artois. It is the most popular of the smooth coats in France today. The English and American Bassets are primarily descendants of this variety.

The Artois distirct, for which they were named, is along the Belgian border. Its neighbor, to the east, is Ardennes, the province in which the Abbey of St. Hubert was located. Do not confuse this with Alain Bourbon's Villa of St. Hubert, built centuries later in Mayenne, to the southwest, and named for the patron saint. St. Hubert settled in the Ardennes area during the sixth century. It was here that he developed the Basset of St. Hubert.

The name of Le Couteulx will always be associated with the Basset of Artois, or Artesien-Normand, as it is now known. It was he who first set about to revive the breed when it had become almost extinct. By 1860, he had successfully built up the strain. Within the next twenty years, there were three types, previously discussed in the chapter on history. These were the Le Couteulx, the Masson, and the Lane, each named for their breeders.

Tristan and Tristeuse, leading couple, Temporal and La Tentatrice, back couple, Artesien Bassets. The portrait from which this drawing was made was painted about 1875 by Charles Olivier de Penne (1831–1897).
Courtesy of *The Chronicle of the Horse*, Middleburg, Va.

The Basset Artesien-Normand.

These little hounds captured the hearts of those in all walks of life. Their versatility made them useful in many ways. They were held in high esteem by those who loved the sport of the chase. Peasants trained them to seek out the truffle, an edible tuber which was an important item in French cuisine. The ladies of the court found their quaintness very amusing, and the Basset became one of the few sporting dogs to be pampered in "madame's chambers." Authors filled their books with lengthy accounts of their abilities in the field. A noted French artist, Charles Olivier De Penne, abandoned the subjects of his award-winning career for the pleasure of painting portraits of animals that he admired before his death in 1897. Many pictures of Bassets are among his works.

The popularity of the Basset Artois continued to grow. M. Leon Verrier became a well-known breeder and perfected a uniformity of type which was accepted in the show ring. He produced many champions, among them Ch. Mosquetaire who was sold to Alain Bourbon. M. Ferdinand Pinel owned Meteore and Galathee. Other leading breeders, through the years, were: M. A. Cann, M. le comte de Champs, M. A. Coste, M. A. Faure, M. Gosselin, M. le vicomte de Peufeilhous, M. le baron de Segonzac who owned Ch. Troubadour, M. Villatte des Prugnes, M. Leparroux, and M. Jean Rothea.

In 1910, the Basset Artois Club was formed. The name was later changed to the Club du Basset Artesien-Normand.

The British and American breedings were directed toward large and heavy dogs. In France, the fanciers aimed for a well-built but not too heavy Basset which was capable of fulfilling its part as a running dog. The variety was used on foxes, as well as rabbits, and actually captured the rabbits.

M. Jean Rothea, current president of the Artesien-Normand Club, wrote that the breedings have been considerably reduced during the 1960s. A sickness has plagued their rabbits. As the Basset has become a specialist at this quarry, there was fear that the rabbit would become extinct unless the number of dogs was minimized. M. Rothea censures the size of American breedings. His sympathies are echoed by M. Abel Desamy, head of the Club du Griffon Vendeen, who states, "I disapprove of your dogs' excessive heaviness, which to my opinion, is a handicap for hunting."

Although earlier descriptions state that these hounds often have small black spots, or ticking, the latest Standard disqualifies any resemblance to a blue-mottled appearance. The Artesien-Normand's size varies greatly, from 10½ to 14½ inches. The depth of its muzzle is much greater than that of the Bleu de Gascogne or of the Saintongeois.

Description of the Basset Artesien-Normand

GENERAL APPEARANCE—a long dog, longer than his size calls for; standing firm, balanced and well made; clearly indicating his great ancestry.

HEAD—domed, of medium width; the cheeks formed, not by muscles as in the Bulldog, but only by skin which makes one or two folds on them; above all, the head must have a lean appearance.

SKULL—the stop marked, but without exaggeration; the occipital bump (la bosse de chasse) prominent.

FOREFACE—of average length; fairly wide, and slightly convex before the nose.

EYES—large, dark, and with a calm, serious expression; the red of the lower eyelid may appear.

EARS—attached low, never above the line of the eye; soft, fine in texture, narrow when coming from the skull, curling inwards, corkscrew fashion at the tips (en tire-bouchonnées), ending in a point.

NOSE—black and large, coming a little over the lip; nostrils full and wide.

NECK—fairly long, with dewlap, but not exaggerated.

SHOULDERS—round, strong, and short; well muscled.

FOREFEET—short, heavy-boned, crooked, or half-crooked, or less than half-crooked provided there is a principal of crookedness sufficiently visible, but never with the pastern displaced in front; the front of the forelegs presents several folds of skin under the articulation of the first joint.

FEET—poised upright, unless toes turn out without malformation of shape from carrying body; the feet of the Basset allow going where difficult terrain prohibits larger dogs; they leave the imprint in soft earth comparable to larger hounds.

CHEST—sternum is prominent; chest has average descent, is wide and rounded.

312

RIBS—rounded, compensating for their lack of depth by their roundness.

BACK—wide and well supported.

LOIN—slightly tucked up.

FLANK—full and descending downward.

THIGH—very muscular; should form with the rump in a spherical mass.

TAIL—well attached, long, strong at the base, tapered to the end, carried upright but never over the back. It is absolutely forbidden to support the tail of the dog while in the showring.

HINDQUARTERS—a little aslant, giving a slight dip to the rump.

HOCKS—slightly bent and strong; often has one or two folds of skin, with a slight projection of skin on the posterior part.

COAT—close, short, not too fine, and waterproof.

COLOR—tricolor, or orange-and-white; the tricolor dogs marked with tan heads, black backs, and tan extremities; white tips preferred but not essential.

SIZE—from 10½ inches to 14½ inches.

GAIT—calm but brisk.

DISQUALIFICATIONS—undershot; straight legs; though not a disqualification, the black spots are not to be encouraged; any resemblance to a blue-mottled effect is a disqualification.

FAULTS—flat head; wide forehead; flat ears, thick where attached; too high or large ears; short neck; sway-back; forefeet touching or knuckled; flat ribs; flat feet; toes separated; twisted or too-long stern; flat or close-set hocks—eyes too bright to give the proper expression.

Hardy de Vendee, owned by M. Abel Desamy in 1963, considered very good type.

Ch. Farino (1901–1909), first dog selected by M. Paul Dezamy, had been chosen as the model of the breed.

24

The Basset
Griffon-Vendeen

THESE sturdy little hounds are the most popular variety of Basset in France at this time. As with the other types, they were named for the area in which they were developed. Vendee is on the west coast, midway between Brittany and Gascony. The terrain is very rugged, rocky, covered with thorny undergrowth, and requires a coat that can withstand such elements. The Griffon-Vendeen is the perfect dog for hunting in this area. The dogs give the impression of the Otterhound in miniature and are very appealing to see. Although there are almost none in America at this time, I am sure if there were more, they would capture the fancy of many who admire both the Basset and the Otterhound.

The Griffon-Vendeen is slightly larger than the Basset Artesien-Normand, which is seldom over 13 inches in France, though the Standard allows 14 inches. The Vendeen is divided into two types: the "petite taille" (small size) ranging from 13 to 14 inches, and the "grande taille" (large size) which are from 14 to 16 inches. They are somewhat more short-coupled than the smooth coat varieties, though still long in comparison to their height. In color, they are tawny, red-and-white, tricolored, black-and-white, and solid color. They are not brilliant in these colors, as are the smooth coats. The shaggy coat often takes on a similarity to the coloring of a rabbit.

The Griffon-Vendeen's description closely resembles that of the Segusian hound of 400 A.D. which was mentioned in an earlier chapter on the History of the Breed. The Segusian, named after a Celtic tribe that inhabited the banks of the Rhone in the second century, was said to be a shaggy little dog, and the most highbred were described as being the ugliest. Though this is not very flattering to the breed, one can visualize that the shaggiest coats and the shortest legs may have seemed unsightly to certain writers. It is quite probable, as with other Griffon varieties of Bassets, that the Segusians were used to develop the variety which became known as the Basset of Vendee.

In 1881, in *The Book of the Dog,* Vero Shaw wrote of the Griffon-Vendeen: "He has straight but short legs; rough, hard coat, with a woolly undergrowth, colour iron-grey, or white with brown markings, or all white. They are powerfully built, not very long, and possess a speed which is extraordinary when one thinks of their shape. A M. d'Incourt de Metz owns a pack of these hounds that run down their hare easily in two or three hours."

Sir Everett Millais wrote of them in 1897: "Some twenty years ago, when I was at school in Paris, I used to frequently adjourn to a dog dealer's, whose shop still exists close to the Arc de Triomphe. I was there not long since, and on asking Mons. Ravry if he could find me a couple of Basset Griffons, such as he used to keep years ago, he informed me that he could not, unless I put my hand very deeply into my pocket. These hounds were like Otterhounds in form and texture of coat, likewise of the same colour, and quite as big as the largest smooth coated Bassets over here (England). About 1874–1875, I used to see a similar type of hound in the variety class at our leading shows, owned first by Dr. Seton, and then by Mr. J. C. Macdona. This hound is registered in the Kennel Club stud book as Romano, and a very handsome specimen he was; hard coated and workmanlike, brown-grey grizzle in colour, and always admired by the hunting men who saw him either on the bench or in the ring.

"Since then I have never seen a hound like Romano in type

and size, except Mrs. Ellis's Rocket, which though not of exactly quite the same character, comes nearer to that mentioned above than the smaller varieties, which might pass better as rough-coated dachshounds than do duty at our show as Basset Griffons.

"In the last class of these hounds which I had the pleasure of inspecting there were no less than four types, and if he included those owned by His Royal Highness, the Prince of Wales, I may, I think, correctly state that there are five different types of Basset Griffons in this country at the present time."

Sir Everett felt that the Griffon fanciers in England had not obtained the cream of the crop, nor bred with such dedication, as did those interested in the smooth coats. The classes were very small even though M. Pussant sent entries from his kennels in France. Some beautiful specimens were seen from the Sandringham kennels of King Edward VII who always had an affection for this variety, using them for work and exhibiting them at the leading shows. His Sandringham Bobs was bred in his kennels and took many first prizes. Both King Edward and Queen Alexandria were very fond of the Bassets kept in their kennels.

At one time, it seemed likely that the Basset Griffon would equal the popularity of the smooth coat variety in England. However, they never "caught on." Special classes were provided for them, but the entries remained scant. The Sandringham entries usually appeared, plus those of Rev. W. Shield, Mr. F. Lowe, Mr. H. Jones, and George Krehl, who kept a few. The strongest kennel in Britain was Mrs. Tottie's, located in Bell Busk, near Leeds. Her Tambour, Truelove, Pervence and Treasure were excellent specimens. Pierrot and Ringwood, owned by Mrs. E. Gerrich, Westbury-on-Tyne, Bristol, were of fine quality. Mr. Krehl's Trompette d'Erpent and Bonnbonneau were very hardy in appearance and carried the Otterhound head. As only a few people found these little hounds interesting, they never became numerous. It is believed that Mrs. Tottie eventually crossed hers with the smooth-coats in her kennel.

In France, the Griffon did not meet with this same fate. A coat such as theirs was needed, in many areas, to protect the dogs from the jagged rocks and thorny undergrowth. Here the variety began to increase. In 1895, the entry was strong at the Paris Exposition. M. Geoffrey Saint-Hilaire exhibited many fine examples. The type

317

of Comte d'Elva commanded attention. A club was formed in 1898, with the count as president.

The Griffon was established. The Vendeen's quality of fascination for the pursuit of the hare was noted. The terrain of the region was very difficult for briquets (Beagles) and impossible for the horse, so it was necessary to go by foot. M. Paul Dezamy chose a large Basset, less rapid than the briquets, but capable of catching the hare, for his breedings. These caused a sensation by their quality of beauty and hunting ability. In 1924 at the trials of Venerie, he won the Grand Prize of Honour of the Venerie Francaise.

The Club Griffon-Vendeen was founded May 30, 1907. M. Paul Dezamy became president, and the Comte d'Elva was made honorary president. A Standard was adopted. Two types were acknowledged: the large, and the small. The Standard, except for the size, was the same for both. M. Dezamy was not, at that time, a strict, uncompromising judge. His standards allowed for a beautiful subject of maximum size. They still say in the French exhibition ring, "Forty-two Dezamy." On St. Hubert Day in 1933, M. Paul Dezamy passed away. The presidency was passed on to his son-in-law, Mr. Abel Desamy (note the difference in spelling), whose young son, Hubert was also bitten by the "canine fever."

M. Hubert Desamy wrote in a recent letter to me, "My father (M. Abel Desamy) concluded very rapidly that the same standard for the large and small Basset was an anomaly. A particular standard was adopted for the small Basset. In order to permit the best selection of the race, the Club Register automatically inscribed the subjects of parents already inscribed. A dog, after one year of age, must be visited by a qualified judge of the Club Griffon-Vendeen to be enrolled on the Club Register. Also, our club preceded, by five years, the Société Centrale Canine Francaise, in the examination of conformation." In short, before a dog is certified, he is examined by delegates from all parts of France. These Bassets are in a large numerical majority, equaling the races of the fourth and fifth groups.

The Grande Basset (large) is the "type Dezamy," an ideal dog for hunting hare. He has a majestic head and a robust body. According to M. Daubigne, "The pace, accuracy, and initiative are natural qualities of the Basset Griffon-Vendeen." The Petite Basset (small)

The Rallye Bocage, 1947: M. Desamy, master of the hunt, and Bassets Griffon-Vendeen.

is above all a good rabbit chaser. His hair protects him and he is impervious to stone, has a good voice, leads well, and is able to keep pace with dogs of larger size.

Standard of the Basset Griffon-Vendeen

Large Size—14 to 16 inches

GENERAL ASPECTS—long structure, but not excessive; straight paw; tail nimble and gay; coat rugged, neither silky nor woolly, on all the body; head is an essential point; ears are long, covered with shorter hair; the eyes are not hidden by the long hair surrounding them.

HEAD—eyes, large, without white, and are intelligent and beautiful in expression; the red of the eyelid is not apparent; the eyebrow is bushy, but does not obscure the eye.

EARS—supple, narrow, and delicate, covered with slightly shorter hair than on the body, yet long; they end in an oval; well rounded inside, reaching under the nose, attached under the line of the eye.

SKULL—deep, long, not too large; pronounced under the eye, moderate stop; well developed occipital bone.

MUZZLE—long, deep, square to the end; slightly arched between eye and nostril; lips encircled by mustache.

NOSE—black; well developed; good openings.

NECK—long and strong; thick near shoulders; without dewlap.

SHOULDERS—flat, lean and sloping; well set to the body.

CHEST—long and deep.

RIBS—round.

FLANK—on the whole descending.

BACK—long, large and straight, beginning to arch at the junction with the loins.

LOINS—solid, full, and agile.

RUMP—very beefy and muscular.

TAIL—set high; large at base, tapering toward tip; carried erect when alert; is long.

FORELEGS—the knees do not touch; the forearm is thick; the wrist agile; the toes longish and slightly separated.

THIGH—well muscled.

HOCKS—large and well bent.

FEET—thick, compressed, and tough; claws solid.

COAT—thick, tough, not too silky and long, nor too woolly; fringe is not too abundant.

COLOR—solid color is tawny, less dark, like the fur of the rabbit in color; two-color is white and orange, white and black, white and color of rabbit fur, white and grey, or white and rust; tricolor is white, black, and tan; white, tan, and rabbit-color; or white, grey, and tan.

HIDE—thick, often marble on the tricolors, white and black, or white and grey.

SIZE—14 to 16 inches, with allowance for exceptional males; the female can be less than two centimeters as tall as the male.

GAIT—walks easily to three gaits.

SERIOUS FAULTS—flat and short head, spotted or discolored nose, light eyes, pointed muzzle, uneven jawbone, flat ears devoid of hair or attached too high, too short neck, not minimum nor maximum size indicated, sagging back, forelegs touching or bowed from supporting too much weight, flat feet, toe variations, too angular or too straight hocks, flat thigh, coat too woolly, silky, or curly.

Small Size—13 to 14 inches

GENERAL ASPECTS—a vigorous little dog with an agile, long body; inclined to haughtiness; coat long and hard without exaggeration; expressive head; ears well set under a line of the eye and furnished with long hair.

EYES—large and intelligent, showing no white, red of eyelid not apparent; hair surrounding the upper lid does not obscure the eye.

EARS—soft, narrow, covered with long hair, ending in an oval; the ear does not reach the end of the nose; it is well attached under the line of the eye.

SKULL—slightly domed, somewhat long, not too large, prominent stop, well developed occipital bone.

MUZZLE—shorter than the Grande variety but nevertheless very long; arched between the eye and nostrils; lips circled by a good mustache.

NOSE—black, well developed, with wide openings.

SHOULDERS—oblique, well moulded to the body.

CHEST—deep but not large.

RIBS—moderately round.

LOINS—well supported and muscular.

CROUP—muscular and full.

TAIL—set high; large at the base and tapering to the tip; not very long; carried erect.

MEMBERS—also strong structure but proportioned to size.

FORELEGS—straight; the forearm thick.

THIGHS—muscular and a little rounded.

HOCKS—large, well bent.

FEET—not very large, tough pad, good claw, tight paws.

COAT—hard, not too silky or woolly, less fringe than the larger variety.

COLOR—same colors accepted as larger variety, tawny color not recommended.

SIZE—13 to 14 inches, deviation of one-half inch allowed.

GAIT—very free and easy.

SERIOUS FAULTS—body too long; head too flat; poorly shaped nostrils, or discolored nostrils; light eyes; uneven jawbone; pointed muzzle; flat or high-set ears with insufficient fur; weak back; crooked forelegs; hocks too straight or crooked; flat thighs; tail too long or too curved; coat of insufficient density, frizzy, woolly, or silky.

Club Rules

All questions on the repertoire of the Club are to be addressed to the secretary and accompanied by:

1. pedigree of dog.
2. lawful inscription.

To be inscribed, the dogs have to earn at least the notice of very good, first or second prize in Open Class in a French exhibition recognized by the Central Canine Society.

3. The dogs are admitted by a special commission of three members, one of which must be a judge qualified by the Club. In case of false declarations, the committee will scratch the dog inscribed and remove from the Club the person who signed the sheet, if there is bad evidence. The right of inscription is ten francs ($2.04) per dog.

Inscription is limited to members of the Basset and Briquet Griffons Vendeens.

Certificate of Hunt—B.C.

Rules: Members of the club, in order to pass for the Certificate of the Hunt, will have to present their pack for our examination. The dogs, maximum three, must enter competition assigned by the club, and be recognized for their qualities of the hunt, by three members of the jury of judges. The secretary must be notified at least one month prior to the examination.

Judges are designated by the committee and chosen from the list of the Société Centrale Canine and by the Society of Venerie for our Group.

Only dogs between the ages of twelve months and six years will be admitted to run for the B.C. They must state whether they are entered for the L.O.F., the R.D.N., or the R.-C.G.V. At each presentation, the number of candidates must be more than three. The owner must accompany them on the chase.

The land for the hunt may be supplied by the owner, if he prefers, and obtains permission. Travel expenses must be paid by the owner. Before awarding a certificate, the examiners take into consideration: age, the quality of the voice, when it is used, how it is used, scenting ability, and if they hold true to the line with few mistakes. The following is a scale of points for judging: temperament, 6; nose, 9; voice, 6; persistence and checking of the track, 9; aptitude to rally with a pack, 6; steadiness and vigor, 6; aptitude to chase and capture the rabbit, 6; what the dog does upon seeing the hare, 5; total 53. The following scale of points applies to shooting-tests: temperament, 6; nose, 8; voice, 7; disposition as a pack-dog and persistence on the track, 8; eagerness and vigor, 8; ability under fire, 8; ability to return, 8; total 53.

The dogs must obtain a minimum of 40 points, to qualify for "Excellent," with the coefficients of 20, 19, or 18. They must obtain a minimum of 35 points, with the coefficients of 17, 16, or 15, to qualify for "Very good," and 30 points, with 14, 13, or 12, to qualify for "Good."

To gain the title B.C., the dogs must have gained one of the awards as mentioned above.

The most important breeders of the Basset Griffon-Vendeen have been: M. Baillet of Rouen; M. de la Brosse of Orvault; and M. Collignon, Ch. Davy, M. Paul Dezamy, M. Gillet, M. G. Lepinay, M. F. Sellier, M. Joulia, M. Abel Desamy plus M. Hubert Desamy, all of Vendee. In the 1920's, M. Dezamy, Comte d'Elva, M. Guillihand, le Marquis de Maulean, and M. Leon Verrier were qualified judges.

Mrs. Mildred Seiffert and Mrs. Wells-Meacham became very interested in the breed and began breeding from, M. Desamy's stock, in England. In the United States, Elizabeth Streeter incorporated them into her Skycastle Pack and the Finn Bergishagens imported one from Mrs. Seiffert.

25

The Basset
Fauve de Bretagne

O NE of the Griffons, the Basset Fauve de Bretagne, is one of the minority varieties in France. Named for the province of Brittany, where it was developed, the dog's rough coat is suitable to the rocky area along the northwest coast. In color, they are fawn or tawny-red, whichever you prefer to call it. These Bassets give one the impression of greater activity and sharpness than the other varieties. Perhaps this is due to their alert expression and short-coupled body, not usually associated with Bassets.

Their lack of popularity may be due to the fact that they are more riotous, harder to break, and do not possess the temperament usually associated with Bassets. They also lack the beautiful voice for which the breed is noted.

Nevertheless, they are useful little hounds in the particular region. A few breeders prize them highly and the strain is kept in its purity. Their interests are guarded by the Club du Basset Fauve de Bretagne, headed by M. Pambrun.

Description of the Basset Fauve de Bretagne

GENERAL APPEARANCE—a coarse, long dog.

HEAD—long; high and domed skull; stop slightly developed; long muzzle; lips not too pendulous.

EYES—dark in color.

NOSE—long and black; nostrils wide open.

EARS—nicely set on, rounded at the tips and slightly folded.

BODY—coarse and long; neck short and heavy; shoulders clean and sloping; chest deep and broad; back long and rather straight; belly slightly tucked up; loins long and broad.

LEGS—nearly straight, thighs beefy and round.

FEET—longish and strong; nails developed; pads hard.

STERN—of medium length, carried upwards.

COAT—wiry and broken; not too long; softer on the skull and ears.

COLOR—tawny red or fawn, white markings.

HEIGHT—at shoulder, about 12 inches.

WEIGHT—about 50 pounds.

26

The Basset Hound
in Australia

THE Basset was known in Australia about 1893. The introduction of the breed in that country was influenced by Sir Everett Millais. For health reasons, Sir Everett visited that country between 1880 and 1884. Soon after, Levity was imported by Mrs. Anderson and Mr. McLoughlin.

The breed, however, became nearly extinct until 1957. Two bitches were then imported, both in whelp, and one dog. The bitches were Grims Caroline and Brockleton Country Maid. The breed was fostered by Mr. John Mackinolty and Harold Spira. According to Keith Goodwin of Wentworthville, New South Wales, Mackinolty's interest was still high in 1964. Though he did not show his dogs, he was considered a valuable judge. Mr. Spira, a distinguished veterinarian in Sydney, continued breeding his Bassets as well as contributing his services as an all-breed judge. Among others, his kennel contained Ch. Grims Vanquish, Fochno Chestnut, and Sykemoor Dauphin, all British imports, at stud. He did a great deal to popularize the breed and progeny from his famous Chevalier Kennels appear at shows throughout the area.

Some of the earlier show dogs in Australia were: Mr. & Mrs. R. Sharpe's male, Garrene Garabaldi; their bitch, Ch. Chevalier Davina; Capt. G. Brandis's dog, Ch. Dewburn Jasper, and his bitch, Ch. Chevalier Undine; Keith Goodwin's male, Ch. Chevalier Walter; S. Goodwin's bitch, Ch. Streatham Matilda; Miss Hamilton's bitch, Chevalier Yvonne; C. Salter's bitch, Rymrac Blanche; P. Warley's bitch, Ch. Chevalier Nicole; and R. Buchanan's male, Ch. Santana-Mendeville My Count, which was imported from the United States.

Many of the bitches had no show career. They were used only for producing litters. Two of these, Mrs. B. Hoares's Chevalier Fiona and Mr. C. Salter's Dewburn Velvet Lady, were considered fine matrons by Keith Goodwin. For many years, there were a limited number of bloodlines with which to work. Improvement was difficult. New blood was imported from the Kelperland stock by Miss Koster. Mrs. B. Walcott, of the Sepaki kennels, imported Grims Compass and some Fredwell stock.

Entries vary greatly in Sydney, ranging from 23 to 40, and even to as high as 100 at the Specialty. The Basset Club holds a point score competition annually. Dogs are judged on points won at designated all-breed shows once a month. For the 1964 season, Capt. G. Brandis's Ch. Dewburn Jasper, five-and-one-half years old and holder of over 100 Challenge Certificates, and Keith Goodwin's Ch. Chevalier Walter were high contenders in males. Miss Hamilton's tricolor, Chevalier Yvonne, led the bitch class.

By 1964, approximately 200 Bassets were being exhibited. The total population ran over 1,000. Field trials, or hunts, had not yet been attempted. The leading kennels included: Chevalier, Sepaki, Leal Ami, Rymrac, Davton, and Goodwin, in Sydney, and the Blandville kennels in Melbourne.

In 1965, the eighth Specialty Show had an entry of 126, judged by Mr. H. R. Spira. Challenge Dog was Mr. and Mrs. H. C. Brown's Ch. Sarnia Pepe and Ch. Chevalier Yvonne, owned by Miss Shauna Hamilton, was Challenge Bitch.

There was also bad news for Australian Bassets in 1965. The breed, and Mrs. Heather Gy, of Eltham, Victoria, suffered a great loss in two of her dogs that died in a fire. One of them was her English import Chantinghall Apollo, one of the four original bitches imported to Victoria.

Ch. Fredwell Tyoro (Ch. Wingjays Ptolemy ex Fredwell Dreamer), an English-bred Basset imported and owned by Mr. C. Harris, won the Challenge for bitches at the 1971 Sydney Royal.

Ch. Wahabi Whimsical (Ch. Sepaki Compass Ajax ex Ch. Sepaki Bettina, CD), owned by Mrs. Janet Beckman, won the dog Challenge at the 1971 Sydney Royal under judge Robert Waters of Canada.

Mrs. J. Harris gained a championship on Sepaki Little Pixie in 1966. The next year, Ch. Kirkarron Argyle gained his final points in Queensland. He was owned by Mr. and Mrs. Benham. Ch. Sarnia Pepe was Challenge Dog at the Royal Easter and both championship shows. Sepaki Little Bonnie, owned by Carole Woolcock, Bonaccord Bluebell and Moongamba Merry Muffin, both owned by Mrs. Judity Leape, of Murwillumbah, all gained their championships.

From 1965 to 1971, a number of new imports were made from Great Britain. Mr. Peter Warby imported Lymewood's Choppette and Sykemoor Hopsack. Dr. and Mrs. Vernon bought Kierhill Donald. Chris and Lyn Harris migrated to Australia and brought Fredwell Tiffy and Fredwell Tyoro with them. Fredwell Chaser went to Western Australia. When a case of rabies was alleged in the United Kingdom, Australia placed a ban on the importation of dogs. Fredwell Pinza arrived shortly before this happened.

By 1971, a number of Bassets had won Best in Show awards at all-breed shows. Several people had taken an interest in obedience work. Mrs. Janet Beckman, the BHC of New South Wales vice-president, was the first to gain a CDX title on her Heathmond Miss Snowy. She gained titles on Wahabi Golden Girl, CD and Ch. Sepaki Bettina. Mrs. M. Parker put a CD on Laurieton Fredericka. Ch. St. Hubert Adorable earned the CD degree and Ch. Langi Larry was well on his way during the late 1960s. Most of these dogs were competing in conformation, obedience and had become members of the hunting pack. The club had established a working branch which was holding successful field meets. It celebrated its tenth anniversary in 1971. The leading kennels, of that time were: the Jasper Park, owned by Capt. George Brandis; Wahabi, owned by Janet Beckman; Sepaki, Mrs. B. Walcott; Laurieton, Mr. and Mrs. Allan Poulton; Broadwater, Mr. and Mrs. C. Harris; Basqueville, Mrs. B. Prosser; Peelsview, Miss C. Woolcock; Houndsleigh, Mr. and Mrs. V. E. Tinsley; Arkda, Mr. and Mrs. K. L. Dark; Kinmonth, Mr. and Mrs. A. K. MacDougall; Vocalique, Dr. and Mrs. R. H. Vernon; and Kiabe, Miss M. T. Blackwell.

The club had been under the leadership of Keith Goodwin during its earlier years. In 1968, because his duties as Secretary of the Australian Engineering Society prevented him from continuing, he declined the office of president. Mr. Alan Poulton subsequently accepted the position. However, Mr. Goodwin's work did allow him and his wife to travel to the United States, on two occasions, visiting the author and attending the BHCA Specialty. Keith Mercer succeeded Alan Poulton as president of the BHC of New ·South Wales. Trevor Shreeve became secretary with Janet Beckman serving as vice-president and Mr. J. Vernon, treasurer.

In 1976, Mrs. Barbara Philpotts-Green sought to further improve the Australian bloodlines by importing a young dog from England. He was from the Langpool Kennels of Dr. Elizabeth Andrews and a grandson of American Ch. Long View Acres Bonza whom we had sent to England several years before.

Ch. Streatham Matilda (Blandville Punchinello ex Huckleberry Antoinette); breeder, Mrs. H. C. Duffell; owner, K. Goodwin.

331

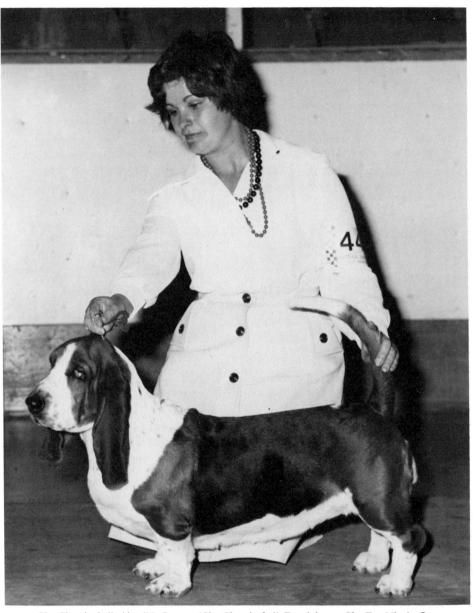

Ch. Chantinghall Airs 'N Graces (Ch. Chantinghall Dominic ex Ch. Eve-Ning's Over the Rainbow), owned by Rosemary McKnight and shown with her handler, Judy Taylor.

Stonham

27

The Basset Hound in Canada

THE first recognized Basset listed in the records of the Canadian Kennel Club was Al's Janet, 143155. Registered May 24, 1936, owned by N. E. Pegg, Janet was the product of two United States Bassets: Al's Chief of Geneseo and Woelk's Beauty. In 1903, however, there had been three Bassets entered in a show. Two types, rough and smooth, were listed in the officially recognized breeds in Canada in 1907. One of the oldest breeders in this country, Miss Dorothy Grant, obtained Maytime Peg O'My Heart from the Fogelsons of Greenly Hall fame.

According to Fred Carter, president of the Basset Hound Club of Canada in 1964, Rosemary Osselton and Mr. Sless are the prominent fanciers in British Columbia. Mr. & Mrs. Stevenson of Portage le Prarie, Manitoba are very active. Many have imported dogs from the United States. Mr. & Mrs. Henderson of Peterboro have become well-known. They imported Lyn-Mar Acres Bojangles from Mr. & Mrs. M. L. Walton. Their Canadian and Bermuda Ch. Gremlyn's Aida has been a familiar entry at the shows. Mr. & Mrs. Ron Purdy of Cheltenham purchased the American and Canadian Ch. Whistle-down's Commando from Milt Stringer of Algonac, Michigan. The Purdys had taken bitches to Commando several times before they bought him. He is the sire of many Canadian champions. The Barlindall kennel of Dick Pike, Maidstone, is known in both the United States and Canada. Mr. & Mrs. A. Digby Hunt of Ottawa based their lines on the Notrenom breedings of Richard Bassett and the Santana-Mandeville line of Paul and Helen Nelson. Fred and Betty Carter purchased Ch. Schauffelin's Logy from the Purdys as a puppy. They imported Ch. Hartshead Fanfare from Emil and Effie Seitz. Their progeny, Ch. Westacre's Queen Valli and Ch. Westacre's Little Nell, as well as Valli's son Ch. Westacres Hugo the Red, have made their mark in the show ring in both Canada and the United States. Ch. Schauffelin's Logy became a top winning Basset at shows in Canada.

The Basset Hound Club of Canada was formed by active fanciers in 1959. The first Specialty show was held in 1960. By 1964 the Basset had risen to great heights in popularity. It was third in Hound registration, preceded only by the Beagle and the Dachshund. An entry of twenty-five was not uncommon at the larger shows. Field trials and obedience work were not much in evidence though interest was being aroused in both of these fields of endeavor.

Ch. Westacres Hugo the Red brought more fame to the Fred Carters in 1965. According to the Phillips system, he was named top winning Hound and fifth top dog of all breeds. He also gained the Mid-east Canada (Ontario and Quebec) Ken-L Award, the first Basset to gain the award in that country. In 1965, "Hugo" was bred to his granddam, Ch. Hartshead Fanfare. Ch. Westacres Fanny Rosa was a product of this mating.

American dogs have done well at the Canadian Specialty show. Barbara Hurry's Am. Can. & Bermuda Ch. Ike of Blue Hill was Best of Breed at three of the four first shows. In 1966, the author judged Am. Ch. Gin Dic's Bit O'Brass, owned by Virginia Lemieux, Best of Breed from the classes. Chris Teeter and Joseph Braun's class entry, Am. Ch. Long View Acres Winston, took the top honor in 1967. He repeated the win, the next year, as a Special. His son, Am. Ch. Braun's Herman of Rambling Rd., owned by Marvin Hartleb, went Best of Winners and gained his title.

In 1967, Jim and Rosemary McKnight moved to Canada from

England. They had founded the Chantinghall kennels in Britain in 1959 with two puppy bitches they purchased from George Johnston's Sykemoor kennels. These were Sykemoor Anabel and Brigit. They provided the McKnights with part of their foundation and also did well in the show ring. That same year, Appeline Serious was purchased from Douglas and Carol Appleton. Although unshown, she is behind one of the all-time greats. In her first litter, bred at Chantinghall, emerged Appeline Dawn, destined to be the dam of the superb English Ch. Dreymin Appeline Coral.

When Jim and Rosemary migrated to Canada, they took with them English Ch. Chantinghall Harmony, her daughter, Chantinghall Amethyst, and a granddaughter, Chantinghall Samantha. Amethyst and Samantha quickly won their Canadian championships and formed the foundation of what was to become one of the top kennels in Canada. In 1969, the McKnights purchased American Ch. Solitude Creek Sophocles from his breeder, Mrs. Alice Lane, in Maryland. His predominately Lyn-Mar bloodlines clicked with those of Amethyst, Samantha and their offspring. Sophocles won his Canadian championship easily and became the top male Basset in Canada in 1971 and top dog in 1972. In 1973, American Ch. Eve-ning's Over the Rainbow was purchased from the Sangsters in California. She also gained her Canadian title easily. Bred to Ch. Chantinghall Dominic, a Sophocles son, she gave the McKnights Ch. Chantinghall Airs 'N Graces, top Basset bitch and number 8 Hound in Canada in 1975 and 1976. Her spectacular career included 56 Group placings, WB and BOS at Westminster in 1977, and Best of Breed from the classes at the Detroit Specialty. In 1977, the McKnights added Am. & Can. Ch. Het's Barney of Whiteside to their kennel. He came from the Glenns, in Texas. The following, all bearing the Chantinghall prefex, gained their championships: in England, Ancestor, Harmony, Flaxen, Jemima, Fredwell Amber, Beatrice, Kitebrook Barley; in Canada, Dragoon, Garnet, Amethyst, Samantha, Daphne, Dominic, Cousin Maud, Beau Brummel, Melody, Viceroy, Pollyanna, Airs 'N Graces, Glory Be, Vanessa, Sweet Adeline, Dewdrop, Blockbuster, Simon Templar, Pricilla, Beulah and Rhapsody; in America, Nan Tucket; in Norway, Sweden, and Denmark, Int. Ch. Chantinghall Lancer; in Brazil, Whinchat; in South Africa, Joshua, Destiny and Miriam.

Ch. Questor's M'Lord Angus, a well-known winner in New Zealand.

28

The Basset Hound
in New Zealand

I N September of 1960, the first Basset Hound arrived in New Zealand. She was three months old at the time, an Australian bitch named Longview Mandy, sired by Fochno Chestnut out of Calumet Camille. Mrs. E. Janee imported her and, later, two more, also from Australia. These were a male, Longview Loyalty, and a bitch in whelp, Ch. Calumet Camille, which had been bred to one of the top Australian studs, Ch. Blandville Bugler. Eight puppies were whelped in December of 1961. These, and their owners, formed the nucleus of the Basset Hound Club which was organized in 1962.

Gallic Jacobite and Lyndhaze Limerick were imported in 1960 from Australia by Mrs. Slade of Christchurch. Dr. J. Hall brought in Chrochmaid Bramble (sire, Barnspark Rakish; dam, Sungarth Bashful) from England.

Further imports were made from England and Australia. Most of them were descended from the Grims line. By 1964, there were about sixty Bassets scattered throughout the North and South Islands according to Peggy Blakeney of Auckland. To that time, all litters were sired or produced by an import.

The New Zealand Basset Hound Club was formed in October 1962 by a group of enthusiastic owners who felt that, in spite of the small number of hounds in the country, the breed should be popularized and an attempt should be made to improve the quality. This eager group tracked down imports, litters, promoted classes at shows, and kept members informed of world-wide Basset news by means of a bulletin. Twice a year they gathered together all available Bassets and held a "ribbon parade." Through the Club's publicity efforts they attracted television coverage and press writeups which brought the breed before the public.

To this time, they held no Working Meets. In 1964, Sqn. Ldr. D. A. Duthie took two hounds, one bred by Mrs. Seiffert (Grims Westward ex Lucky) and the other by Miss Keevil (Vanguard ex Welfare), from England to New Zealand. With the help of Duthie and his trained Bassets, plans were made to form a Working Branch.

The breed is judged under the English Standard. To become a New Zealand champion, eight C.Cs. (Challenge Certificates) under five judges are required. The first New Zealand-bred champion was Mr. P. Blakeney's Grantham Daveau, followed by Mrs. D. Cavanaugh's Tartarin Fleurette. Many were capable of capturing Challenge Certificates, Best Sporting Dog, Best Puppy in Show, Best Hound in Show, and Best in Show, at all-breed shows.

Some of the more prominent owners were: J. Ward of Auckland, who owned Tartarin Isadore (Chevalier Hillary ex Carillon Garland); Mrs. Andrew of Paparimu, owner of Napoleon de Bramble (Ch. Gallic Jacobite ex Chrochmaid Bramble); Mrs. Cox of Warkworth, owner of a litter by Fivefold Bounty ex Bertie of Haven; B. Norris, owner of Tartarin Honore; Mr. & Mrs. Mechaelis of Wellington; and Mr. David Fifield.

The 1970s surge of winning dogs began with a litter bred in 1970 by Mr. and Mrs. F. Lister, of Wellington. Their Australian import, Ch. Baswyler Emma Lou was bed to Ch. Rosston Warrington. Under the Questor prefix, the resulting litter of eight did well in the show ring. Questor's M'Lord Ajax became the first New Zealand-bred Basset to gain a title in both New Zealand and Australia, and four others finished. New Zealand and Australian Ch. Questor's M'Lady Arlette gained these titles while still a junior and became the foundation bitch of Mrs. Maree McKenzie's Longfellow kennels. The Listers bred their Australian import, Heathlyn Bellella to an Australian dog named Longview Muscat, producing their "B" litter and a 1972 English import, Fredwell Phayre to New Zealand Ch. Questor's M'Lord Angus for the "C" litter. Mrs. McKenzie bought Questor's M'Lady Constans to mate to her Australian import Jasperpark Jamie. This produced a very successful litter from which Ch. Longfellow Bronson came. He has been the top-winning New Zealand Basset during the latter half of the 1970s. In 1976, Bronson sired Ch. Longfellow Carlos, owned by Mr. J. Wilson, who became a champion at eleven months of age, the youngest in the country to do so.

From 1970 to 1974, the Questor stock continued to dominate the show ring. For the next three years, most show winners could be traced back to this kennel.

In 1974, the Basset Hound Club held its first championship Show. Best in Show was Ch. Questor's M'Lord Angus.

Mrs. Rowett-Johns, of England, sent Ch. Wingjays Polygon to Mr. and Mrs. J. Valter in 1973. He gained his New Zealand title the following year. Mr. and Mrs. Morritt returned from Australia with their Australian Ch. Lyndhaze Nebula. She gained her championship in 1975. By 1977, four dogs had gained titles in two countries. The Australian and New Zealand titles were held by Questor's M'Lord Ajax, Questor's M'Lady Arlette, and Lyndhaze Nebula. Ch. Wingjay's Polygon holds titles in England and New Zealand.

The Club had grown to over 200 members throughout the country. A branch of the Club was formed in Wellington in 1969. It holds championship shows annually, alternating between Auckland and Wellington. The members meet regularly for educational, competitive, and social affairs. Three Club members became judges in New Zealand and two of them held cards internationally for the Hound Group.

The most prominent breeders in New Zealand have been: Mr. and Mrs. G. Carrick, Glenmire Hall Kennels, Wellington; Mr. and Mrs. A. Drake, Erleigh Kennels, Wellington; Mr. and Mrs. M. Duffy, Greystokes, Auckland; Mr. and Mrs. R. Faulk, Barrams, Wellington; Mr. and Mrs. C. Flipp, Belvoire, Wellington; Mrs.

L. Hay, Crozet, Auckland; Mr. and Mrs. F. Lister, Questor, Wellington; Mr. and Mrs. R. McKenzie, Longfellow, Auckland; Mr. and Mrs. I. Morritt, Bayloud, Auckland; Mr. and Mrs. E. Steel, Chantor's Bay, Kumeu; Mr. and Mrs. J. Stein, Whittinghame, Auckland; Mrs. J. Wilson, Tarabas, Hawkes Bay.

American breeding was introduced when Mr. and Mrs. C. Flipp imported Verwood Woodsville from England. This dog is a son of American Ch. Lyn-Mar Acres Endman.

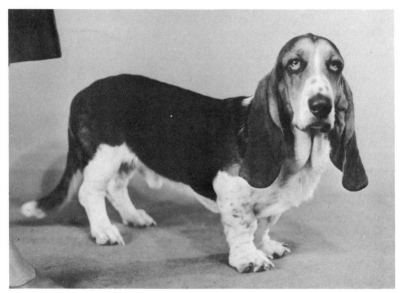

Hubert d'Andagium (Napoleon de Bramble ex Longview Mandy), from the first litter sired by a New Zealand dog; breeder, Mrs. Joyce Beasley; owner, Peggy Blakeney.

29

The Basset Hound
in Other Countries

THE first Basset in Iran was Dixie's Darrus Darling H-772297 (Ch. Bradley's Southern Rebel ex Dixie Queen Suzette), registered with the American Kennel Club. In 1957 her breeder-owners, Mr. & Mrs. William Cox, were sent to Iran by their employer, an American oil company. Their young female puppy went with them. Her dam remained in the United States. There were few dogs of any breed in Iran, no veterinarian, no dog food, no other supplies commonly taken for granted. As Abby (Dixie's Darrus Darling) advanced in years, the Coxes felt the need to add more Bassets to the household. In 1963, they imported Braun's Jolly Nicholas (Ch. Trojan Echoes Erebus ex Trojan Echoes Persephone) from your author's kennel. The Coxes undertook to raise a litter of puppies. Abby and Nicky produced three males and four females in 1964. Many of the puppies were sold to other Americans who would one day return home; some went to British owners; two remained with the breeders.

In South America, there are two known breeders: Juan Pedro Jacobsen and Luis Rueda-Gomez, both in Bogota, Colombia.

Colombia

Juan Pedro Jacobsen introduced the Basset Hound in Colombia, South America, in 1960. He had met Chris Teeter in Detroit, Michigan, and had become fond of the dogs. His first import was Long View Acres Sweet Jane, better know as "Campanita," bred by Richard Pike of Canada. She gained her Colombian championship and lived until 1968. Soon after his first import, Mr. Jacobsen obtained Long View Acres Miranda, "Congoja," and Long View Acres Ambassador, "Agobio," from Mr. Teeter. Congoja was a daughter of Ch. Long View Acres Lazy Bones. Both these dogs also gained their Colombian titles.

The all-breed club in that country is the *Club Canino Colombiano* and is affiliated with the Federation Cynologique International in Thuin, Belguim. There are four or five shows each year in Colombia. At least two of them are considered International and are controlled and authorized under the supervision of the FCI. As in European countries, the CACIB award system is used. To become an International champion, a dog must win at least three CACIBs, in at least two different countries. One male and one female may receive a CACIB at each International show. The award would compare to Winners Dog and Winners Bitch in the United States.

In 1963, Mr. Jacobsen visited Paul Marischen in Cincinnati, Ohio. Here he purchased Marischen's Lonesome George to take back to his friend and colleague Luis Rueda Gomez. This dog, whose kennel name was "Guayabo," became the first Basset Hound in Colombia to gain an International championship. He also became a Colombian, and Venezuelan, champion and won seven Best in Show awards in Bogota, Medellin, and Caracas, by 1971.

Mr. Jacobsen has also been associated with Longhaired Dachshunds. He adopted the kennel name de Bonjour Tristesse, in honor of Long View Acres Kennels and bred several Bassets that finished in Colombia and gained CACIBs. Among these was his Melancolia de Bonjour Tristesse. He obtained Isolda de Bogota from Mr. Alvaro Hernan Mejia who had joined Mr. Jacobsen and Mr. Gomez as a serious Basset breeder. By 1971, Mr. Alonso Restrepo de Leon had also taken a great interest in the breed. However, there were still only approximately forty Basset Hounds in the country with about fifteen being shown.

By this time, a few Basset Hounds began to appear in Venezuela and Peru in addition to those in Colombia. Luis Bustamante, of Caracas, Venezuela, has had Basset Hounds since 1968.

Dominican Republic

Roland L. Royalty, a missionary from California, owned the ninth Basset to be registered in the Dominican Republic. This was his first Basset, purchased from Joan Smith, of Homestead, Florida, in 1972. She was Royal Duchess III. After her death, and that of her mate, Pancho, the Royaltys purchased Temecula Tami, by Ch. Ranchound's Oliver A ex Ranchound's Gretchen Biehler, from Paul and Renee Clinton of Temecula, California, while they were visiting the area. Although the Royaltys did enter one show, time and finances did not allow them to pursue the sport. They hope to produce a litter or two to help improve quality in the breed in the Dominican Republic.

Africa

The breed was known to have been owned in the Transvaal in 1924 and a few dogs were in Cape Province in the early 1930s. Most of these, it is believed, were brought there by German settlers who migrated to Southwest Africa.

Between 1957 and 1959, four hounds were imported from England and the breed's popularity began to grow. When Mrs. S. Fletcher moved to Johannesburg, from England, she took with her Tess of Linacre. In 1961, Tess was bred to Ch. Grims Williwaw. Kelperland Potwalloper Daffodil was imported, in 1960, by Mrs. Fletcher, and bred to Sykemoor Westward in 1962. One of the resulting puppies, Deschamps Ginger Lloyd, did very well at the shows and gained his championship at fourteen months of age. He proved to be a producer of quality when his sons and daughters also gained their championships. Mrs. Fletcher later imported Rowynan Rachel and Dremin Persephone. Mrs. Julie Miles, of Transvaal, was winning with her Ch. Gayrob's Kensington Armstrong Angus, bred in Africa by Mr. S. R. C. DeLacerda. She also owned "Angus's" sister, Gayrob's Kensington Bonita. A mating of "Angus" and Ch. Dreymin's Clancy of Pevans produced Horace of Pevans and Rupert of Pevans, owned by Mrs. Val Evans.

343

In the late 1960s, the Basset Hound Club of South Africa was organized by Mrs. Newby-Fraser, Mrs. Val Evans, and Mrs. S. Fletcher. They were supported by other breeders of the era, such as: Mr. Clark, who had the Maitland hounds in Lyttleton; Mrs. Eales, Hatherleigh Kennels, Pretoria; Mrs. Behrman, Mrs. Scott and Mr. deRidder. Bloodlines had been brought in by importing Rowynan Legacy from Rosemary Goodyear in Great Britain, Sykemoor Dulcet and Ch. Fredwell Varon Vandal bloodlines, also from England, and Chantinghall stock from Rosemary McKnight of Scotland. Mrs. Nardone had imported Chantinghall Joshua and Destiny.

Although Margaret Holding, of Nairobi, had seen an occasional Basset from Tanzania in the show ring, she imported the first to arrive in Kenya in 1966. These were Hardacre Oliver and Nicety from the kennels of Mrs. Anne Matthews in England. By 1967, "Oliver" had gained his championship and "Nicety," after rearing a litter, gained her first C.C. Oliver was undefeated until Mrs. Ambler imported and showed Woelven Penelope. She was obtained from Major C. Newlove's bloodline. Three dogs out of the first mating of "Oliver" and "Nicety" were shown extensively. One female was bred back to her sire and another was mated to Kierhill Fergus. Unfortunately, Mrs. Holding suffered a great disappointment when a few long coats appeared in her breedings but she quickly set about to remedy this. In 1968, a promising dog of Rosemary Goodyear's Rowynan bloodline arrived in Kenya from Great Britain. Another pair of Bassets was taken to Uganda. These represented most of the bloodlines in East Africa over the next several years.

Belgium

The main governing body, the Federation Cynologique Internationale, is located at 14, rue Leopold 11, 6530 Thuin, Belgium. All show approvals and breed Standards are kept here. Each country of origin for the breed approves the Standards. The American Standard represents the Basset. The FCI keeps records of all CACIBs and applies them to a dog's International championship title. A dog must win three CACIBs in as many countries under at

International Ch. Tarza Beau Monde, owned by Donald and Nancy Berg, holds titles in the United States, Belgium, and France in addition to the FCI international designation. He is shown here with Mrs. Berg.

least two judges. Hunting dogs must also pass a *travail test*. The first one for Bassets was run in 1976. The Basset must follow a trail 1000 meters long (approximately 3900 feet) through the woods. The trail is of wild boar blood, laid 24 hours before the trial. It must include at least three right angle turns. The dogs are allowed to stray three meters to either side of the trail. The handler is also allowed to put the dog back on the trail once. At the end of the trail, the wild boar's body is laid. The dog must not show fear at finding it. If the dog passes the test, it gains a title of CQN and is the holder of a hunt certificate. Having passed this test, a dog may be entered in the travail or hunt class in any FCI-approved show. Dogs with a CQN have an edge because the judge knows that they are capable and can gain a title. Before becoming a champion, a dog must pass the travail test.

There is a new Belgian Hound Club. Donald Berg, an American, is on the Board and is vice-president. Mrs. Philip DeSchutter is the secretary. The Club is striving to hold its own shows and travail classes.

Donald and Nancy Berg moved to Belgium in 1974. They obtained their first Basset, from the author, in 1961. After spending the next four years in Illinois, they moved to California where they became very active in the Basset fancy. When their first dog died, Sam Dickerson, then president of the Southern California Club, helped them find a dog that was to become their first champion, American & Mexican Ch. Tarza Dewey, CD. After eight years, they moved to Belgium taking with them "Dewey," Am. & Mex. Ch. Tarza Basil of Sussex, Am. & Mex. Supai's Daffodil of Sussex, Ch. Tarza Beau Monde, Tarza Dahlia of Sussex, and Ellenbusch Blossom C. Lee, plus three children and one cat.

The Bergs attended the Antwerp show as spectators, and later they began showing, making entries in five countries. Ch. Tarza Beau Monde began winning for them on the Continent. By 1977, he had American, Belgian, International, Dutch, and French championships. He was Best of Breed twice at the Orleans Basset Specialty, the second time under judge Joan Wells Meacham. European bitches, from many countries, were bred to him. The Bergs' Supai's Daffodil was also shown sparingly. She was eventually bred to "Beau" and the resulting puppies were much in demand by European breeders.

At first, winning with the American-style dog was a bit difficult. The judges were used to seeing dogs with more daylight under them. However, as the type caught on, the dogs began to do exceptionally well.

Judging may take over an hour for each dog. Each receives a card with a written comment. Dogs are rated from not acceptable, poor, good, very good, to excellent. Only dogs rated excellent compete further for the CAC or CACIB designations.

Germany

After World War II there were only a few imported Bassets in Germany. The first regular breeding program was started by Mitzel Droemont in Bad Godesberg. A great part of her work is still in German bloodlines. In November of 1958, she bought a bitch whose dam was American, and the following year she purchased Rossingham Emerald from England. She had no stud dog at this time, but used a hound named Pierre of Saigon. He was owned by a Mr. Bigelow, an attache from the American Embassy. This dog was strongly bred on Santana-Mandeville bloodlines, so the first modern dogs to be bred and campaigned in Germany were largely from American and British bloodlines. Frau Droemont's campaigning brought the breed to the attention of others who became interested in Bassets. After her death, Frau Droemont's daughter, Wilma, carried on the work. Their kennel name was Vonn Herzogtum Juelick.

Within a few years, Erika Schlick and her husband became interested in the breed. In 1965, they owned one male and three females. Among these was Sykemoor Irka, imported from George Johnston of England.

The Bassethound Klub was founded in 1967 with thirty members. By 1977, it had grown to 300 and there were plans for a regional group in Berlin. The Horst Kliebensteins, the Helmut Haeussners, Peter Strecker and Johannes Ulmmann were active members as were Mrs. Haeussner, L. Helbig, and W. Steinhausen. Members were importing dogs from America, South Africa, England, Poland, Denmark and France. Mrs. Hassi Eppelsheimer's bitch, Beacontree Flory Mata, an English import, was the first CACIB by winning in France, Belgium and Germany.

347

Holland

The main registration body is the *Raad van Beheer op Kynologisch Gebied in Nederland,* Emmalaan 16, Amsterdam Z. Dutch Basset fanciers also belong to the *Nederlandse Brakkenclub,* brakken meaning scent hounds. Among the 2200 member total in this club, the Basset Hound (as we know it) and Basset Artesien-Normand are the more popular breeds. The club puts on an all scent hound show each Spring. If there are at least ninety Bassets entered, the Winners Dog and Winners Bitch can each gain two points and the Reserve can also pick up a point toward the Dutch championship. A dog must have four wins under at least two different judges to become a champion. No travail, or working test, is required. In order to gain an International title, a dog must do its hunting work in some other country that requires it. The wins in Holland must be accumulated within a year's time.

To stick to true type and to eliminate faults in the breed, there is a breeding commission. People who need it can have information about pedigrees and the ancestors of given dogs, their positive and negative qualities from this body. Because both Basset Hounds and Bassets Artesien-Normand are represented, breeders can learn a great deal about both breeds. The best Artesiens in Holland trace back to the old pre-war de Barly, de Jaulzy and de Bourceville lines.

Mr. John Hiddes, the most prominent Dutch judge and student of Bassets, writes that type varies enormously. Some of the best dogs one sees are rather heavy but also Artesian-like in type. He believes this is largely due to the French influence in English stock brought to Holland. Some important dogs brought over by Mrs. Thomassen were Ch. Rollinhills Jolly Roger and a bitch, Rollinhills Peppermint. Mrs. Gerber-Niedenzu imported, among others, a very prepotent sire, Beacontree Why Not. Mrs. Van Terheydin imported Langpool Likely Lad and Langpool L. Lancelot, going back via both grandfathers to American Ch. Longview Acres Bonza who was sent 'to England by the author. She also imported a bitch, Langpool Mary Rose. All were balanced hounds, with excellent fronts, bone, good toplines which were badly needed, and apple-rounded hindquarters. Mr. Hiddes feels it was up to the breeders to make proper use of the first-class material imported.

348

Scandinavia

Finland, Sweden, Norway, and Denmark all have a four-month quarantine period for dogs from all over the world except England. Consequently, most imports are from Great Britain. Niles Roed, of Copenhagen, did purchase a puppy from the Donald Bergs of Belgium. This was the first Basset in Scandinavia with all American bloodlines.

Although Queen Alexandra, whose Sandringham hounds were so famous, was a native of Denmark, it seems odd that the breed was not known to exist in the Scandinavian countries until relatively recent times. Mrs. Ries, of Holte, Denmark, founded her Riesbo kennel in 1959. She and her daughter imported several dogs from Great Britain and campaigned them throughout Scandinavia. The breed slowly attracted a few admirers who joined Mrs. Ries in a breeding program. Although the Danish dogs were mostly from British imports, they developed a considerable amount of blue-mottled coloring. Riesbo Agathe and Riesbo Ajax, both blues, were consistent winners. As interest increased, Mr. Parkild and Dr. Krasilnikoff, who were influential members of the Danish Kennel Club, assisted Mrs. Ries and the newer breeders. The Standard used in Britain, was adopted in Denmark. The Standard used in Sweden and Norway is the American.

One of the earliest breeders, in Sweden, was Mr. Petersen of Odeshog. His hounds were known by the kennel name of Astors. Mrs. Rose-Marie Hartvig was also an interested Swedish breeder who imported some American bloodlines to help the breed along. As more Bassets were shown, by exhibitors seeking International titles, the breed slowly caught on and the ranks of Basset fanciers increased.

In Norway, Inger Bjorg Stenhaugen, Dogcastle Kennels, obtained her first bitch, Mende's Amanda, from Mende Kennels in Sweden. In 1968, Liv Schoyen also obtained a bitch, Alandia's Isabella, from the Alandia Kennels, also of Sweden. In 1972, Amanda was bred to Swedish & Norwegian Ch. Moonman, owned by Kennel Bazett, producing Dogcastle's Blue Light and Dogcastle's Burley. Burley was later bred to Alandia's Isabella. Kasper and Bazett's Helena were purchased by Mr. and Mrs. Sveinall from Kennel Bazett, in Sweden. Mrs. Elisabeth Knap obtained them, and their daughter

349

Verwood Hyacinth, owned by Frau Elfriede Krok, Dusseldorf Germany.

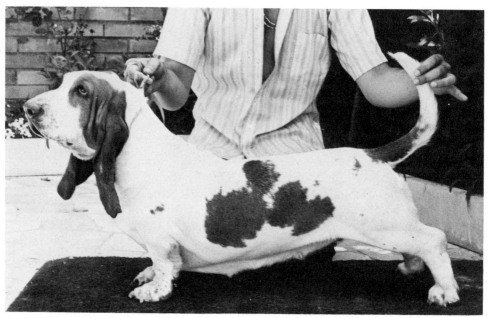

Torella Del Canedoro, owned by Francesco Lamarca, Naples Italy.

Frida, in 1973. In 1975, she imported Lyn-Mar Acres Top Brass from the American kennels of Mrs. M. Lynwood Walton. The following year he gained his Norwegian title having been shown only four times. He sired litters bearing the Baseknap prefix out of Norwegian Chs. Frida and Wingjay's Poppy.

Italy

Early in the 1960s, two dogs were sent to Italy by Clip and Helen Boutell from their Double B Kennels in Connecticut. Anna Maria Caravaggi eventually became the owner of one of these named "Angela." Mr. and Mrs. Locatelli owned a stud dog and Mr. G. Benelli imported Hardacre Wildaway Willow from Mrs. Matthews in England. "Willow" proved a strong winner on the Continent with a record of 30 CACs won in 1966. Mr. Benelli then imported Hardacre Zueika and Classic, followed by a bred bitch, Hardacre Juno, who presented her new owner with a litter of nine by Hardacre Valorous. He also obtained Hardacre Clementine from Mrs. Matthews. As these dogs began to produce, and more imports were made, the breed began to flourish in Italy. Admirable Admiral of Heathrow was obtained from Mr. and Mrs. R. C. Waterhouse, Vancouver, B.C., Canada.

In 1968, Rita and Vittorio Belli and Mrs. Belli's mother, Lida Rossi, became interested in the breed and obtained their first Basset. By 1972, their Fredwell Flirtatious, a litter sister of their English Ch. Fredwell Flick, had the title. Flick also gained his championship in Austria and Yugoslavia and became an International champion in 1973. Fredwell Prickle and Fredwell Petite gained titles as well. These dogs had been imported from Mrs. Joan Wells Meacham in England. The Bellis and Mrs. Rossi adopted the name Arlica as a prefix, and the homebreds Arlica Florinda, Flipper and Fayre finished in 1975 at 17 months. The Arlica breedings became well-known for the high quality of the winning dogs they produced.

A cause for concern developed in Italy over a general lack of quality in the majority of Italian Bassets. Of some 150 hounds imported, and 500 litters produced, perhaps only four or five dogs were considered worthy of being shown and bred. As president and

351

secretary of the newly formed club, *Societa Italiana Basset Hound,* Mr. and Mrs. Belli are trying to encourage greater control in importing and breeding. One of the methods used is to limit importations to dogs for personal use only. In other words, a breeder may not sell a dog that he imports, at the risk of losing his kennel affix immediately. The Italian club is trying to arrange for possible exchanges of stud dogs between club members and the importation of quality American bitches. The latter objective has met with some difficulty.

Japan

Like several other foreign breeds, the Basset Hound caught the eye of Japanese fanciers. Prior to illness, Hisashi Yobuzaki owned Bassets for about fifteen years. Nobuji Suzuki owned American Ch. Syrclesee's Coke out of Ch. Kazoo's Fredie the Freeloader ex Ch. Manor Hill Greta. American Ch. Moal's Sam Weller was owned by Kimio Orima. Sam was out of Nancy Evans Tina Marie, sired by Bayberry's Calhoun. Hidetaka Chikaraishi owned American Ch. Senator Sloopy of Addison who was out of Ch. Peppy's Top Serenade of Shadbo ex Lady Bird Klutch. Hisashi Yabuzaki had a granddaughter of Sloopy. Her dam was Ch. Arabella vom Grau Haus whose ancestry went back to British breedings. Mr. and Mrs. Chiba exhibited Fredwell Dodee. Ardel of Camrose, bred by the Chibas, was shown by Mr. Takeo Azumakawa. Mr. Michizoh Ikoma showed Algler Chummy of Bassetology whom he had obtained from Mr. Yabuzaki.

THE BASSET HOUND

published
by

THE BASSET HOUND CLUB OF AMERICA
Member AKC Since 1937

This publication developed under the auspices
of the Education Committee of BHCA
written by John A. Hackley

HISTORY OF THE BREED

There are many theories abroad about the true origin of the Basset Hound. Ultimately, the present day Basset Hound enthusiast must study the various theories of origin posed by the several authoritative writers about the breed and through his analysis of the evolutionary theories offered, and his own historical preferences, come to his own conclusion as to which theory he finds most appealing.

In terms of the present day American Basset Hound, there is little of true relevance to be gained by a speculation about whether the modern day American Basset Hound is a descendant of a long-bodied strain of dogs known to man as early as 2200 B.C. or, if the Basset Hound is a direct descendant of the St. Hubert Hound. Admittedly, at least for the more sophisticated enthusiast, there is real intellectual challenge in pursuing a comparative study of the various theories of origin developed by many writers of both the 19th and 20th centuries.

The most pertinent historical development in the breed for the present day American Basset Hound breeder and fancier is that of the breed since its appearance upon the American scene. Suffice it to say that by the turn of the 18th century the Basset Hound had become broadly recognized throughout France as a valuable working breed and was employed extensively in game hunting by the aristocracy and laboring classes alike because of its suitability for hunting on foot.

Subsequently, this interest and also specimens of the breed were transported across the channel to England where the interest and activity in the breed prospered. Later, English nobility and near-nobility brought their enthusiasm and some of their Basset Hounds with them in the colonization of America. As could be expected, here again the interest in hunting as a sport as well as a necessity fostered the growth and proliferation of the breed in North America to the extent that legend has it that even George Washington possessed a pair of Basset Hounds which he prized. The interest in and devotion to the Basset Hound in the United States and all of North America has been so substantial and enduring through the last several generations that the Basset Hound is considered in most quarters to be a breed of quite superior quality.

THE BASSET HOUND CHARACTER

"What is a Basset Hound?," you ask! Yes, he is long and low. In youth he may seem humorous because of his apparent discoordination. He may step on his long velvety ears as he walks. His rear may wag in unrepressed happiness while his wrinkled brow and grave eye may simulate a professional mourner. Can he truly be the brave hunter, fearless and stout of heart, when he simultaneously seems so tranquil and easygoing?

Perhaps the most sensitive word portrait of the Basset Hound can be found in The Complete Basset Hound (Howell Book House) wherein the words of Mercedes D. Braun we read:

> "We must not forget that it is the Basset's versatility that brought him fame. He is perhaps best known for the lovable nature which led him to be dubbed, 'the armchair clown.' Do not be fooled when you see him sound asleep on his back or sprawled on his favorite chair (which he has taken away from you). Put a lead on this same dog, take him to a show, and he can give a polished performance with a 'Don't you love me, Mr. Judge?' attitude that will command applause from the ringside. Take him to the field and he can show you how a scent-hound should perform -- over, under, and through rough ground, never tiring all day long.
>
> At home the Basset will assume his subtle manner of 'ruling the roost.' He refuses to accept the fact that he is a dog by devious methods. He can effect poor hearing when he doesn't want to obey or pretend to sleep so soundly that you do not have the heart to disturb him. But his alertness miraculously returns if you open the refrigerator door ever so stealthily. He is a built-in babysitter, an ideal family pet. A Basset needs firm convincing that his big brown eyes will get him nowhere. But first convince yourself of this, if you can. He is smart enough to be very adept at playing dumb. He will do his best to outmaneuver you to gain his own way, and he will make you like it. You need only one Basset to fill the house with laughter, the woods with beautiful music, and the show with an approving ovation. Small wonder the breed has attained such popularity and owners readily admit, 'I am owned by a Basset.'

CHOOSING A PUPPY

A Basset Hound puppy should have sound temperament, be in good health and conform to the breed standard as much as a very young dog can be expected to do. If possible, spend some time with the litter, observing the individual characteristics of each puppy in action with littermates. Puppies should be outgoing, aggressive and show no signs of shyness. Noises should not be an upsetting factor. An indication of good socialization is a pup's eagerness to approach strangers.

Insist upon seeing the dam of the litter and also see the sire or at least a picture of the sire. How do they conform to the Standard of the breed? Often times a pup cannot be expected to develop into a substantially better specimen of the breed than its parents. Remember that observable faults in a pup do not disappear with maturity -- rather, they become more pronounced as the puppy grows. An excessively faulty or stunted puppy may tug at your sympathetic nature but it is a serious mistake to choose any but the very best specimen from among those available to you.

The best safeguard is to contact your local Basset Hound club or the Basset Hound Club of America for the names and addresses of reputable breeders in your area. Local all-breed clubs may also be able to provide helpful leads to sources of good quality breeders and animals.

"The Basset Hound" has been prepared at the instruction of the Board of Directors of BHCA under the auspices of the Education Committee of the Basset Hound Club of America. Every owner, breeder, exhibitor, enthusiast or admirer of the Basset Hound will find this new official publication of interest. This publication about the Basset Hound, copyrighted 1975 by The Basset Hound Club of America, is made available to its membership and the public at cost as a service to the breed and its fanciers.

PRICE, including postage:

    1 - 10 copies . . . . 25¢ each

   11 - 20 copies . . . . 23¢ each

  21 - 100 copies . . . . 20¢ each

BASSET HOUND ACTIVITY

The four kinds of licensed events which constitute the full spectrum of recognized activities for the Basset Hound are: conformation showing, field trialing, obedience trialing, and tracking tests. The Basset Hound was bred to be a determined and deliberate trailer, slow but blessed with great physical stamina. The Basset is a multi-purpose dog, a marvelous and devoted companion, and a classic individualist.

Conformation competition seems to be that activity in the sport of dogs with which the public and novice enthusiast are most familiar. Dog shows, as conformation competition is generally known, are intended to promote the physical improvement of the breed. Since judges are required to judge the conformation of competing Basset Hounds according to the Standard for the breed, it follows that breeders must breed to produce dogs that evermore closely approximate the ideal Basset Hound as described by the Official Standard.

Field Trialing is at the very heart of Basset Hound activity -- it could be no other way, for the Basset is a scent hound and he was born for the trail; the breed was developed to hunt small game. In this same way tracking, the fourth official activity in Bassetdom, is equally fundamental to the purpose and unique characteristics of the breed. Just as conformation competition encourages the continual striving to breed Basset Hounds that evermore closely approximate the ideal physical specimen - so also field trialing and tracking encourage the breeding of the Basset Hound that is true to the real purpose of the breed.

Obedience trialing is a licensed event which provides stimulus for and recognition of diligence, discipline and intelligence. The natural intelligence of the Basset Hound plus its loyalty, sense of competition, extreme devotion to its master, and sincere desire to please, make the Basset Hound a very suitable candidate for obedience training and competition.

STANDARD FOR THE BASSET HOUND

The Standard is a word picture of the representative dog of a breed as approved by the American Kennel Club. Essentially it describes the features and characteristics that establish the uniqueness of this breed from other breeds. The present Standard for Basset Hounds was accepted by the American Kennel Club in January of 1964. Revisions had been made upon the recommendations of the Basset Hound Club of America to clarify the prior Standard and to reinforce the emphasis on the utility and true purpose of the breed.

The AKC Standard for the Basset Hound

The Basset Hound

General Appearance -- The Basset Hound possesses in marked *degree* those characteristics which equip it admirably to follow a trail over and through difficult terrain. It is a short-legged dog, heavier in bone, *size* considered, than any other breed of dog, and while its movement is deliberate, it is in no way clumsy. In temperament it is mild, never sharp or timid. It is capable of great endurance in the field and is extreme in its devotion.

Head -- The head is large and well proportioned. Its length from occiput to muzzle is greater than the width at the brow. In overall appearance the head is of medium width. *The skull* is well domed, showing a pronounced occipital protuberance. A broad flat skull is a fault. The length from nose to stop is approximately the length from stop to occiput. The sides are flat and free from cheek bumps. Viewed in profile the top lines of the muzzle and skull are straight and lie in parallel planes, with a moderately defined stop. The skin over the whole of the head is loose, falling in distinct wrinkles over the brow when the head is lowered. A dry head and tight skin are faults. *The muzzle* is deep, heavy, and free from snipiness. *The nose* is darkly pigmented, preferably black, with wide-open nostrils. A deep liver-colored nose conforming to the coloring of the head is permissible but not desirable. *The teeth* are large, sound, and regular, meeting in either a scissors or an even bite. A bite either overshot or undershot is a serious fault. *The lips* are darkly pigmented and are pendulous, falling squarely in front and, toward the back, in loose hanging flews. *The dewlap* is very pronounced. *The neck* is powerful, of good length, and well arched. *The eyes* are soft, sad, and slightly sunken, showing a prominent haw, and in color are brown, dark brown preferred. A somewhat lighter-colored eye conforming to the general coloring of the dog is acceptable but not desirable. Very light or protruding eyes are faults. *The ears* are extremely long, low set, and when drawn forward, fold well over the end of the nose. They are velvety in texture, hanging in loose folds with the ends curling slightly inward. They are set far back at the base of the skull and, in repose, appear to be set on the neck. A high set or flat ear is a serious fault.

Forequarters -- *The chest* is deep and full with prominent sternum showing clearly in front of the legs. The shoulders and elbows are set close against the sides of the chest. The distance from the deepest point of the chest to the ground, while it must be adequate to allow free movement when working in the field, is not to be more than one-third the total height at the withers of an adult Basset. The shoulders are well laid back and powerful. Steepness in shoulder, fiddle fronts, and elbows that are out, are serious faults. *The forelegs* are short, powerful, heavy in bone, with wrinkled skin. Knuckling over of the front legs is a disqualification. *The paw* is massive, very heavy with tough heavy pads, well rounded and with both feet inclined equally a triffle outward, balancing the width of the shoulders. Feet down at the pastern are a serious fault. *The toes* are neither pinched together nor splayed, with the weight of the forepart of the body borne evenly on each. The dewclaws may be removed.

Body -- The rib structure is long, smooth, and extends well back. The ribs are well sprung, allowing adequate room for heart and lungs. Flat-sidedness and flanged ribs are faults. The topline is straight, level, and free from any tendency to sag or roach, which are faults.

Hindquarters -- The hindquarters are very full and well rounded, and are approximately equal to the shoulders in width. They must not appear slack or light in relation to the overall depth of the body. The dog stands firmly on its hind legs showing a well-let-down stifle with no tendency toward a crouching stance. Viewed from behind, the hind legs are parallel, with the hocks turning neither in nor out. Cowhocks or bowed legs are serious faults. The hind feet point straight ahead. Steep, poorly angulated hindquarters are a serious fault. The dewclaws, if any, may be removed.

Tail -- The tail is not to be docked, and is set in continuation of the spine with but slight curvature, and carried gaily in hound fashion. The hair on the underside of the tail is coarse.

Size -- The height should not exceed 14 inches. Height over 15 inches at the highest point of the shoulder blades is a disqualification.

Gait -- The Basset Hound moves in a smooth, powerful, and effortless manner. Being a scenting dog with short legs, it holds its nose low to the ground. Its gait is absolutely true with perfect coordination between the front and hind legs, and it moves in a straight line with hind feet following in line with the front feet, the hocks well bent with no stiffness of action. The front legs do not paddle, weave, or overlap, and the elbows must lie close to the body. Going away, the hind legs are parallel.

Coat -- The coat is hard, smooth, and short, with sufficient density to be of use in all weather. The skin is loose and elastic. A distinctly long coat is a disqualification.

Color -- Any recognized hound color is acceptable and the distribution of color and markings is of no importance.

Disqualifications

Height of more than 15 inches at the highest point of the shoulder blades. Knuckled over front legs. Distinctly long coat.

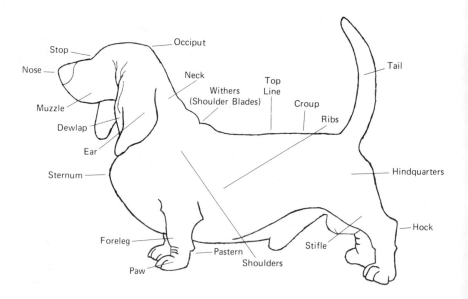

BASSET HOUND CLUB OF AMERICA

The purpose of the Basset Hound Club of America is to protect and foster the interests of purebred Basset Hounds. The BHCA was responsible for developing the revised conformation standard for the breed in 1964. The BHCA publishes a news magazine bimonthly for its membership, thereby providing nationwide information of events in all areas of Basset Hound activity.

Although the Basset Hound Club of America, Inc. has been a member of the American Kennel Club since 1937, there were several intervening years before the breed became popular enough to stimulate the organization of smaller clubs, under the jurisdiction of the national organization. The first such local club was recognized by the AKC and BHCA in 1954. By the end of 1975 there were 32 recognized regional or local Basset Hound Clubs in the United States.

ORGANIZATION OF A BREED CLUB

For any group of enthusiasts, whatever their breed of interest, the most important tenet for them to follow when contemplating the formation of a breed club is to adhere strictly to the guidelines and sequence of steps set forth by the American Kennel Club. Fortunately the AKC has recently published a brochure specially designed to provide this essential guidance to those planning to form a new dog club. This publication is "The Formation of Dog Clubs"; it is published by and available from the AKC, 51 Madison Avenue, New York, New York 10010. A single copy is free upon request.

Persons interested in organizing a local Basset Hound club should first familiarize themselves with the requirements and recommendations of the American Kennel Club. Additional information and helps may be obtained from other local and regional Basset Hound clubs within the allowable proximity to the interested group. Of course, the Basset Hound Club of America can be of substantial assistance in advice and counsel to a newly forming club. A letter to the secretary of BHCA will secure a description of the ways in which the Basset Hound Club of America is prepared to be helpful as well as the names and addresses of other Basset Hound clubs in the area that may be contacted for help and advice.

A SELECTED BIBLIOGRAPHY

There are many, and an ever-increasing number of books and journals, periodicals and other publications which are available and can be of interest to the Basset Hound enthusiast. No bibliography could be truly exhaustive and current for any measurable period of time. However, that is not even the intent of this selected bibliography. Included here are merely the few publications which are either considered basic to Basset Hound literature or fundamental to the regulations of activities in the sport of dogs.

Pure-Bred Dogs - American Kennel Gazette
published monthly by The American Kennel Club
51 Madison Avenue, New York, New York 10010

The Complete Dog Book
The Official Publication of The American Kennel Club,
published by Howell Book House Inc.,
730 Fifth Avenue, New York, N.Y. 10019

The Complete Basset Hound, by Mercedes D. Braun
Howell Book House
730 Fifth Avenue, New York, N.Y. 10019
1969, 1967, and 1965

The Basset Hound, by George Johnston
Popular Dogs Publishing Company, Ltd.
178-202 Great Portland Street, London, W.I., Great Britain
1968

Beagling and Basseting, by James Fagan Schamberg,
The Old Dominion Press
Richmond, Virginia
1973

All About the Basset Hound, by Jeanne Rowett Johns
Pelham Books Limited
52 Bedford Square, London, W.C.I., England
1973

The Basset Hound Club of America, Inc., Bylaws (as amended 10/5/68)
The Basset Hound Club of America, Inc.

Sample Constitution and Bylaws for a Local Specialty Club
January 1971, The American Kennel Club
51 Madison Avenue, New York, New York 10010

Regulations for Record Keeping and Identification of Dogs
November 1970, The American Kennel Club
51 Madison Avenue, New York, New York 10010

Rules Applying to Registration and Dog Shows
(amended to May 1, 1973)
The American Kennel Club
51 Madison Avenue, New York, New York 10010

Regulations for Sanctioned Show Matches, Sactioned Obedience Matches
Publication Number E-19-2
The American Kennel Club
51 Madison Avenue, New York, New York 10010

Obedience Regulations
January 1, 1972
The American Kennel Club
51 Madison Avenue, New York, New York 10010

Regulations for Junior Showmanship
(amended to September 11, 1973)
The American Kennel Club
51 Madison Avenue, New York, New York 10010

Basset Hound Field Trail Rules - and Standard Procedures
Effective December 10, 1974
The American Kennel Club
51 Madison Avenue, New York, New York 10010

Dogs Steps -- Illustrated Gait at a Glance, by Rachel Page Elliott
published by Howell Book House, Inc.
730 Fifth Avenue, New York, New York 10019

Dog Standards Illustrated
Howell Book House Inc.,
730 Fifth Avenue, New York, N.Y. 10019
1975

The name and address of the Basset Hound Club in your vicinity is:

For further information about the Basset Hound and/or Basset Hound Club of America, write to:

The Basset Hound Club of America
Mrs. Jean Sheehy, Secretary
822 Danbury Road
Georgetown, Connecticut 06829
Telephone: 203/544-8257

For more copies of this brochure, please write:

The Basset Hound Club of America
John A. Hackley, Treasurer
P.O. Box 99237
Tacoma, Washington 98499